Lights and Shadows of American History
by Samuel Griswold Goodrich

Address:
HardPress
8345 NW 66TH ST #2561
MIAMI FL 33166-2626
USA
Email: info@hardpress.net

Lights and shadows of
American history

Samuel Griswold Goodrich

LIGHTS AND SHADOWS

OF

AMERICAN HISTORY.

BY THE AUTHOR OF

PETER PARLEY'S TALES.

Saml Griswold Goodrich

———·oo✗oo·———

BOSTON:
THOMPSON, BROWN & COMPANY.
23 HAWLEY STREET.

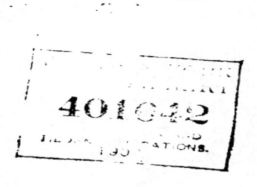

CONTENTS.

Lights & Shadows of American History

THE continent of America stretches from the polar regions of the north, almost to the frozen zone of the southern hemisphere. Its whole length is nearly nine thousand miles, and, bent upon the surface of the globe, embraces more than one third of its entire circumference. It occupies about one third of the land upon the earth. Its inhabitants may be estimated at forty-five millions, or one twentieth part of the entire population of the globe.

In comparison with the eastern continent, America is marked with a scale of grandeur in several of its physical features. The great chain of mountains which extends through both portions of the continent, from Cape Horn to the borders of the Arctic ocean, is the longest in the world. Lake Superior has a surface exceeding that of all the fresh water lakes of Europe, Asia, and Africa. The river Amazon bears to the ocean as great a volume of water as the united streams of Europe. The mountains of South Amer-

1*

ica rise to an elevation of more than five miles, and tower above all others, save only the peaks of Himmaleh. The two hundred volcanoes of the Andes and Cordilleras, present a spectacle of sublimity unrivalled by all the other volcanic phenomena of the earth.

The history of America properly begins with its discovery by Columbus, in 1492. The Scandinavians had indeed established feeble colonies in Greenland, and made discoveries along the coast of New England, about five centuries before; but the knowledge they acquired was not imparted to Europe, and the existence of this western world continued to be a profound secret. Abraham, Isaiah and St. Paul, Alexander and Aristotle, Cicero and Cæsar, Charlemagne and Chaucer,—patriarchs, prophets, apostles, princes, poets and philosophers,—had lived, flourished, and passed away in ignorance of the fact that another continent than their own existed upon the face of the globe.

In the time of Columbus, the enlarged knowledge of mankind had led to the conception of the true form of the globe, and the possibility of the existence of undiscovered lands in the western ocean. Coming events seemed indeed to cast their shadows before; but it was reserved for Columbus to withdraw the curtain from the mighty secret. The events which immediately followed are among the most striking and romantic in the history of mankind. A voyage across the Atlantic was at that period a matter of high adventure. None but the bold and daring would undertake such an enterprise, even after Columbus had led the way. Stimulated by the desire of making discoveries, the expectation of amassing gold, silver and precious stones, or the hope of achieving some great and brilliant exploit, a multitude of daring spirits were attracted to the New World. Their imagination was wrought up to the highest pitch. The days of chivalry presented no hopes or expectations so brilliant or alluring. Here were mighty empires of simple, unwarlike people, whose temples glittered with gold, whose common utensils were of silver, and whose persons were decorated with every variety of precious gem. Such were the gorgeous spoils that tempted the cupidity of these European adventurers. No dainty scruples interposed to prevent them from taking possession of whatever came within their grasp. They professed to be Christians, and by a monstrous perversity of judgment, they deemed the heathen but as their inheritance. Beside, the pope had given these western empires, kingdoms, and nations to his majesty of Spain ; and thus, according to the philosophy of that day, under the banner of the cross, and in the name of Jesus Christ, the stupendous system of murder, rapine, and devastation was carried on and consummated.

Fernando Cortez, who appears to have united in his character a singular mixture of religious fanaticism and greedy avarice ; of heroic courage and mean duplicity ; a love of glory worthy the days of chivalry, with a cruelty befitting an inquisitor, led a small band of about six hundred men into Mexico, and conquered an empire of eight millions. Pizarro, a vulgar, brutal soldier, inspired by the enthusiasm of the age, and lifted above himself, with a still smaller force, mastered the great empire of the Incas. Other Spanish leaders, like a flight of eagles and vultures, pounced upon different portions of the carcass, tearing it limb from limb; and thus, Florida, Mexico, the isthmus which joins the two continents, and the entire peninsula of South America, with the exception of Brazil and Guiana, fell into the greedy grasp of Spain. Cuba, the finest island on the face of the globe, and some other of the West India islands, fell also to the share of that kingdom.

While Spain thus reaped the largest part of the harvest, the other European powers seized upon the remainder. The West India islands were distributed among France, England, Denmark, Spain and Holland. Brazil, a territory nearly equal to all Europe, and enjoying unrivalled advantages of soil and climate, was appropriated by Portugal. The great valley of the St. Lawrence was taken by France, and our Atlantic borders were settled by the English. Thus, America was partitioned out among the powers of Europe on the principles of a scramble, in which each of the parties seizes upon what he can get without scruple, or inquiry even as to the rights of possession thus assumed. One principle seems to have been adopted in all these measures, and that is, that enlightened, civilized and christianized man may usurp the mastery over his savage brother, and compel him to submission even at the point of the sword. Our English forefathers seem indeed to have entertained some notions of justice towards the savages, for they pretended to recognize their independence, and to purchase their lands ; but the result of intercourse between them has been, not the improvement and civilization of the Indians, but their gradual extirpation from the homes of their fathers. Among all the arts which Christianity and civilization brought to these western shores, the art of improving the social condition of the Indian was not to be found. The course of events in the Spanish portions of the continent was marked with atrocities toward the natives, the recital of which fills the mind with horror. A few pious priests devoted themselves with energy and success to the instruction of certain Indian tribes ; but with these slight exceptions, the march of Spanish power upon this continent was everywhere traced by the blood of the native masters of the soil. A retribution as fearful as the crime itself has followed in the lapse of centuries. Spain, four centuries ago a leading power in Europe, after being gorged by the spoils of her transatlantic dominions, sunk into a long nightmare of ignorance and fanaticism, to be at last awakened by the terrific scenes which followed Bonaparte's invasion nearly forty years ago. The echoes of those shrieks which filled the valleys of Mexico, the heights of the Cordilleras, and the table-lands of Peru, four hundred years before, were now heard in the cities and plains of Spain herself. Her driveling monarch, as weak as Montezuma, bargained away his crown, and while his people were butchered, and his capital plundered, he contented himself with weaving fantastic garments for the image of the Virgin. Since that fearful day, this unhappy country has been the constant scene of civil warfare, and, at the same time, the brightest colonial jewels in the crown, Mexico, Peru, Chili, one by one, had dropped away, till not an inch of land remains upon the American continent in the possession of that power beneath whose flag the New World was discovered. The conquests of Cortez, Pizarro, Almagro, and Valdivia, mighty as they were, have proved as baleful as they were wicked, and at last have vanished from the grasp of the spoiler. How stupendous is the lesson which Providence has thus afforded, that even in the history of nations, as in that of individuals, violence, fraud, and perfidy are connected with inevitable retribution.

Among the most interesting phenomena of American history are those events which relate to our own country. In the year 1776, the thirteen United States of America declared themselves independent; and since that period, we have maintained our stand among the sovereign nations of Christendom. We have since been making a great experiment in political philosophy, which is to determine the question whether the people of any country are competent to govern themselves. The prevailing theory of former ages has been, that the great body of the people were too ignorant, corrupt and degraded to be entrusted with power, and that the many must therefore be governed by the few. This theory has led to the establishment of monarchical institutions, which prevail in almost all countries throughout the globe. But, as the reformers in Europe were protestants against the spiritual dominion of papacy, so were the founders of our political institutions, repudiators of kings and princes. They denied the divine right of certain individuals to reign over mankind they asserted that the end of government was the greatest good of the governed, and that the people were at once the only safe depositary and legitimate source of political power.

Upon these principles, they proceeded to erect the fabric of government, the foundation of which is laid in our admirable constitution. This went into operation in 1789; and after an experiment of almost sixty years, we may fairly assume, in the face of the world, that this great experiment, upon which we entered, has been attended with complete success. There may be, and indeed there doubtless are, other nations which surpass ours in certain refinements; but if we regard the general happiness of the great mass of the people, our country is without a rival. If we are without the palaces of Europe, so we are without its paupers. If we have no princes of the blood, no titular nobility, and consequently no courtly standard of etiquette, so we have no starving millions perishing for the staff of life. If we have no costly galleries of paintings or statuary, we have the substantial comforts of life in abundance. If we have no architectural monuments which carry us back to remote antiquity, we have present content, and happy prospects for the future. Most of the blessings which government seems competent to bestow, have flowed from our political system; and the great question, whether the people of this country are competent to govern themselves, may be regarded as triumphantly determined in the affirmative.

Our example has not been without its effect upon

Europe, and thus young America has taught lessons of great import to the Old World. Throughout Europe, the high claims of legitimacy have been weakened. The rights of man are more extensively recognized, the obligation of the governing power to secure the happiness of the people at large, is generally admitted.

But while the republican institutions of these United States have resulted in securing the peace and happiness of this nation, it must be admitted that other experiments of the kind on this continent have been attended with less happy results. Within the last thirty years, ten republics have sprung up from the Spanish dominions in America; yet it is to be remarked that in none of these have the people enjoyed the blessings of good government. All of them have been torn by faction, shaken by revolution, and desolated by civil war. It is evident, therefore, that republican institutions alone are not competent to confer happiness. These are indeed but instruments, and are good or ill, as they are used by wisdom or folly. In the hands of a sagacious and virtuous people, they bring peace and prosperity; but entrusted to the ignorant and vicious, they are even worse than despotism. In considering the question why the southern republics of America have thus resulted in failure, we shall easily discover the answer in the fact, that the people at large are ignorant, fanatical, and profligate. In all these countries, a religious system prevails, which enslaves the mind of the mass, keeps them studiously in ignorance, and fits them to be the tools of intriguing and aspiring leaders. It is a fact not to be overlooked, that it is only in countries where the Protestant religion predominates, that the people have been raised, by education and freedom of inquiry, to that pitch of intelligence and virtue, which are indispensable to the success of liberal institutions.

It is sometimes said by European critics, that society in these United States is far behind the highest standard of civilization in the other hemisphere. We have already admitted that in some things we cannot rival the refinements of Europe, but if the whole mass of society be weighed in the balance, we maintain that the people of these United States will show a higher average of all the elements of civilization—of knowledge, art, comfort, virtue, and power, physical, moral and mental, than any other nation on the face of the globe. In comparing our progress with that of the old and luxurious countries of the eastern continent in the refined arts of poetry, painting, sculpture, music and architecture, our inferiority must be admitted ; but in all that belongs to the substantial business of society, the master spirits of the western world have shown themselves competent to cope with those of the eastern ; and measuring nation by nation, the comparison is incontestably in our favor.

We are sometimes spoken of as without a history and deficient in those elevating emotions which spring from the memories of the mighty past. This may be true, yet we have our compensation in the inspiring hopes presented by the brilliant prospects of the future. In respect to those, who watch our progress with jealous and disparaging hostility, the era of youth is past ; the present institutions of Europe must be regarded as on the wane, and tending to dissolution. The glory of crowns, and thrones, and dynasties, must be sought, not in the present or the future, but in the days that are forever gone. With us, the career of improvement and of glory lies in the near and certain prospect before us. Under these circumstances, we may easily bear the gibe of the scoffer; and while he, standing in the midst of decay, points to the splendors of the past, we, in the midst of present prosperity, shall find ennobling inspiration in the cheering anticipations of a happy future.

We are aware that there are persons among us who indulge more desponding views than these. There are individuals in all countries, who are disposed to judge the world only by its clouds and its tempests, those who never seem to bear in mind that in all lands there is more sunshine than shadow. These maintain that we are sinking rather than rising in the scale of civilization. In their view, vice and crime are on the increase. The people are becoming less intelligent, and the heart of man grows more and more perverse. The obliquity of these views will appear manifest by the consideration of a few obvious facts.

Let us look, in the first place, at the provision already made for education. Not only are the higher seminaries increased throughout the country, but in almost every state of the Union a system of common school education has been adopted. Throughout New England, every child has the opportunity of obtaining instruction, free of charge, in the ordinary branches of an English education. In the state of New York, the same system prevails, and there are more than ten thousand district schools in active operation there. In other parts of the country, a similar state of things exists, or measures are in progress to ensure this result. Everywhere, the importance of education is appreciated, and everywhere education is easily obtained.

What a mighty contrast does this view present, when compared with that which this country exhibited at the opening of the present century. New England was then the only portion of the nation which had undertaken to educate the whole mass of the people. In the other states, universal instruction was either regarded with aversion, or as a mere chimera. Nor are these facts the most striking evidence of change and improvement upon this subject. Not only are the means of education extended, but the standard of instruction is far more elevated. Forty years ago, grammar, geography and history, were excluded from most of the common schools of the country. They are now introduced into nearly all. There are at least a dozen popular geographies in use among us, and nearly half a million of these are annually sold for the use of our public seminaries. Beside this, in the larger towns throughout the country, there are numerous schools, accessible to all, where higher branches of instruction, such as rhetoric, natural and moral philosophy, botany and chemistry, are taught. Thus, the sciences, which forty years ago were but as a sealed book, except to a favored few, are now laid open, and within the reach of nearly all. In our public schools, the children are taught more of the wonders of science than were revealed to Sir Isaac

Newton, for they enjoy the results not only of his profound researches, but those of Herschel and La Place. At the opening of the nineteenth century, there were not probably ten expert chemists in the United States, and there are now many thousands. A botanist, forty years ago, was a great rarity among us; but botany is now as familiar as household goods. In short, the mysteries of science are mysteries no longer. The mass of the people have broken into the arcana of nature, and possessed themselves of its wonders. Knowledge is everywhere diffused; the standard of education is elevated; a love of learning has pervaded the whole mass; our very streets are teeming with literature, to be devoured by the quickened multitude. The toiling million are rising from their prostrate condition upon the earth, and are becoming reading, thinking, reflecting men.

These are incontestable facts; and how are they to be reconciled with the ideas of retrogradation which have been suggested? The truth is, society is advancing with the force of an irresistible tide in its intellectual career. Already, it has made great progress. Forty years ago, the steamboat was but a dream of the schemer; it is now familiar to all. Fifteen years since, the railroad was but a chimera; it is now as common as the highway. The whistle of the locomotive, once so wild and startling, excites as little emotion now as the rumbling of the wagon-wheel. These mighty improvements are apt illustrations of the progress we have made in science and art. In the year 1800, we travelled on foot or on horseback, at the rate of five miles an hour; we now glide along in the locomotive's train, almost with the swiftness of the eagle.

Such is the onward march of society in less than half a century. Nor let it be supposed that we have reached the end of improvement, or that the age of discovery is over. A short time since, the arts and sciences were confined to the few; they are now in the hands of the many. A hundred thousand ingenious heads and strong hands are this day thundering at the gates of knowledge, and demanding entrance into its hidden places. Upon the sea and upon the land, in field and mine and cavern, in alkali and acid, in the fleeting air and subtle gas, in mineral and metal, in light, heat and electricity, in the cloud and the tempest, in the bowels of the earth, and at the extremities of the poles—everywhere, human philosophy is at work with its crucible and its blowpipe, its microscope and telescope, its hammer and wedge, seeking the discovery of new facts, or the solution of old phenomena. Let it not be supposed that these researches can be in vain. The temple of science is of boundless dimensions; and we have reason to believe that hitherto we have only trod its threshold.

Nor do we think that the moral advancement of society is greatly less than its intellectual. The institutions of religion, formerly obtaining a reluctant support by law or the stern guardianship of authority, are now better sustained by the free will of the community. The general standard of morality is higher than in former days. The discipline of the churches is more strict, the requisitions of society are more exalted. Conduct that was tolerated thirty years ago,

B 2*

especially in public men, would be fatal to their standing now. The cause of temperance has not only wrought a great change in the community by partially removing the chief source of vice and crime, but it is evident that society itself, before it could sustain such a cause, must have been greatly purified and exalted. We do not mean to assert that vice and crime have ceased to exist; we do not mean to say that dark stains do not continue to rest upon the bosom of humanity; but we affirm that wickedness is becoming more and more rare, and virtue more and more common. Two things are now clearly settled in the community. Vice of every kind is looked upon with general reprobation, and virtue with open approval. There is no party, no sect, no body of men, who will dare, in the light of the present day, to be the advocates of the former, or the enemies of the latter. The moral vision of society is distinct and clear, and distinguishes truth from error in all important things, as readily as the eye distinguishes between light and darkness. If there are still evils among us; if prejudices are indulged, and wrongs perpetrated by society, we may entertain the confident hope that they wil. ere long be obliterated, or at least softened by the united force of that intelligence and virtue which are now diffused among us and constitute the basis of public opinion.

In stating our present condition and future prospects, we should not neglect to notice the improved state of society in respect to the comforts, conveniences and luxuries of life. Our country has ever been happily free from the melancholy spectacles of beggary and pauperism, which afflict the heart of the traveller in every portion of the Old World. Here, each person, with moderate industry, may enjoy the comforts of life. Nothing is more common than to see whole villages in our country, where almost every individual is the independent proprietor of the roof beneath which he dwells. Such scenes are not to be witnessed in any other part of the globe. Nor is the condition of society in these respects stationary; year by year, there is improvement—old evils are constantly being mitigated or removed, and new comforts introduced. The houses are better than they were twenty years since; the furniture more abundant and tasteful. With the advance of knowledge and the improvement of the arts, a higher estimate is put upon life, its comforts, enjoyments and duties; and this results in an onward march toward that standard of perfection, which humanity may reasonably hope to attain.

If we may be permitted to look to the future, and consider the probable destiny of our country, in a political aspect, we cannot fail to indulge in the brightest anticipations. Already are these states the asylum to which the oppressed of all lands are flying for deliverance from sorrow, and for the enjoyment of peace and prosperity. The thousands that flock .o our shores, are so many living witnesses in behalf of our country, and afford an overwhelming refutation of the slanders poured out upon us by the enemies of liberty and human rights. It is vain to deny that we have attained a state of general happiness realized by no other country. Under the genial influence of our institutions, our population is doubled in five-and twenty years. Many who are now living will doubtless see it reach fifty millions ; the wave of emigration has already swept over the Rocky Mountains, and broken upon the shores of the Pacific. Ere thirty years are past, we have reason to believe that the mighty valley of the Mississippi will be teeming with an abundant population — that the streams which centre in the Columbia will turn the busy wheels of the factory, and waft the abundant agricultural harvest to a metropolis yet to rise at its mouth — that a continuous line of railroad will extend from the Atlantic to the Pacific, and that a journey from one ocean to the other will be a familiar incident with our citizens. The wires of the magnetic telegraph will speedily be extended to the Mississippi ; and before the present generation has passed away, by the magic power of this amazing invention, the inhabitants of Astoria will read at noon an account of the events which have transpired in the morning, of the same day, along the shores of the Atlantic. With such anticipations, is it not a privilege to be an American ? — and who shall not feel himself bound, by its enjoyment, to such a course of action as may promote the glory and prosperity of his country ?

GREENLAND.

GREENLAND is well known as the most northern tract of land lying between Europe and the continent of America; but its nearer propinquity to the latter justifies us in regarding it as a part of the western world. Considering its vast extent in comparison with the small portion yet known, it may justly be enumerated among the unexplored regions of the north. It was long supposed to be connected with the American continent; but the discoveries of Parry, Ross, Back and others have recently proved that the waters of Baffin's Bay and the Arctic Ocean to the northwest are united by a continuous channel, thus separating Greenland from the continent, and forming it into an island.

The name of *Groenland,* or *Greenland,* was be-

stowed on the eastern coast of this country by its discoverers, the Norwegians and Icelanders, from its
uncommonly verdant appearance. This side, now
called Ancient, or Lost Greenland, is at present almost
entirely unknown to us, having been inaccessible, on
account of the ice, for a long period of time. The
tales of Icelandic writers, who describe in glowing
colors the fertility of ancient Greenland, and the
beauty of its villages and churches, are generally
thought to be mere fictions, or exaggerations. It is,
notwithstanding, a fact that traces of a superior state
of cultivation have been observed along the western
coast, and the remains are still to be seen there of
dwelling-houses and churches, probably erected by the
Norwegians long since.

West Greenland is inhabited by people of European descent, between the 62d and the 71st degrees
of north latitude. The shore is lofty, rugged and
barren, rising close to the water's edge into tremendous precipices and lofty mountains, crowned with inaccessible cliffs, which may be discerned from the sea
at the distance of a hundred miles. All the mountains and hills, except where the rocks are smooth
and perpendicular, are covered with eternal ice and
snow, which accumulate particularly on elevated
flats, entirely filling many of the valleys, and probably increasing from year to year. Those rocks on
which the snow cannot lie, appear at a distance, of a
dusky gray color, and without any sign of vegetation ;
but upon a nearer inspection they are found to be
streaked with numerous veins of colored stone, with
here and there a little earth, which affords a scanty

nourishment to some hardy species of heath. The valleys which contain small brooks and ponds, are overgrown with low brushwood. The whole coast is indented with deep bays or *fiords*, which penetrate a great distance into the land, and are sprinkled with innumerable islands of the most fantastic shapes. At about the 63d degree of latitude is a remarkable place called the *Ice Blink*. This is a large and lofty sheet of ice, which casts by its reflection a brightness over the sky, similar to the northern lights, and which may be discerned at a great distance from the land. The mouth of an adjoining bay is blocked up by ice, driven out by the ebb tides, and so wonderfully piled up by the waves, that the space between the islands is completely vaulted over, and the whole presents the sublime spectacle of a stupendous bridge of ice eighteen miles long and nearly five in breadth. Under the arches of the bridge, which are from twenty to sixty yards high, boats may enter the bay, though threatened with destruction by the masses impending from above.

This coast is often beset with icebergs, or enormous islands of ice, which float about in the sea, and exhibit an endless variety of shapes. Some look like churches or castles, adorned with turrets and spires, others like ships under full sail, and so close is often the resemblance that pilots have been deceived, and have rowed off to them in order to guide the imaginary ships into port. They are composed of extremely hard ice, perfectly transparent, and generally of a pale green color, though some pieces are found of a sky blue: when melted, and frozen a second time, the ice is white. Twenty or thirty of these icebergs may often be seen after a violent storm, chasing each other in and out of Davis's Strait. Some of them frequently aground in the shoal water near the coast, and remain there for years, till at last they break to pieces, or are forced off by the wind and currents. Most of them are finally carried down to the latitude of Newfoundland and Nova Scotia, when they melt under the beams of the summer sun.

No trees grow in Greenland, yet the country is plentifully supplied with fuel. The streams of the ocean bring with them immense quantities of wood, and deposit it upon the islands along the shore. Among this drift timber are often found great trees torn up by the roots, which, by driving and dashing many years amidst the ice, have been stripped of their bark and branches, and eaten through by the worms. These trees are chiefly pine and fir. The cold in Greenland is so intense, that in February and March the stones are split, and the sea smokes like an oven. This is called *frost-smoke:* it raises blisters on the skin, and congeals into minute particles of ice, which are driven before the wind, and cause so sharp a cold that it is scarcely possible to stir out of doors without having the face and hands frozen. At such times the Greenlanders are in danger of starvation. In summer, the heat is often so powerful as to melt the pitch on the decks of the vessels, but this is never of long continuance. Above the 66th degree, the sun does not set for many days before and after midsummer, and in all parts of the country it is so light during the summer nights, that the smallest print may be read, and the mountain-tops are continually gilded by the sunbeams. During the period in which the sun never sets, he ceases to dazzle a few hours after noon, and is entirely shorn of his powerful beams, appearing only like a full moon, which the eye may dwell upon with impunity. The winter nights, on the contrary, are proportionally long, and at Disko Bay the sun never rises from the 30th of November to the 12th of January. The inhabitants enjoy then only a clear twilight, caused by the reflection of the sun's rays from the cold, dense atmosphere and the icy summits of the mountains. In Greenland, it is never so dark at any season as in more southern regions. The light of the moon and stars, shining through the clear cold air, is so brightly reflected by the snow and ice, that common sized print may be read at all times of the night : and when there is no moon, her loss is more than repaired by the Aurora Borealis, which illuminates the heavens in a most beautiful manner. Sometimes nearly the whole sky appears like one vast dome of burnished gold, which is presently transformed, with the rapidity of lightning, into all sorts of fantastic shapes, often presenting the appearance of a glorious amphitheatre splendidly fitted out with dazzling furniture, and decked in all the colors of the rainbow. This fire-built structure does not last many minutes. All its parts soon acquire a tremulous motion, and the rays cross and intermix with inconceivable velocity, dancing sportively through the heavens with a constant interchange of coloring, and in the most wonderful variety of forms, til the approach of the sun closes the magical exhibition. The suddenness with which the scenes shift resembles the rapid succession of different forms produced by shaking a kaleidoscope.

The aboriginal Greenlanders vaguely term themselves *Innuit*, that is, men or natives. The Icelanders, who first discovered and colonized the country, bestowed upo_ ·hem the contemptuous appellation of *Skrællings*, expressive of their dwarfish and imbecile appearance. Their stature rarely exceeds five feet, and their appearance promises little bodily vigor. They have a dark skin, but this is probably not natural to them, as their children are born white. Their uncleanly habits, their continual use of blubber, their smoky houses, and their total neglect of washing, soon change their complexion. They have universally long, coarse, and coal-black hair, and are so fat that they can bear an extreme degree of cold with slight clothing. They are very nimble-footed and strong. A man who has eaten nothing but seaweed for three days, will manage his *kajak* or skiff in the heaviest sea; and a woman will carry a whole reindeer eight or ten miles. They consider themselves the only civilized people in the world, and the highest praise they bestow upon a European is to say, " He is almost as well bred as we."

A Greenlander in his *kajak* is an object of wonder. His sable sea-dress, shining with rows of white bone buttons, gives him a striking appearance. He rows with a celerity almost incredible, and when charged with letters from one settlement to another, will go fifty miles in a day. He dreads no storm; and as long as a ship can carry her topsail, he braves the mountain billows, darting over them like a bird. and even when completely buried in the waves, he soon re-appears, skimming along the surface. If a breaker threatens to overset him, he supports himself in an erect position by his oar, or if he is actually upset, he restores himself to his balance by one swing of that instrument. But if he loses the oar, it is certain death.

If we use the name of savage to imply a brutal, un-social and cruel disposition, the Greenlanders are not savages. They are not intractable, wild or barbarous, but mild, quiet, and good-natured. They live in a state of natural liberty without formal government, but in social communities of a republican character. These societies, which consist of several families in one house, or of several houses on an island, are not kept together by fixed laws and an organized power to enforce them, but by a certain order mutually under-stood and spontaneously agreed to. They have in this way subsisted for several centuries, with more quietness than any community in Europe. Few materials can be collected for the history of this peo-ple, as they have no oral traditions of any importance, nor are there any records or monuments of antiquity among them. All they know of their ancestors is this, that they expelled the *Kablunat*, or former colo-nists of the country.

According to the Icelandic chronicles, Greenland was first visited by Europeans in the ninth century. Eric, the son of Thorwald, was obliged to flee from Iceland to avoid the consequences of a murder. He had been informed that a certain Gunbiœrn had discovered a new country in the west, and he steered in that direction. He first came in sight of the land at Herjolf's Ness; then coasting along to the southwest, he wintered in a pleasant island, and named the strait adjacent, Eric's Sound. The following summer he spent in examining the mainland, and returned in the third year to Iceland. The glowing description which he gave of the verdant meadows, the woods and the fisheries of this newly discovered territory, which he called *Greenland,* allured such multitudes, that twenty-five ships full of colonists followed him thither in the ensuing spring, with a large stock of household goods, and all sorts of cattle. New swarms of settlers followed in subsequent years from Iceland and Norway, and planted their colonies thickly along the eastern and western coasts. One hundred and ninety villages on the eastern, and a hundred and ten on the western shores of Greenland, are enumerated by contemporary writers.

A short time after these events, the Icelanders renounced their Scandinavian creed and embraced Christianity. Greenland was continually receiving new colonists, and ere long, the Christian population became numerous. A bishop was sent thither from Denmark in 1122, and fixed his residence at Gardar. The commerce of the country was now considerable. Cattle, peltry, fish, butter and cheese were exported in large quantities.

There appears to be no evidence that Greenland was inhabited when first discovered by the Icelanders. In the fourteenth century, the *Skrællings* suddenly made their appearance in West Greenland, where they killed several of the people and captured others. Ivar Beer, the Greenland justiciary, was sent by the bishop with some ships to expel them from the coast, out on landing, he found all the invaders had fled, and left behind them a large drove of sheep and oxen. Nothing more was heard of this body of Skrœllings.

All accounts of the state of Greenland draw to a close soon after this date. The eastern coast was shut in by immense masses of ice, which have never since dispersed, and this territory bears the name of "Lost Greenland." In the west, the Skrœllings again appeared, and the settlers fled before their encroachments. Presently we lose all sight of the country. Some traces of the colonists were however discovered long afterward. About the year 1530, Bishop Amund, of Skalholt, in Iceland, on his return from Norway to that island, was driven by a storm so near to the coast of Greenland, at Herjolf's Ness, that he could see the inhabitants driving home their cattle. He did not land, but bore away before a favorable gale which immediately sprung up and carried him on his voyage. A Hamburg seaman was thrice driven among the islands on this coast, where he saw huts like those of Iceland, but could discover no people. Fragments of shattered boats have been frequently stranded on the coast of Iceland, and in 1625, an entire canoe was driven ashore, compacted with sinews and wooden pegs, and smeared over with blubber. An oar was also found, inscribed in Runic characters with the words, " Oft was I tired while I drew thee."

The name of Greenland was almost forgotten, when the discovery of America by Columbus and his successors revived among the Danes a recollection of this lost colony. Frederic II., in 1578, sent the famous navigator, Magnus Hennington, in search of it. After many perils from storms and ice, he succeeded in gaining sight of the land, but returned home with the marvellous report, that the ship all at once stood still and could not by any means be forced onwards, although it blew a fair and strong breeze, and there was an unfathomable depth of water. He ascribed this mysterious obstruction to a submarine rock of loadstone. Others affirmed that a *remora*, or sucking-fish, had seized the ship with its teeth. Fear of the ice on the part of the navigator, is a much more probable explanation of the matter.

Martin Frobisher, who was sent by Queen Elizabeth, two years before, to make discoveries in the northern seas, is supposed to have seen Greenland. His description of lands that he discovered, agrees very well with that country. But he also informs us that the natives were a very civilized race, and their king, Cakiunge, was covered with gold and jewels. Such a fiction impairs our belief in his narrative. John Davis, in 1585, and the two following years, explored a considerable part of the western coast, and traded with the natives. The Danes were roused to new exertions by these discoveries, and sent three ships to Greenland in 1605, under John Knight, an English seaman of long experience in the Greenland seas, and the Danish Admiral Lindenow. The admiral anchored on the eastern coast, but distrusting the savages, he remained there only three days, bartering for skins. Seizing two of the natives, he returned to

Denmark. Knight sailed with two other ships to the western coast, where he found inhabitants much more barbarous than those at the east. He also met with rich silver ore. He took five of the Greenlanders prisoners, one of whom he killed in order to terrify the rest into submission.

The king of Denmark was so much encouraged by the success of this expedition, that he sent out the admiral in the following year, with three of the Greenlanders as interpreters. They arrived in Davis' Strait in May, 1606. At their first attempt to hold intercourse with the natives, the latter kept aloof. At the second place where they landed, they were received with a show of hostility. At a third place, where the natives absolutely rejected all intercourse, one of the admiral's men ventured on shore in hopes of conciliating them by presents. But no sooner had he set foot on land, than they fell upon him with their wooden knives, and, before he could receive any assistance, hewed him in pieces, in revenge of the violence committed by the Danes the preceding year. The commander losing all hope of opening a communication with the natives, returned home.

The fate of the Greenlanders who were carried to Denmark, was most melancholy. Though they received the kindest treatment and were well supplied with the dainties of their own country, fish and train oil, they frequently looked with longing eyes and heart-breaking sobs toward the north. At length they escaped to sea in their boats, intending to find their way home across the ocean; but being driven back by a violent wind to the coast of Schonen, two of them died of grief. Two of the survivors again attempted to escape, and only one of them was recovered. This forlorn being was observed to weep most bitterly whenever he saw a child hanging on its mother's neck, whence it was supposed, for no one understood his language, that he had a wife and children in his native country. The remaining two lived ten or eleven years in Denmark, and were employed in the pearl fishery; but were so rigorously tasked, even in winter, that the one died, and the other fled to the sea in his boat; but, being recaptured above a hundred miles from land, he likewise pined away and died of home-sickness.

The Danes continued their attempts to explore Greenland. Some of their ships could not approach the land on account of the ice, and others failed in the enterprise from various causes. In 1636, a company of Copenhagen merchants fitted out two vessels, which reached Davis' Strait, and traded with the natives. One of the sailors discovered on the beach a glittering kind of sand, which was of a golden color and extremely heavy. The crew believed they had discovered another Ophir or Peru, and loaded both ships with it. On their return to Copenhagen, it was examined, and pronounced to be of no value. The whole was therefore thrown into the sea; but not long afterward, a foreign artist succeeded in extracting grains of gold from a sand found in Norway, precisely similar. The captain of the Greenland expedition now died of vexation, and no other person was able to find the place where the glittering sand had been obtained.

The Danes seem to have given up Greenland in despair, when, about the year 1715, Hans Egede, a clergyman of Vogen, in the north part of Norway, had his sympathies strongly excited on reading in the Danish histories that Christian inhabitants formerly lived in Green.and, all knowledge of whom was lost, and who had probably sunk into paganism. It appeared to him to be the duty of every philanthropic Norwegian to search out his lost countrymen, and reclaim them to Christianity and civilization. Being of an enthusiastic and persevering temper, he succeeded in engaging several other persons in the enterprise, which at length received the sanction of the king; and in May, 1721, he sailed from Copenhagen, with a company of forty settlers, for Greenland. They encountered great perils from the ice on the western coast; but at length, on the 3d day of July, they landed at Baal's river, in the sixty-fourth degree of latitude, and immediately began to build houses. This was the first settlement in Greenland, which has continued to the present day. By judicious exertions in conciliating the natives, they were brought into friendly relations with the settlers, and new establishments were formed along the western coast, which are still in a flourishing condition. More than a thousand of the Greenlanders are now, nominally at least, of the Christian religion

c

THE NORTHMEN IN AMERICA.

Dighton Rock.

THE remarkable fact that in the tenth century, the continent of America was visited by Europeans, who founded settlements on the shores of New England, seems to be fully substantiated by the Icelandic histories which have been brought to light within a few years. According to these documents, the authenticity of which seems indisputable, the Northmen, who settled Iceland and Greenland, pushed their discoveries south as far as the coast of Massachusetts and Rhode Island; to which countries they gave the name of *Vinland*, from the wild grapes which they found growing there.

The first discoverer was Biarne, a young Icelander, who, on returning home from a voyage at the end of

the summer of 986, found that his father had gone to
Greenland. He sailed in pursuit of him, although he
had never voyaged in that quarter, and was unacquainted with the route. For three days his voyage
was prosperous; but then the sky became overcast, a
strong wind blew from the north, and he was tossed
about for several days, driving he knew not whither.
At length, the sky grew clear, and after a day's sail,
they descried an unknown land covered with woods
and hills. Biarne sailed for several days along the
coast, after which the wind shifted to the south, and
he made his way north to Greenland.

This adventure was no sooner reported to Leif, the
son of Eric the Red, a bold and enterprising young
chief, than he determined upon an expedition to this
newly-discovered region. He set sail, with thirty-
five men, and, following the direction pointed out by
Biarne, arrived in view of the unknown land. It was
rude and rocky, with mountains covered with snow
and ice. He named it *Helluland*, or the land of
rocks. He next came to a flat region covered with
forests, which he called *Markland*, or the woody
land. Sailing still farther onward, and favored by a
north wind, he reached a delightful island near the
continent. The soil was fertile, the ground was covered with bushes which bore sweet berries, and there
were a river and lake, amply stored with salmon and
other fish. The grass was covered with dew, sweet
as honey. A German, named Tyrker, penetrated
into the country, and came back in great exultation, announcing that he had discovered grapes. He
showed them the fruit and they gathered large quan-

tities; with which, and the timber they felled, **they** loaded their vessel, and returned home, naming **the** country Vinland.

The next adventurer was Thorwald Ericson, **who** sailed for Vinland in 1002. He arrived at a spot where Leif had built some huts, and to which **he** had given the name of *Leifsbooths*, spent the winter there, and caught fish. The next spring, he sent a party in his longboat to make discoveries to the southward. They found the country beautiful and well-wooded, the trees growing nearly down to the water's edge. There were also extensive ranges of white sand. In 1004, Thorwald sailed eastward and then northward, pas ·ng a remarkable headland enclosing a bay; opposite to which was another headland. He called it *Kialarnes*, or Keel Cape. He then proceeded along the eastern coast to a promontory overgrown with trees, where he landed with all his crew. He was so well pleased with this place that he exclaimed, "This is beautiful; here I should like well to fix my dwelling." On the beach they found three canoes, and a number of Indians, whom the Northmen call *Skrœllings*. They came to blows with them, and killed all but one, who escaped in his canoe. Afterwards a countless multitude came out of the interior of the bay against them. They endeavored to protect themselves by raising battle-screens on the ship's side. The Skrœllings continued shooting arrows at them for a while, and then retreated. Thorwald was mortally wounded, and gave orders that they should bury him on the promontory, and plant crosses at his head and feet. From this circumstance the place was named *Krossares*, or Cross Cape. The following year his men returned to Greenland.

Thorfinn, the brother of Leif and Thorwald, not discouraged by the fate of his kinsmen, fitted out another expedition in 1007. It consisted of three vessels, and one hundred and sixty men. They took with them various kinds of live stock, being determined to form a settlement if possible. In Helluland and Markland, they found much wild game. Sailing a great distance southwesterly, they arrived at Kialarnes, where they found long beaches and hills of sand, called by them *Furthurstrandir*. The land now began to be indented by inlets, and they found grapes and wild grain. They continued their course till they came to a bay penetrating far up into the country. At the mouth of it was an island, where the current ran very swiftly. Here the eider-ducks were so numerous, that it was scarcely possible to walk without treading on their eggs. They called the island *Straumey*, or Stream Island, and the bay *Straumfiord*, or Stream Firth. They landed on the shore of this bay, and made preparations for their winter residence. The company afterwards separated, and one party sailed further south to a place where a river falls into the sea from a lake. Opposite the mouth of the river, were large islands. They steered into the lake, and called the place *Hop*, (Hope.) Grapes and wild grain were growing on the low grounds. Here they erected houses and spent the winter. No snow fell, and the cattle pastured in the open fields.

One morning in the beginning of 1008, a number of canoes were seen approaching. One of the Northmen held up a white shield as a token of peace, and the savages joined them and commenced trading. They were very fond of red cloth, and gave furs in exchange. They would have bought swords and spears, but these the Northmen would not sell. While the traffic was going on, a bull, which had been brought from Iceland, came out of the wood and bellowed loudly; which so frightened the savages, that they all ran to their canoes and paddled off. Towards winter, they came again in great numbers: the Northmen caused the red shield to be borne against them, and they joined battle. The savages had a sort of war slings, and there was a furious discharge of missiles on both sides. The Indians then hoisted a huge ball upon a pole, and swung it from their canoes over the heads of the Northmen, upon whom it fell with a terrible crash. This struck them with a panic, and hey fled, till they were rallied by a female named Freydisa, who displayed the most intrepid courage, and caused the savages to fly in their turn. The hostilities of the natives caused them to abandon this place, and they sailed for Kialarnes, from whence they steered northwesterly. The land was covered with thick forests as far as they could see, and some high hills were discerned in the interior, which they considered to be part of a range connected with the heights of Hop. They spent the next winter at Straumfiord, and afterwards returned to Iceland.

These voyages, and many others which the Northmen made to Vinland, and of which the narratives are so minute and authentic as to place their truth beyond a doubt, render it an indisputable fact, that a considerable part of the coast of America was known to these navigators. By a diligent examination of the routes pursued by them, and a comparison of the same with the coasts of Nova Scotia and New England, it appears that their excursions extended as far as Rhode Island. The bearings, distances and general description of the territories seen by the Northmen, correspond remarkably with the actual situation of the country. *Hellerland* is Newfoundland ; *Markland* is Nova Scotia ; *Kialarnes* is Cape Cod, and *Furthurstrandir* is the long sandy beach of that peninsula ; *Straumfiord* is Buzzard's Bay ; *Straumey* is Martha's Vineyard, and *Hop* is Mount Hope Bay, in Rhode Island ; *Krossanes* is either Point Alderton at the entrance of Boston harbor, or the Gurnet at Plymouth. The heights seen in the interior are Milton Hills.

In Rhode Island and the neighborhood, there are still extant some remarkable relics of antiquity, which many persons regard as belonging to the age of the Northmen.* At Dighton, on Taunton river,

---

* The Royal Society of Northern Antiquities, at Copenhagen, have bestowed great care in the investigation of the Rhode Island antiquities, the result of which may be seen in their great work entitled *Antiquitates Americanæ*. The Newport Tower is supposed to have been an ancient baptistry ; the figures on the Dighton Rock, which correspond in form to those used by the Northmen during the middle ages, they conceive to mean in substance as follows :

Thorfinn, with a hundred and thirty men, took possession of this spot.

This seems to coincide with the account found in the Icelandic Skin Books, which states that in A. D. 1007, Thorfinn.

which falls into Mount Hope Bay, is the famous
" writing rock," covered with sculptured characters,
which have afforded much scope for the ingenuity of

antiquarians. At Newport there is, yet to be seen
the most remarkable architectural ruin in the United

with several ships and a hundred and sixty men, sailed for Vinland, for the purpose of establishing a colony there. He also
took with him cattle, and all such articles as would be needed
in an infant settlement. They reached their place of destina-
tion, and made a settlement at Hop, supposed to be Mount
Hope ; but in consequence of frequent annoyances from the
Indians, they returned to their native country, A. D. 1009.
Beside the inscriptions upon the Dighton Rock above trans-
lated, there are other sculptures, among which are two human
figures, representing, as some conjecture, Gudrida, the wife of
Thorfinn, in a sitting posture, and Snorre, their son—the first
person of European parentage born in this country, to whom
the genealogy of the great sculptor, Thorwaldsen, is traced

States. It consists of the lower portion of a circular tower, built of rubble stone, and resting on arches and pillars. No structure of the kind has ever been known in any other part of the country, nor is there any account, either in writing or tradition, of the date of its erection. It is evidently, of high antiquity and is supposed to be of Scandinavian origin. At Fall River, on Mount Hope Bay, there was discovered, in 1834, the skeleton of a man, who is supposed to have been one of the settlers of Vinland. The body was brought to light by digging down a hill. On the breast was a plate of brass much corroded, but which was evidently a shield or breastplate; and below this, was a curious belt of brass tubes. In the grave were found many arrow-heads of brass, of a fashion entirely unknown among the Indians. There were also appearances of embalmment about the body. In our account of the Pilgrims, we shall have occasion to mention a similar discovery at Cape Cod. These and other relics scattered along the coast are generally regarded as vestiges of the Scandinavian adventurers.

The more recent settlers in Vinland became involved in bloody civil contentions, which had a most disastrous effect upon the colony. In 1121, Bishop Eric, of Greenland, embarked on a missionary voyage to Vinland, the result of which is not known. Men-

ack. There is also a shield of the form peculiar to the ancient Scandinavians, and similar to some used at the present day by the inhabitants of Iceland, the lower portion being fashioned like the tail of a fish; likewise a helmet inverted, typical of the peaceful state of the colony; a quadruped is also seen, which is an emblem not unusual in ancient Icelandic inscriptions, indicative of domestic life.

4*

tion is made of a voyage to Markland as late as **1347**
exactly a century before the birth of Columbus.   After
this, the country appears, for some unknown reason
to have been abandoned by the Northmen, and Vinland gradually became forgotten.

The ancient accounts of these voyages, to borrow the
language of an able writer,* " contain nothing which,
when rightly considered, ought to impair their substantial credibility, on the score of extravagance.
They present many of the characteristics of the legen-
dary tales of rude ages, of the narratives of credulous
mariners, relating their exploits in distant and newly
discovered countries.   The German Tyrker, whose
discovery of the grape gave the name of Vinland to
the region, is represented as having lost his way from
the exhilarating effect of the fruit which he had eaten.
In the image of a German sea-rover intoxicated with
eating fox-grapes, there is indeed a ludicrous extravagance.   So, too, the savage who shot Thorwald is
described as a one-legged animal, a phenomenon
which awakens a burst of poetic admiration on the
part of one of the company.   On the death of Thor-
stein, in Greenland, while his wife, Gudrida, is holding
the lyke-wake, the dead body enters into conversation
with her, and relates her future fortunes in the style
of the epic visions of Greece and Rome.   These are
the ornaments with which a traditionary tale is clothed
by minstrels and rhapsodists ; they are the supersti-
tions of a credulous age ; they are the romantic crea-
tions of weather-beaten mariners, sitting with their
skinny-handed crones around a driftwood fire, during

* N. A. Review, No. 98.

the long Arctic night, and rehearsing the wonders of the sea. Rude but vigorous fancy redeems the frozen and homely poverty of real life. The poor seaman's cabin, excavated under the comfortable lee of a glacier, one half sunk into a frozen soil, the other covered with eternal snow, warms and flashes up with strange pageantry. Its inmates have seen spirits dancing on the northern lights ; they have beheld wild eyes glaring out of the ice-blink, have looked with amazement at the sea-serpent as he curled up and overtopped the mainmast, and have cast their anchor into the small ribs of the kraken. Regarding the age and the region in which these Icelandic traditions must have circulated for two or three generations, we think they have suffered less than might have been expected from the credulity and extravagance, the superstition and the ignorance of their narrators."

COLUMBUS.

FEW things show more strongly the contrast between ancient and modern times, than the science of
navigation. The boldest and most skilful of the ancient seamen confined his enterprise almost entirely
to the practice of timidly creeping along the shore,
while the most ordinary navigator of modern times
boldly adventures across the wide ocean. There is
but a single instance of this in ancient times. The
Alexandrians, in the most advanced state of their skill
and enterprise under the Roman empire, made voyages across the Indian Ocean, from the m·uth of the

Red Sea to the coast of Malabar. The voyage was always performed under the influence of a favorable monsoon, which rendered it safe and certain; and a circuitous route along the coasts of Arabia and Persia had been followed for ages, ere some daring sailor ventured to strike across the ocean to a coast, the situation of which was already known.

The most skilful and adventurous sailors during the middle ages were the Northmen. In the south, navigation received little improvement under the Saracen conquerors. Although for several ages they were the most civilized, intelligent and enterprising people in Europe, yet, having been bred originally in the interior of the Asiatic continent, they never acquired any strong maritime habits. The idea of the termination of the ocean in darkness, which had only floated in the minds of the ancients, was formed by them into a regular creed. The whole circuit of the sounding ocean of the earth, appears in their maps under the appellation of the " Sea of Darkness." A region to which such a name was affixed was not likely to prove inviting even to enterprising navigators. There is, however, the record of a voyage westward from Lisbon, while that city was under the dominion of the Saracens. It was performed by two brothers, called Almagrurim or the " Wanderers," and led to the discovery of some islands at a considerable distance westward, which were probably the Azores. These islands were settled by the Portuguese, who in the fifteenth century were celebrated as the first navigators in the world; yet the whole extent of the Atlantic remained a " sea of darkness," till a bold and enterprising genius arose, and formed a new era in the history of mankind, by tearing away the veil which shrouded the mysterious region, and disclosing a New World to the astonished eyes of Europe.

Christopher Columbus, the person who accomplished this great undertaking, was born in the republic of Genoa, about the year 1447. His father is represented by some writers as a wool-comber, and by others as a bargeman. Humble as was his condition, he nevertheless sent his son to school, where he studied Latin, geometry, cosmography and astronomy; sciences for which he showed an early predilection. He went to sea about his fourteenth year, and his first voyages were in the Mediterranean; but his enterprising spirit, not contented with such narrow bounds, carried him into the northern seas, probably in one of the fishing vessels which then began to frequent Iceland and the polar regions. It is highly probable that in these voyages some tradition of the expeditions of the Northmen to Vinland came to his ears, and proved the origin of those speculations and researches which fired him with the ambition of making discoveries in the west. He afterwards sailed with a famous Genoese corsair of his own name and family, and spent many years cruising against the Mahometans and Venetians, till the vessel in which he served took fire in an engagement, and he with difficulty saved his life by swimming ashore.

Having thus acquired a considerable degree of nautical skill and experience, he repaired to Lisbon, then the great resort of naval adventurers, where his brother Bartholomew seems to have been already established in the business of making maps and charts. Here Christopher married the daughter of a sea captain, employed in voyages of discovery by Prince Henry, of Portugal; thus he obtained access to his journals and charts, and gained a knowledge of all that had been done by the Portuguese in exploring the coast of Africa and the adjacent islands. He made a voyage to Madeira, and for some years traded to that island, the Canaries, the Azores, and the settlements in Africa. From the information which he was thus enabled to obtain, and from profound meditation on the theory of the globe as it was then known, assisted doubtless by the Icelandic traditions, Columbus became fully convinced, not only that there must be inhabited lands farther west, but that a shorter passage to the East Indies, then the great object of the Portuguese navigators, might be found by steering in that direction, than round the continent of Africa. From the letters which passed between him and Toscanelli, a Florentine physician of great skill in cosmography, it appears that he had entertained these ideas as early as 1474.

The ambition of making this great discovery now stimulated Columbus to incessant action. He laid a plan for the voyage before the senate of Genoa, but narrow conceptions, and the want of an enterprising spirit, caused his proposals to be rejected by that body, as chimerical and impracticable. His next application was to John II., of Portugal, who received him favorably, and appointed commissioners to examine his plan. These persons were mean enough, while they pretended to be discussing the matter, to fit out privately a small vessel, the master of which, furnished with the charts of Columbus, was to proceed in the track which he pointed out, and endeavor to anticipate him in his discoveries. This adventurer lacked both the skill and courage requisite for such an undertaking, and was soon compelled to return. Columbus, irritated at the meanness of this transaction, abandoned Portugal, and proceeded to Spain, where he laid his scheme before Ferdinand and Isabella. The kingdom was then involved in a war with the Moors of Granada, and the council to whom the project of Columbus was referred for examination, were not sufficiently enlightened to comprehend his arguments. He was, therefore, exposed to the chagrin of another rejection; and his only hope seemed now to rest upon England, whither he had despatched his brother to lay his proposals before Henry VII.

Columbus was about leaving Spain, when an intimate friend, who had a just estimation of his character, Marchena, the guardian of a monastery near Palos. prevailed upon him to make a second attempt at court. By means of his credit with Isabella, he found means to interest her in behalf of Columbus. But the cold prudence of Ferdinand again caused his rejection, and Columbus was on the point of embarking for England, when the interposition of some zealous patron wrought a sudden change in his favor. The queen now offered to pawn her jewels to raise funds for the enterprise, and a treaty was immediately concluded. Columbus was to be high admiral in all the seas discovered by him, and viceroy in the territories, with a tenth part of the profits accruing from the discoveries. A fleet was immediately fitted out; but the whole adventure of the kingdom of Spain on this great occasion, consisted of but three small vessels, carrying ninety men in all.

With this insignificant equipment, which was destined to accomplish an achievement tenfold more important than that contemplated by the Invincible Armada, Columbus set sail from the small seaport of Palos, in Andalusia, on the 3d of August, 1492. He first directed his course toward the Canaries, where he was obliged to refit his crazy barks, which even in this short run were found unseaworthy. Having accomplished this, he boldly launched into the unknown regions of the Atlantic, on the 6th of September, and stood due west. Scarcely had the fleet lost sight of land, when the courage of his crew, which had hitherto continued firm, began to give way before the terrors of the "sea of darkness." When they found themselves on a trackless ocean, without a chart of the mysterious waste into which they were plunging, doubts and apprehensions began to appall them. Some fell to sighing and weeping, and exclaimed that they never should behold the land again. The variation of the needle, a phenomenon now for the first time observed, struck them with new terror. Columbus, however, continued resolute; he was constantly on deck with the sounding line or astrolabe in his hand, observing every uncommon appearance in the sea and sky, and noting down everything with philosophical accuracy.

Three weeks passed in this manner; no land was

seen; the trade-wind was hurrying them westward, and they had already proceeded to a great distance—greater indeed than they suspected, as Columbus kept two reckonings, the one accurate, for his own use, and the other with diminished computations of each day's sailing, which was open to the inspection of his men. By this artifice, and his ingenuity in explaining every unusual appearance that alarmed the crews, he kept them tolerably quiet for some days longer, when, no signs of land appearing, their terrors were renewed, and a mutinous spirit began to show itself. Some talked of throwing their commander overboard, should he persist in an undertaking which must prove fatal to them all. Columbus, with admirable patience, firmness, and dexterity, by the employment of persuasions, arguments and threats, quelled this rebellious spirit, and continued boldly steering to the west. At length, on the evening of the 11th of October, a light was discovered ahead, and soon after land was seen by the foremost vessel. The fleet lay to, and when the morning dawned they descried a flat and pleasant island, full of limpid rivulets and abundance of green bushes. The crews were filled with the liveliest transports of joy; they threw themselves at the feet of their commander, begging pardon for their past conduct, and almost considering as divinely inspired, the man whom they lately reviled as a visionary and an impostor.

This island was Guanahani, one of the Lucayas or Bahama Islands. Columbus named it San Salvador. This, as well as the neighboring islands, and the still greater ones of Cuba and Hayti, which he visited in

this voyage, were found to be inhabited by an innocent people, in the simplicity of pure nature ready to believe that the Spaniards were superior beings, and too unsuspecting to regard with jealousy any proceedings undertaken by these wonderful strangers. At Hayti, which Columbus named Espanola, he lost one of his vessels by shipwreck. The humanity of the natives enabled him to save all her equipment, and he built a fort on this island, where he left a body of his men, and sailed for home, carrying some of the natives and specimens of the productions of the country, among which was a sufficient quantity of gold to stimulate highly the avarice of the Spaniards. On the voyage to Spain, he encountered a violent storm, in which his two shattered vessels were menaced with destruction. While all his men were overwhelmed with a sense of personal danger, Columbus was meditating on the means of preserving a record of his great discovery. Retiring to his cabin, he wrote a succinct account of all he had seen and done, which he carefully inclosed in wax, secured in a tight cask, and committed to the ocean, in hopes that chance might land it on the coast of Europe. Happily, however, the storm abated, and Columbus, after touching at the Azores and Lisbon, arrived at Palos, after an absence of seven months and eleven days from that port.

His safe arrival was hailed with general rejoicing and unbounded admiration. He was received by the king and queen with all the honors due to one who had accomplished so important an enterprise. His family was ennobled, and every degree of respec was sh... ...im by the court and the grandees. A second expedition was planned, on a much larger scale than the first; and Columbus soon set sail with a fleet of seventeen ships and fifteen hundred men, well equipped for the foundation of a colony. On this second voyage, he fell in with the Caribbee Islands, which he found peopled with a fierce and warlike race of savages, who never permitted the Spaniards to land without a spirited opposition. On reaching Espanola, he found the little garrison which he had left there totally extirpated; a catastrophe brought on by their own ill-conduct toward the natives. The foundation of a town was now laid, named Isabella; expeditions were despatched into the interior in search of gold. The island of Jamaica was also discovered. The avarice and cruelty of the new settlers soon brought a dreadful train of wars upon the unfortunate natives. The outrages of the Spaniards drove them to hostilities. The superiority of the Europeans in arms, discipline and courage, soon triumphed over countless multitudes, and the wretched natives were either put to death, or reduced to servitude.

Columbus having returned to Spain, in order to silence the complaints which the discontented colonists had sent home against him, again embarked in 1498. On this third voyage, he stood farther to the south than before, and discovered the island of Trinidad, at the mouth of the Orinoco, the vast size of which river assured him that it must take its rise in a continent. He next touched upon various parts of the coast of the Spanish Main, which he, however, imagined to be an island. On arriving at Espanola, he found the settlement in a most unprosperous condition, and threatened with a civil war. These troubles he composed as well as he was able; but such a rancorous spirit was excited against him, that his enemies succeeded in persuading the queen to revoke his commission of viceroy, and appoint Bovadilla in his place. This officer, on his arrival in the New World, placed Columbus and his two brothers in irons, and sent them prisoners to Spain. So gross an outrage shocked every honest mind in the kingdom. Blushing for their own ingratitude, and the stain thus thrown upon Castilian honor, the king and queen instantly liberated Columbus, and invited him to court, where he was received with all external civility. Nothing was done, however, to re-instate him in his office; and so deeply did the insult he had sustained sink into his mind, that he always carried about him the fetters he had worn, hung them up in his chamber, and gave orders that they should be buried with him. His passion for discovery, however, induced him to propose another voyage, of which the leading purpose was his original idea of opening a new track to the East Indies.

On this voyage, accompanied by his brother Bartholomew and his son Ferdinand, he set sail for the New World, the last time, in May, 1502. When he arrived at Espanola, he found a fleet of eighteen ships, richly laden, about to sail for Spain. The experience which Columbus had acquired in navigating these seas, enabled him to foresee an approaching hurricane. He requested permission to enter the harbor of St. Domingo, and at the same time warned the fleet not to sail. His request was refused and his warning disregarded. The hurricane came on. By proper precautions, he escaped its fury; but it fell with such destructive violence on the homeward-bound fleet, that only two or three ships were saved. Bovadilla, and several other inveterate enemies of Columbus, perished, with all their wealth; and it was considered remarkable that the ship in which were embarked the remnants of the property of Columbus, was one of those that escaped the general destruction.

He proceeded on his voyage, and explored the coast of the isthmus of Darien, in search of a passage to the South Sea. He then coasted along the continent to the north, where his fleet was shattered by a series of terrible storms. After incredible sufferings, he steered toward Jamaica, and was barely able to keep his ships from sinking long enough to reach that island. Here they were run aground, so completely eaten up by the worms as to be incapable of repair. In Jamaica, Columbus suffered great distress from the mutiny and desertion of his men, and the disaffection of the natives, who withheld their supplies of provisions, till, by the prediction of an eclipse, which immediately followed, he obtained a complete authority over their minds. At length, he was delivered by a squadron which had sailed from Espanola, and, after a short stay at San Domingo, he returned to Spain, in December, 1504.

He had now the mortification of finding his best friend, Isabella, dead; and Ferdinand, always preju-diced against him, was little disposed to redress his injuries. Though received with cool civility, his repeated petitions for a restitution of the dignities and emoluments to which he was entitled by treaty, were neglected or evaded, and he was even insulted with a proposal that he should renounce them for a pension. At length, overwhelmed with cares and disappointments, he closed his life in poverty, at Valladolid, on the 20th of May, 1506. Such were the dishonesty and ingratitude of the Spanish court to the man who, in the language of his epitaph, " gave a new world to Castile and Leon." His eldest son instituted a lawsuit against the king, and compelled him to render that justice which he had denied to his father. The descendants of Columbus have existed in Spain to the present day, under the title of the Dukes of Veragua.

The discoverer of the New World was not only defrauded of the profits of his great achievement, but likewise of the glory of giving his name to the territory which he discovered. Amerigo Vespucci, a Florentine navigator, made several voyages to the New World after Columbus, and published accounts of them, in which, either by a designed fraud or unconscious error, he represented himself as being the first European who saw the main land. Columbus, on his third voyage, made the first discovery of the continent at the mouth of the Orinoco; but the misrepresentation of Vespucci was not exposed till the name of America was given to the northern portion of South America, which he pretended to have originally discovered. Vespucci himself had not the smallest conception of the enormous extent to which this misapplication of his name would spread. America would have been the name of a territory no larger than Cuba or Jamaica, had the region of Paria been an island; but the unbroken extent of the continent caused the name to be gradually applied to larger portions of the New World, till it became a general appellation for a whole quarter of the globe Never before did chance make a man's name so celebrated.

In our concluding remarks, we shall copy the language of Mr. Irving. "Columbus was a man of great and inventive genius. The operations of his mind were energetic but irregular; sallying forth at times with that irresistible force which characterizes intellects of this order. He had grasped all kinds of knowledge connected with his pursuits; and though his information may appear limited at the present day, and some of his errors palpable, it is because knowledge in his peculiar department of science was but scantily developed in his time. His own discoveries enlightened the ignorance of that age, guided conjecture to certainty, and dispelled numerous errors with which he himself had been obliged to struggle. His conduct as a discoverer was characterized by the grandeur of his views and the magnanimity of his spirit. Instead of scouring the newly-found regions like a grasping adventurer, eager only for immediate gain, as was too generally the case with contemporary discoverers, he sought to ascertain their soil and pro ductions, their rivers and harbors. He was desirous of colonizing and cultivating them, and civilizing the natives, of building cities, introducing the useful arts, subjecting everything to the control of law, order and religion, and thus of founding regular and prosperou.

empires. In this glorious plan, he was constantly defeated by the dissolute rabble which he was doomed to command, with whom all law was tyranny, and all order restraint.

"He died in ignorance of the real grandeur of his discovery. Until his last breath, he entertained the idea that he had merely opened a new way to the old resorts of opulent commerce, and had discovered some of the wild regions of the East. He supposed Espanola to be the ancient Ophir which had been visited by the ships of Solomon, and that Cuba and Terra Firma were remote parts of Asia. What visions of glory would have broke upon his mind could he have known that he had, indeed, discovered a new continent, equal to the whole of the Old World in magnitude, and separated by two vast oceans from all of the earth hitherto known by civilized man! And how would his magnanimous spirit have been consoled amidst the chills of age and cares of penury, the neglect of a fickle public, and the injustice of an ungrateful king, could he have anticipated the splendid empires, which were to spread over the beautiful world he had discovered, and the nations and languages which were to fill its lands with renown, and to revere and bless his name to the latest posterity!"

EL DORADO

THE first conquerors of the Spanish Main, as they penetrated into the interior, received information from the various Indian tribes, which worked strongly upon their excited imagination and avaricious feelings. They were assured that by marching a considerable distance to the south, they would come to a region on the shores of a broad lake, inhabited by Indians of a peculiar character, known by the name of Omegas. These people were represented as highly civilized, living under regular laws, principally in a large city, the houses of which were covered with silver. According to the accounts, the magistrates and ministers of religion wore habits of massy gold. All their fur niture was of gold and silver. The nation, equally populous and warlike, kept on foot armies so formidable as to render them the terror of the surrounding tribes. In every part of Venezuela and Caraccas, to which the Spaniards directed their steps, they received similar accounts, and from Indians too far separated by distance to have combined in the invention of the tale. It did not appear that superstition had any share in these traditions, for no supernatural virtue or power was attributed to the Omegas.

These accounts were confirmed by information from other quarters. In Peru, Pizarro and his followers received intelligence of the existence of a nation called the Omaguas, on the borders of a lake to the northeast of that country. The representations agreed with those of Venezuela, respecting the riches of these people, their power and policy. It was said that after the destruction of the Incas, a younger brother of Atahualpa had fled from Peru, carrying with him the greater part of the royal treasures, and founded a greater empire in the north than that of which he had been deprived. Sometimes, this emperor was called the Great Paytiti sometimes the Great Moxo, sometimes the Enim or Great Paru. It is undeniable that Manco Inca, the brother of Atahualpa, made his escape to the regions east of the Cordilleras; the remainder of his history is not clearly known.

An Indian at Lima affirmed that he had been in the capital of this country, the city of Manoa, of which he gave a minute description. Three thousand workmen were employed in the street of the silversmiths. The columns of the emperor's palace were of porphyry and alabaster; the galleries of ebony and cedar; the throne was of ivory, and the ascent to it by steps of gold. The palace stood on a small island in the lake. It was built of white stone. At the entrance were two towers, and between them was a column twenty-five feet in height; on the top of this was a large silver moon; and two *pumas*, or American lions, were fastened to the base with chains of gold. Beyond the place occupied by these was a quadrangle planted with trees, and watered by a silver fountain, which spouted through four golden pipes. The gate of the palace was of copper. Within, a golden sun was placed on an altar of silver, and four lamps were kept burning before it, day and night.

This territory obtained the name of El Dorado, which means " the gilded," and is variously derived. According to some accounts, it refers to the costume of the emperor, who was anointed every morning with a certain precious and fragrant gum, after which gold-dust was blown upon him through a tube, till he was encrusted with gold. This the barbarian thought a more magnificent and costly attire than could be afforded by any other potentate in the world. According to others, it was the chief priest who was gilded. All these stories found a ready belief in the minds of the Spaniards, fashioned to credulity by the wonders of the New World, and the obscurity in which much of it long remained involved. They who could believe in the existence of a fountain whose waters had the virtue to restore to youth and beauty the old and decrepit, could have no difficulty in giving their faith to the golden marvels of El Dorado, a region which differed from the known part of the continent only in enjoying a superiority in wealth. The accounts of Peru itself had been equally incredible before being verified by the conquest.

No geographical fiction ever occasioned so vast an expenditure of human life. The attempts to discover this wonderful region, cost the Spaniards more men and treasure, than all their substantial conquests in the New World. A history of the expeditions in search of El Dorado, would form a most singularly curious and interesting volume. There is nothing in romance to surpass the wonderful dangers, privations and sufferings endured by the adventurers in these undertakings. Yet neither the disasters, nor even the almost total destruction of many of the bands, prevented others from following them. New adventurers were found to follow in quick succession ; although the former had returned discomfited and disappointed, the last always flattered themselves with the hope that the discovery of El Dorado would be accomplished by them. The mania continued for ages, and was considered by some of the Spanish religionists as a device of the devil to lure mankind to their destruction.

Among these daring spirits was Philip Von Hutten, whose expedition is so much the more worthy of notice, as it was very nearly successful, and actually substantiates a part, at least, of the story of El Dorado. As this singular and interesting portion of American history is probably not familiar to most of our readers, we shall dwell with some minuteness upon its details, particularly as they furnish materials the least equiv ocal which can be found, respecting the explanation of the great mystery. Von Hutten was one of those German adventurers who formed the first expedition of the Welsers to Venezuela, in 1528. Less savage than his companions, he did not yield to them in ambition and intrepidity. From the time of his arrival in America, to his death, a period of fifteen years, he seemed scarcely to have enjoyed a single instant of repose. Always on the march, fighting the Indians, living on wild fruits, exposed to all the extremes of an insalubrious climate, his life was a tissue of dangers and sufferings. In the course of his expeditions into the country in 1541, chance led him to a place where he learned that Quesada, one of the conquerors of Santa Fe de Bogota, had just passed with a body of infantry and cavalry, in quest of El Dorado. The news was true. Quesada marched a long distance, suffered much, and discovered nothing. Von Hutten determined to follow in his track, in order to obtain at least a part of the riches of El Dorado, should he arrive too late to share in the conquest.

After many days of incredible fatigue, he reached the province of Papamena. He found there an Indian equally distinguished by his rank and superior understanding. Von Hutten told him of his design. The Indian answered, with every appearance of good faith, that by continuing his march in that direction, he would only find uninhabited countries and deserts, where his men would starve to death. But if he wished, the Indian added, he would conduct him in person to a region abounding in gold and silver; this country was to the east, on the Guayuava, near the

Lake of Parima. The Indian even showed him some apples of gold which his brother had lately brought from thence. Von Hutten saw fit to discredit this account, and pursued the route followed by Quesada, taking the Indian with him as a guide. But after a march of eight days, amid all sorts of difficulties and obstructions, the Indian, seeing that nothing could change the resolution of the Christians, took the opportunity of a dark night to escape. His flight, together with the badness of the roads, excited murmurs against the leader of the band, who, however, continued obstinately bent on pushing forward. All the soldiers complained of him for not following the advice of the Indian. He alone remained immovable in his resolution.

A few days after, they discovered a mountain resembling that at the foot of which El Dorado was said to be situated; but, on exploring it, their hopes were disappointed. The army, now reduced by intense fatigue and suffering, were obliged to pass the rainy season here, and endure the most cruel effects of hunger. Ants and reptiles were their only food. Many of the men swelled up and died in the most excruciating agonies; others lost their hair, their eyebrows, eye-lashes and nails. As soon as the favorable season returned, Von Hutten began his retreat to Coro, then the capital of Venezuela. On his march he was obstructed by inundations, and halted, till the waters should subside, at a village called Nuestra Senora de Fragoa. While his men were reposing themselves, and thought only of the pleasure of returning home, their commander, irritated at his disappointment, fixed his mind upon new endeavors to retrieve his fortunes. From the Indians of the neighborhood, he learnt that there was a region in a certain quarter, richer by far than any that had yet been discovered. The inhabitants, called the Omegas, were represented as a warlike and ferocious race. Other Indians called them Itaguas, but they all agreed as to the topographical situation of the country.

Fired anew with brilliant hopes, Von Hutten determined to march immediately for the Omegas. His army was now reduced to forty men; but as soon as the plains were clear of water, he moved forward. The Indians offered to conduct him safely to the banks of the Guayuava, and they kept their word. He marched to the river by roads tolerably commodious, and there acquired fresh information. The natives told him that the city of Macatoa, through which he must necessarily pass, was on the other side of the river; this he could not cross without a canoe. One of these Indians appeared to him so sincere, that he commissioned him to go and apprize the inhabitants that he was there with forty men, on his way to more distant provinces; and that he requested a passage and the friendship of the natives, to whom he offered his own. The Indian fulfilled this commission, and returned the next morning with the son of the cacique, who was sent by his father to offer his friendship and hospitality to the strangers. Von Hutten, with his men, proceeded to Macatoa, and was received in the kindest manner.

The cacique, being told of their design, informed them that the country of the Omegas was in fact full of gold and silver, but that its population was so great, and so disciplined to war, that their attempt, with so small a body of men, was most rash and impracticable. No prospect of danger or difficulty, however, could shake the inflexible determination of the commander; and he therefore continued his march. The cacique furnished him with guides as far as the next town, which was distant nine days' journey, and gave him also recommendations to the cacique, who was his friend. This march was performed with tolerable comfort, as the roads through the wilderness were well wrought. The second cacique received the strangers with great affability. Like his friend of Macatoa, he told the general that his undertaking was utterly extravagant and desperate; but he also assured him that all which had been related of the Omegas was true. No nation had ever attacked them with success, and it was contrary to common sense to suppose that forty men, even though they had the strength and courage of lions, could subdue a whole nation highly populous and warlike. These representations, however, did not stagger the obstinate and self-willed leader; and the cacique, finding him resolved to make the attempt, consented to guide him to the country he was seeking; but warning him and his men, at the same time, to bear in mind that he had done his utmost to avert their calamitous fate. All this was heard with coolness and indifference; nothing was thought of but the region of gold and silver.

After four days' march, they arrived at a mountain, on the skirts of which they saw four or five villages surrounded by well-cultivated fields, further off their eyes were ravished by the prospect of a broad and most delightful valley, in which stood a city so extensive as to stretch beyond their view. The streets appeared to be regularly laid out, and the houses well and compactly built. " There," exclaimed the cacique, ' is the capital of the Omegas. Behold this famous region whose riches the Spaniards so ardently covet. That edifice in the centre of the city is the dwelling of the governor, and the temple of a number of gods. The population of the place is immense, and the order that is preserved there is admirable. The houses which you see scattered on the sides of the hills round the city, are inhabited by those who practise agriculture, while the others exercise the trade of war. Now that you yourself see the strength of these people, you can reflect anew on the temerity of your project. If you persist, I must withdraw, and pray to the gods to protect your lives."

Nothing could now repress the ardor of the adventurers, inflamed by the sight of the object which they had been so long pursuing. They took leave of the cacique, and marched immediately to the city. On approaching some houses, they met a few of the Indians, who, struck with surprise at the sight of men with beards, white faces, and in strange dresses, instantly took to flight. These were pursued, and Von Hutten unfortunately overtook and seized one of them. The Indian was armed with a lance, and instantly aimed a blow at his adversary, who, finding himself severely wounded between the ribs, quitted his hold, and the Indian escaped. The adventurers soon heard in the city a great noise of drums and other instruments of war, mingled with the most terrific cries. Night was now approaching, and they retreated, carrying off their wounded commander in a hammock.

They passed the night on a neighboring mountain, and the next morning beheld an army of several thousand Indians marching out of the city in pursuit of them. Von Hutten was unable to fight, and resigned the command to his chief officer, Limpias. A battle now ensued, similar to the conflicts between the soldiers of Cortez and the Mexicans. The superior arms, valor and resolution of the Spaniards, enabled them to resist the attacks of an immense throng of assailants. Not one of them was killed; and the Omegas retreated, leaving the field of battle covered with heaps of their slain. But the Spaniards were now convinced of the desperate character of their undertaking, and unanimously agreed that the conquest of the Omegas could not be effected without a much stronger military force. They returned to the cacique who had acted as their guide, and here reposed themselves for some days. The general was cured of his wound, and, after obtaining from the cacique all the information necessary for rendering a second journey more rapid and easy, he took his departure for Coro, intending to organize a new expedition against the Omegas; but before he reached that place, he was assassinated at the instigation of a usurper named Carvajal, who by means of a forged commission had seized upon the government of Venezuela, and did not think himself secure in his usurpation till he had got rid of Von Hutten, who, it seems, had been appointed lieutenant general. His most faithful adherents were also assassinated with him. Such was the close of this memorable expedition, which occupied the space of four years.

Among the numerous adventure s who shared in the expeditions for the discovery of El Dorado, was Sir Walter Raleigh, an Englishman of the highest talent and character. A man of his chivalrous feelings could not but be filled with admiration at the courage and energy which had been exhibited by the Spaniards in the pursuit of this romantic and brilliant object. Having also a firm belief in the real existence of El Dorado, he determined to make an attempt to discover it himself. The multiplied failures of the Spaniards produced in him a strong conviction, not that they had wasted their strength in pursuit of a phantom, but only that they had missed the right way. In classing Raleigh, however, with the knights-errant of El Dorado, we must in justice to his memory state, that his aims were of a far higher order than those of other adventurers. A part of his design was to conquer and colonize Guiana, and thus to extend the sphere of English industry and commerce.

In February, 1595, Raleigh sailed from Plymouth, with five vessels and above a hundred soldiers. On arriving at Trinidad, he made prisoner of the governor, Berrio, who was himself preparing an expedition for El Dorado on a magnificent scale. From hence he sailed to the mouth of the Orinoco, the navigation of which was entirely unknown to the English, bu which it was necessary to ascend in order to reach the grand object of the voyage. A hundred men embarked in boats, as the ships drew too much water to proceed up the stream. In these they continued to advance for a month, exposed to the open air, sometimes under a burning sun, sometimes amid torrents of rain, with no shelter, and no resting-place but the hard boards of their boats. Raleigh's account of their progress through the labyrinth formed by the numerous outlets of the great stream, of their alternate hopes and fears, wants and fortuitous supplies, the aspect of the country and its productions, the natives and their chiefs, and of their entrance at last into the grand channel of the magnificent Orinoco,—is full of interest and variety, and occasionally presents descriptive passages of great beauty, joined also with traits of most extravagant credulity.

After ascending the river about a hundred and eighty miles, the rapid and terrific rise of its waters compelled them to descend. Raleigh firmly resolved soon to return, took formal possession of the country, and made the caciques swear allegiance to Queen Elizabeth. He returned to England at the end of the summer, and published an account of his voyage, containing, in addition to ascertained facts, many marvellous tales which he had picked up among the Indians. His determination to visit America again was inflexible, yet it was not till 1613 that he sailed on his new expedition. This was more disastrous than the former, but we have not room to give the particulars.

The belief in the existence of El Dorado could not be eradicated from the minds of the inhabitants in that quarter. So late as the year 1780, a wild Indian presented himself before the governor of Spanish Guiana, declaring that he came from the borders of Lake Parina. He was plied with questions, which he answered with as mich perspicuity and precision as could be expected of a savage who spoke mostly by signs. He succeeded in making them understand that on the banks of that lake was a city whose inhabitants were civilized and well disciplined in war. He said much of the beauty of the buildings, the neatness of the streets, the regularity of the squares, and the riches of the people. The roofs of the houses were of gold or silver, and the high priest he said was powdered with gold dust. The Indian sketched on a table with a bit of charcoal a plan of the city. The governor was fully convinced of the truth of his representations, and engaged him to serve as a guide to the place.

A body of Spaniards immediately set out for the discovery. They travelled nearly five hundred leagues to the south, by the most difficult and often frightful paths. Hunger, the swamps, the rocks and the precipices, soon wore them out, and most of them died. When the remainder thought themselves within four or five days' journey of the city, their guide disappeared in the night. This utterly dismayed them. They knew not where they were, and after wandering about for some time, all of them perished except Don Antonio Santos. The idea of disguising himself as an Indian occurred to him. He threw off his clothes, stained his body with *roco*, and introduced himself among the savages by means of the knowledge he possessed of many of their languages. He continued a long time among them, and at length fell into the hands of the Portuguese on the Rio Negro. After a long detention, they sent him home, and he died in Guiana, in 1796.

It is impossible not to entertain a great curiosity as to the true origin of a story which led to such results as we have related. Men of intelligence, judgment, and acuteness, some of whom have resided many years in that country, have announced their serious opinion that the story of El Dorado is not destitute of foundation in reality. Unless we suppose the account of Von Hutten to be a complete fabrication, which does not appear warrantable, occurring as it does in the work of a respectable historian, we have evidence at least of the existence of a warlike nation, more civilized than the rest of the Indians, who had built on the borders of Lake Parima a large and handsome city. The eminent traveller Humboldt adopts another method of solving the mystery. While engaged in exploring the countries upon the upper Orinoco, he was naturally led to direct his attention to the origin of a tale of such celebrity, which was still credited in that quarter. " When near the sources of the Orinoco," he says, " we heard of nothing but the proximity of El Dorado, the Lake Parima, and the *ruins of its capital!* " He attempts to account for the tales of El Dorado in a geological way. According to his conjecture, there may be islets and rocks of mica-slate and talc within and around the lake, which, reflecting from their shining surfaces the rays of an ardent sun, appear to form a gorgeous city, whose temples and houses seem to be overlaid with gold and silver. He supposed that this scene was thus formed by the imagination into the gilded metropolis. Humboldt attempted to penetrate to this spot, but was hindered by the Guayacas, a tribe of Indian dwarfs.

The story of El Dorado remains, therefore, still involved in deep obscurity. We cannot, however, withhold our belief that it had some foundation in truth. The reader, perhaps, will be surprised to learn that the region which is pointed out as the locality of this celebrated place, has never, to this day, been traversed by a European. Its great distance from the sea, and the impassable wilderness that surrounds it, have repelled the arms of the conqueror from its borders, while the bravery or ferocity of its inhabitants forbids every traveller to approach it. Is it improbable that a great city, or the ruins of one, should exist in this unknown territory? A few years ago, who suspected that the plains and forests of Central America and Yucatan contained those immense and magnificent ruins brought to light by the researches of modern travellers? Cortez, in his march to Mexico, passed within ten miles of the great city of Copan, without hearing of it.

Mr. Stephens does not hesitate to avow his opinion that aboriginal cities may yet be found, in the unexplored regions of South America, peopled by unconquered natives. The probability of such facts is still greater in respect to a district more remote from European establishments, and which possesses positive traditions attesting their existence.

MIRANDA HURTADO.

A TALE is interwoven in the history of the first establishment of the Spaniards on the banks of the Paraguay, which is so much in the romantic and chivalrous taste of the Spanish literature of that period, that some persons have questioned its authenticity. It is as well attested, however, as any fact in the annals of the country, and is, in itself, so interesting an episode, and relieves so effectually the dryness of historical detail, by varying the scene from public and general events to those of a domestic and personal nature, that it would scarcely be excusable to omit it in this volume.

Sebastian Cabot, in 1526, discovered the great river where the Spaniards obtained the first silver seen in America, and which, on that account, received the name of the Rio de la Plata, or "River of Silver." He sailed up this river, and on the shore of the Paraguay, one of its main branches, he built a fortification, which he named the fort of Espiritu Santo. Here he left a garrison of a hundred and twenty men, under the command of Nuno de Lara, and returned to Spain. Lara, seeing himself surrounded by nations of savages, from whom he could expect no friendship, except in proportion as he showed himself friendly to them, made exertions to gain the good will of one of the nearest and most powerful tribes, the Timbues

A friendly intercourse was soon established between these Indians and the Spaniards, which speedily led to consequences which had never entered into the conception of either party.

One of Lara's principal officers, Sebastian Hurtado, was accompanied by his wife, Lucia Miranda, a lady of singular beauty. Though the American Indians in general have shown themselves little susceptible of the tender passion, yet this has not been uniformly the case. Mangora, the cacique of the Timbues, in the course of his frequent visits to the Spaniards, became deeply enamored of this fair Castilian. It was not long before she perceived it, and knowing how much was to be feared from a savage chieftain, with whom it was for the interest of all to live upon good terms, she endeavored by all the means in her power to avoid being seen by the cacique, and to guard against any surprise. Mangora, on his part, revolving the means by which he could get her into his power, often pressed her husband to pay him a visit, and to bring his wife with him. Hurtado had been informed by Miranda of the passion with which the savage chief was smitten, and the apprehensions she felt for the consequences. With a policy suited to the emergency, he declined the cacique's invitation, alleging that a Spanish soldier could never leave his camp or garrison without the permission of his commander, nor could with honor ask that permission except to fight the enemy.

The cacique was sufficiently shrewd not to be deceived by this reply and soon became sensible that, for the accomplishment of his purpose, the removal of the husband was a necessary step. Nourishing his passion with the utmost ardor, he was incessantly brooding over schemes for the attainment of the object of his desire. By watching every movement of the Spaniards, he discovered at length that Hurtado had been sent out of the fort with a company of fifty men to collect provisions. This seemed o offer a favorable opportunity for making an attempt to seize the lady, as it not only removed the husband, but weakened the garrison. He determined to practise a stratagem for the surprisal of the place. He selected four thousand of his best warriors, and posted them in ambush in a marsh not far distant. Himself, with thirty others, then set out for the fort, loaded with provisions. On arriving at the gates, he sent a message to Lara, informing him that he had heard that the garrison were in want of supplies, and he had brought a quantity sufficient to last them till the return of the foraging party. The commander received the treacherous cacique without suspicion, offered him every possible mark of friendship and confidence, and insisted upon giving an entertainment to him and his followers.

This was precisely what Mangora had expected, and accordingly he had given his men instructions how to proceed, and appointed signals for the ambush in the neighboring marsh. The feast was spread, and the entertainment lasted till beyond midnight; when, just as the Spaniards were rising to bring it to a close, the magazines of the fort were discovered to be on fire. The signal had been given, and the Indians had rushed from their ambush, and entered the place. All was now confusion and slaugh-

ter: the Spaniards, whether sleeping or waking
were everywhere put to death. Lara, however, revenged himself upon the author of this bloody treachery. Having received a severe wound, he sprang
upon the cacique, and running him through the body,
laid him dead at his feet, but was himself immediately overpowered and slain by the Indians. Of all
the Spaniards in the fort none remained alive but
Miranda, the innocent cause of this terrible catastrophe, with four other women, and as many children,
who were all pinioned and carried off to the residence
of the Indians.   —

Siripa, the brother of Mangora, succeeded him as
cacique. He also became deeply enamored with
the beautiful Miranda, and reserving her to himself,
he relinquished the other captives to his attendants.
He entreated her not to think of herself as a prisoner,
and solicited her favor with a gentleness and address
that love alone could inspire in the breast of a savage.
He compared the situation of her husband with his
own: the one a forlorn fugitive in the forests of a
hostile country, the other the chief of a powerful nation, and possessing unbounded wealth and luxuries.
But the virtue of Miranda was proof alike against
persuasion, and the fear of slavery and death. Siripa's offers were scornfully rejected; and her behavior
towards him was marked by a degree of acrimony,
intended to excite his rage, and impel him to put her
at once to death, by which she hoped to escape a more
fearful danger. Her conduct, however, had a very
different effect, and contributed to heighten the passion of the savage lover, by increasing his esteem of

her, and enhancing the value of the expected conquest by throwing new difficulties in his way. He treated her with moderation and gentleness, and showed her more civility and respect than could well have been expected of a chieftain little accustomed to control.

In the mean time, Hurtado with his troops had returned to the fort, where they found only a heap of smoking ruins and the dead bodies of their countrymen. Ranging the neighborhood to learn the cause of this fatal calamity, he fell in with some Indians, from whom he learnt that the Timbues had been the authors of the deed, and that his wife was a captive among them. He could not doubt of the motive which prompted this act of treachery, and was aware of the danger which threatened him, should he place himself in the power of their perfidious chief; but his conjugal affection prevailed over his fears, and he immediately sought the place where he hoped to meet his unfortunate spouse. On his arrival among the Timbues, he was made prisoner, and Siripa, indignant at his presumption, as well as feeling the bitterest hatred toward the man who alone possessed the affections of Miranda, and was, as he conceived, the sole obstacle to his happiness, instantly ordered him to be bound to a tree, and shot to death with arrows.

But the power of beauty again prevailed, and the eloquent intercessions of Miranda soothed the fierceness of the savage. The life of Hurtado was spared, and he was unbound; but nothing could induce the cacique to release his wife. Tormented with various passions, he seemed at times determined to sacrifice

7*

the husband to his jealous rage; but at other periods the desire of gaining the good will of his fair captive so far overcame his enmity, that the husband and wife were even permitted to see each other. Their interviews became gradually more frequent and unrestrained, but one fatal interdiction marred their happiness. The cacique warned them against any indulgence in such caresses as might awaken his dormant envy. But vain were the considerations of prudence, and vain the resolutions which they had formed to treat each other with a coolness and reserve that might allay the jealousy of the savage inamorata. Siripa one day surprised them in each other's arms, and, in a paroxysm of ungovernable rage at their contempt of his orders, and their presumption in committing this outrage upon his feelings, he instantly ordered them both to execution. This sentence was carried into effect without delay. Hurtado died by the punishment from which he had before escaped; and Miranda perished in the flames.

THE TYRANT AGUIRRE.

THE legend of El Dorado is in some measure connected with the history of Lope de Aguirre, a man who figured in the adventures referred to in the preceding pages, and whose bloody deeds obtained for him the name of *El Tirano*, or the Tyrant, by which he is remembered to this day in those countries which formed the theatre of his exploits. He was born at Onate, in the province of Guipuzcoa, in Spain, and was of noble blood but of poor parents. In the early part of his life he served in the lowest employments, and grew up with a very bad reputation. At what period he left his native country for the New World, is not known; but even among the infamous adventurers who, in those days, swarmed in Peru, he was notorious for his evil deeds. In all the revolts by which that country was disturbed after the conquest, he bore a part; sometimes engaged on one side, and sometimes on the other, and acquiring an ill fame with all. Alone, he is said to have lacked courage; but to have been brave even to rashness when surrounded by his companions. He was short and meagre, lamed by a wound which he had received in the king's service, and mean in aspect, with a restlessness of eye which indicated a suspicious and perturbed spirit.

This man became the chief actor in one of the

most singular tragedies in American history. Abou
the year 1560, a horde of Brazilian savages, wandering first in search of some resting-place beyond the
reach of the Portuguese, and then flying before the
enemies whom they provoked on their march, made
their way, after ten years' travel, into the provinces
of Quito. Here they gave out that they had passed
through the territory of the Omaguas, which they
found full of large towns, the streets of which were
teeming with goldsmiths; to these, they added other
particulars of their adventures, highly exciting to the
avarice of the Spaniards. This occasioned a great
sensation in Peru. The Marquis de Cañete, their
viceroy, was solicited to send out an expedition for
the conquest of El Dorado, which it was now supposed would surely be discovered. He was glad of
an occasion to rid the country of a troop of turbulent
spirits, who were already too numerous, and from
whom new rebellions were to be apprehended. Nor
is it unlikely that the viceroy himself partook of the
general credulity. He therefore furnished money for
the expedition from the treasury, and some on his
own account. Pedro de Orsua, a knight of Navarre,
and a man of talent and experience, was appointed to
the command.

The force raised consisted of three hundred Span
'ards, and a hundred mestizos. Forty of the Spaniards
were men of rank; but of the remainder, so many
had borne a part in the late rebellions, that the government, seeing them thus collected, began to fear the
consequences of its own policy. Orsua's friends were
alarmed for his safety; and one of them wrote to him,

warning him against some of his men, among whom was Aguirre. He besought him, also, not to take with him a beautiful widow, who was his favorite, Dona Inez de Atienza; as such a proceeding might draw after it the most fatal consequences. This advice was given in vain. Orsua, as if impelled by an evil genius, set out on his expedition, carrying with him the two individuals who speedily proved his ruin.

The sufferings of Pizarro's army had warned Orsua against attempting to proceed by land; he therefore determined to build two brigantines and nine flat-bottomed boats, on the head streams of the Amazon, and sail down that river, which he expected would conduct him to the land he was seeking. While these vessels were on the stocks, he sent thirty men forward, with orders to proceed twenty leagues down to the province of the Caperuzos, or hooded Indians; there to collect what provisions they could, and wait for another detachment; then proceed in company to the river Cocama, and remain laying in stores till joined by the main body of the corps. Instead of following these instructions, the detachment went more than two hundred leagues down the river, past the mouth of the Cocama, and landed on an island. By this time, they were in a starving condition, having been forced to feed on alligators by the way. They now fortified themselves with a palisade; and the natives, after suffering severely in repeated attacks upon them, sent a party to them with a present of provisions and a peace-offering. The adventurers, always suspecting treachery, because they were ever ready to perpetrate

F

it themselves, decoyed the unsuspicious Indians into a hut, fell upon them, and massacred more than forty of them. This cruelty terrified the inhabitants of the whole country; all the natives, who thought themselves within the reach of the Spaniards, abandoned their dwelling-places, and the party were enabled to procure subsistence for three months, till they were joined by Orsua.

That chieftain had met with disasters at his very outset. Six of his boats proved useless, and he was compelled to leave behind the greater part of his baggage, and most of his live stock. Of three hundred horses, he could embark only forty; the rest were abandoned to run wild. The whole expedition now fell down the river. The natives along the banks generally abandoned their houses and fled; but in some places they held intercourse with the Spaniards. Orsua gave strict orders that no trade should be carried on with them except in his presence, that he might be certain that no injustice was practised toward the Indians. Notwithstanding this, some of his men plundered and robbed them without scruple By this time, he had begun to perceive what a set of desperadoes he had collected together; and it was not long before symptoms of mutiny were disclosed. A man named Alonzo de Montoya was detected in a plot to steal some of the canoes and stores, and make his way, with a band of accomplices, back to Peru. Orsua inflicted no heavier chastisement upon him than to secure him for a time with an iron collar. His mode of punishing other offences was to make the offenders pull at the oar for a certain number of days, a labor which was probably at other times performed by the unfortunate Indians, whom they carried along with them.

The expedition proceeded, according to their own computation, seven hundred leagues down the Amazon; sometimes passing deserts, and at other times populous countries; they also encountered every kind of adventure with the Indians. No tidings were yet heard of El Dorado, and the hopes of the most ardent were desponding. Murmurs arose, and the men whispered to each other, that it was better to return to Peru, lest they should all perish. These discontents were instigated by a party whose original object in joining the expedition was to turn back, under some leader, and attempt to seize the government of Peru, that the old days of anarchy and the sword might be resumed. Aguirre, Zalduendo, Vandera and Chaves, the men against whom Orsua had been especially warned, were among the foremost of this party. Zalduendo and Vandera had both set their eyes upon Orsua's mistress. One of the complaints which they urged against him with most effect, was, that he doted upon this woman as if she had thrown over him a species of enchantment; that she, and not Orsua, commanded the army; that the men were condemned to the oar like galley-slaves, only that they might row her canoe; that the commander was dallying with her, when he ought to be attending to the welfare of his men; and that, instead of lodging in the midst of his army, as his duty bade him, he always took up his quarters apart, that he might not be disturbed in his amusements. A strong party of conspirators was now formed; they were all of low birth, and a leader was wanting respectable enough to give some show of authority to their proceedings. The men of rank were attached to the general, but at length they prevailed on Don Fernando de Guzman to come into their plot. A secret council was held; and a proposition was made to put Orsua and Vargas, his lieutenant, to death; to return to Peru; to seize upon the government and make Guzman its lord. He had neither the virtue nor the understanding to take alarm at this desperate proposal, but, drunk with ambition, he consented to the measures which these wretches advised. The proposed sentence of death was passed.

By this time suspicion was excited among the general's friends, though none could foresee the extent of the treason. They warned him that there was mischief impending, and besought him to have a trusty guard about his person. But, as this would have prevented him from being alone with Dona Inez, he gave no heed to the advice. "These precautions are needless," said he; "there are so many men of Biscay and Navarre in the army, that I have only to speak a word in Basque, and I am safe." A more emphatic warning might have roused him, had it but reached his ear. Juan Gomez de Guevara, an elderly man of high character, and one of his best friends, was at a late hour enjoying the freshness of the night air before his lodging, which was next to that of the general, when a figure passed him in the shade, and he presently heard a voice exclaim, "Pedro de Orsua, governor of Omagua and El Dorado, God have mercy upon thee!" Guevara followed the image but it was gone. He supposed it to be supernatural, and when he communicated the warning to some of Orsua's friends, they, having the same belief, agreed not to mention it to the general, because he was at that time indisposed. It was on the night after the murder had been resolved upon, that the voice was heard; most probably one of the conspirators, conscience-smitten, took this measure to put the victim on his guard.

The night of New Year's day was fixed upon for the execution, because, that being a festival, it was supposed less caution would be observed than usual. It would almost seem that some good angel made one more effort to save the infatuated leader. A negro of Vandera's discovered the plot, and, at the risk of his own life, found means to go to Orsua's lodging to tell him of his danger. He was alone with Dona Inez when the negro arrived. Even on such an errand the man could not obtain admittance; he dared not wait, and imparted his intelligence to a black slave of the general. The latter, perhaps being in the conspiracy, or, it may be, hating his master, never delivered his message. When it was night, the chief conspirators assembled, and sent a mestizo in Guzman's name to beg a little oil of Orsua, a pretext for discovering whether he was alone. At a late hour, they sallied out, and found the chieftain in his hammock, conversing with a page. He demanded what they wanted at such a time; they replied by plunging their daggers into his bosom. Vargas was despatched immediately afterward, and the conspirators shouted " Liberty! liberty! long live the king! the tyrant is slain! "

VII.—8

By threats and promises, all the soldiers were forced into the ranks of the mutineers; no man daring to resist, because each felt himself alone, and knew not upon whom he could rely. Guzman was declared king, and all allegiance to the king of Spain was formally renounced. The new monarch immediately appointed his household; he had his chamberlain, his high steward, his carver, his pages and his gentlemen, to all of whom he assigned salaries upon the treasury of Peru. He was served at table with the pageantry of a real court, and his orders were issued in the name of "Don Fernando de Guzman, by the grace of God King of Terra Firma and Peru," and heard hat in hand. The plan of the campaign was now arranged. They proposed to proceed to the island of Margarita, where they knew no resistance could be made, and where they could obtain a supply of provisions. From hence, they were to cross the isthmus of Darien, seize upon Panama, and all the ships in the harbor. They expected to be joined here by many volunteers from Veragua and Nicaragua, and by the negroes who were then in insurrection. With a force thus collected, and the artillery which they expected to obtain at Panama and Nombre de Dios, they intended to invade Peru, where there were no troops capable of resisting such a force. So great was their confidence of success, that grants of land were solicited and bestowed; the ruffians adjusted every 'hing beforehand, that there might be no disputes after the conquest.

Aguirre was the master spirit in all these proceedings, and Guzman was only a feeble puppet in his hands. The latter soon became sensible of this, and fear overpowered his ambition. He felt that his only safe course was to discard his crown, return to his allegiance, pursue the original object of the expedition, and by his services make atonement for what had been done. In this opinion his friends concurred, and in a secret consultation it was resolved to put Aguirre to death. Unfortunately, this was deferred till they should all be embarked in the brigantines which they were constructing to transport them to Margarita. The infatuated usurper did not perceive that Aguirre was constantly taking measures to strengthen himself, by remodelling the army, and placing his trusty adherents in authority. Those whom the crafty conspirator desired to get rid of, he ordered to be strangled. Zalduendo, his ancient associate in crime, was put to death among others. It was told him that on the preceding day, when Dona Inez was weeping at the funeral of a mestiza child, she had exclaimed, "God be merciful to thee, my child! thou wilt have many companions before many days are over!" This was sufficient provocation for a wretch who delighted in murder, and he immediately assembled his ruffians. Zalduendo, whose favorite Inez had now become, knew for what purpose they were collected, and hastened to Guzman, to entreat his protection; but Aguirre with his assassins slew him in the presence of the king. He then despatched two desperadoes to take the life of Inez. These executed their bloody commission, and seemed to take delight in defacing the beautiful form which had been the cause of so much trouble.

From this hour, the wretched Guzman never lost

the deadly paleness which came over him on witnessing these horrible deeds, nor ever again smiled or made a show of cheerfulness, but wore the countenance of one struck aghast with despair; neither had he sense or courage to take any measures against the outrageous tyranny of Aguirre, or make one struggle in his own defence. This pusillanimity accelerated his destruction. Two of his friends who had been of a secret council where the death of Aguirre was resolved, believing that such a secret could not long be kept, thought to escape the consequences of discovery by betraying it themselves to the dreaded tyrant. This intimation startled him, for till now he had despised Guzman too much to think of him with fear. His measures were soon taken for the assassination of the mock king. A few days after, Aguirre, with a band of adherents, burst into Guzman's lodgings early in the morning; he was in bed, but starting up at their coming, and seeing Aguirre, he exclaimed, "What is all this, my father?" for by that term he was accustomed to call him since the contract of a marriage between Aguirre's mestiza daughter, who accompanied the expedition, and the brother of Guzman, who had been left in Peru. The wretch bade his excellency fear nothing, and passed on to the inner apartment, where he slew four of Guzman's friends; meantime the others discharged their arquebuses into the body of their victim, thus concluding his miserable and disgraceful mockery of royalty.

Aguirre now became the nominal as well as real chief of the band. They sailed down the stream, plundering the Indians when they did not find them too numerous and warlike. No considerable number of days could be passed by Aguirre without some execution. He feared every man who seemed to have a friend; and whenever an officer became popular in the army, he was speedily strangled or stabbed. After a long and wearisome voyage down the river, they reached the ocean, and steered towards Margarita. In seventeen days, they came in sight of the island, and anchored in a port which is still called Traitor's Harbor, in remembrance of that event. Scarcely had the vessels anchored, when, upon some pretence, the tyrant ordered two more of his men to be executed. One of them cried out so loudly for "confession" while they were endeavoring to pass the cord round his neck, that the executioner, fearing that his cries would be heard on shore and excite alarm, stabbed him to the heart. Aguirre landed in the evening, and in the morning sent one of his men to the city of Margarita, to inform the inhabitants that they had come down the Amazon, and were in great distress for want of provisions. The people, suspecting nothing, exerted themselves to relieve the necessities of the strangers. Aguirre landed a strong body of his musketmen, and by an artifice decoyed the governor into his presence and made him prisoner. The adventurers then pushed forward to the city, crying "Liberty! liberty! Lope de Aguirre forever!" They took possession of the citadel, then scoured the streets, disarming all the inhabitants, and committing whatever outrages they pleased. Aguirre went into the public square and ordered his men to cut down the gallows : but it was made of lignumvitæ, and they broke their axes upon it to no purpose.   Next he proceeded to the treasury, forced the doors, broke open the royal chest, seized all the gold and pearls which it contained, which were of considerable amount, and destroyed the records.

His next measure was to issue a proclamation, ordering every inhabitant of the island to appear before him with all his arms of whatever kind, on pain of death, and forbidding any one to go out of the city without his permission, on the same penalty.   An inventory was made of all the goods in the city, and the owners were forbidden to touch any part of them as they valued their lives.   While Aguirre was thus intent on plunder, he was not unmindful of more important measures ; he ordered all the boats and canoes of the island to be broken up, that no person might carry intelligence of his designs to the main. These were but the beginning of miseries to the wretched inhabitants of Margarita.   The greater the excesses of Aguirre's ruffians, the more he seemed to be pleased, and they who were the most-savage were his favorites.   He used to say that the soldiers who told their beads were not fit for his service ; he wanted fellows who would throw dice with the devil, and stake their souls upon the cast.   Upon their fidelity he could have no reliance, and therefore he encouraged them to commit crimes, which he thought would make them faithful to him by cutting off all hopes of pardon.

After a stay of forty days in Margarita, during which every deed of wanton and diabolical cruelty

was committed, Aguirre passed over to the continent.
He had three banners made of black silk, bearing
bloody swords laid across, to signify the slaughter he
should make, and the mourning which would follow.
In one of his strange humors, he caused these banners
to be consecrated in the church, and then delivered
them to his captains, charging them to respect the
women and the churches, but in other things to follow
their own inclinations. He landed at Burburata with
a force now reduced to one hundred and fifty men.
The houses had all been abandoned, for the alarm was
general along the coast, and as soon as his vessels
appeared in sight, all the inhabitants fled. He burnt
the vessels and quartered his troops in the town, proclaiming war with fire and sword against the Spanish
authorities, declaring that every person who did not
voluntarily join him should be executed, and ordered
his men to give no quarter, on pain of death to themselves. He then began his march into the interior.
Everywhere the terrified inhabitants fled into the
woods, and every step of his progress was stained by
blood. It would be tiresome and disgusting to detail
the freaks of this mad wretch. At length, a strong
military force was collected by the Spaniards to
check his progress. Aguirre's followers deserted one
by one, and at last he was besieged in the town of
Baraquicimeto. All his dreams of conquest were
now over; most of his men had deserted, and only
a handful of veteran miscreants remained. They
killed their dogs and horses for food, and after some
days, Aguirre, finding himself in danger of starvation,
determined to make a desperate effort to retreat to the

coast.   On the morning of the fifth day of the siege, he ordered their arms to be taken from most of the soldiers, and loaded upon the beasts that remained, and prepared to set out.   This last act of suspicion completed his ruin : the men asked if he was leading them to slaughter, that they were thus to go forth unarmed.   Their pride also was wounded : it was disgraceful, they said, to turn back, as if they wanted courage to proceed.   These things were said so loudly, and discontent was so nearly ripening into open mutiny, that the falling tyrant restored the arms of the men, craving pardon for what he had done.   There were some who sullenly refused to receive their weapons till Aguirre condescended personally to entreat them.

The besiegers, having been informed by deserters of the intended retreat, advanced up to the fort, and called out to the soldiers, warning them not to be deceived any longer by the traitor, but to come over at once to the king's standard, while a free pardon was yet to be obtained.   A body of fifteen arquebusiers sallied out as if to attack the besiegers, but, watching a favorable opportunity, they went over to them with the cry of "Long live the king."   The main body of Aguirre's men, seeing this, thought that all hope of resistance was over, and that not a moment was to be lost in securing their own pardon.   With this intent they all advanced.   The tyrant imagined they were going to attack the enemy, but in a few minutes he saw them mingle in the opposite ranks, and heard them shout, "Viva el Rey."

The unhappy wretch now perceived that his career of crime was at an end.   Not one of his companions

In atrocity remained except Llamoso, a miscreant who had even exceeded his master in guilt: but he was faithful to the last to the tyrant whom he had sworn to serve. Aguirre asked him why he also did not go and receive the king's pardon. He replied that he had been his friend in life, and would be so in death. Aguirre made him no answer, but went into a chamber where his daughter was sitting in company with a young woman who had come with her from Peru. " Say thy prayers, child," said he, " for I must kill thee!"—" Why?" she exclaimed. He replied— " That thou mayst never live to be reviled, and called the daughter of a traitor." Thus saying, he drew his dagger and stabbed her to the heart. Shortly after, his enemies burst in upon him. Aguirre begged for his life, stating that he had matters to communicate which were of importance to the king's service. But his own men were desirous that he should not live to make confessions which might show how deeply they were implicated in the atrocities which had been committed, and he was immediately shot. At the first discharge, he exclaimed, " That 's badly done ;" at the second, " That will do," and instantly expired.

The character of this sanguinary monster has hardly a parallel even in the blood-stained pages of South American history. Aguirre is still spoken of 'ong the Spanish Main by the name of " The Tyrant ; and it is the popular belief that his spirit, perturbed and restless now, as when it animated his body, still wanders over the scenes of his guilt, in the form of that fiery vapor which is frequently seen in the island of Margarita and the savannas of the continent, ever fleeing at the approach of man.

A BUCCANEER.

THE BUCCANEERS.

THE West Indies in the sixteenth century gave rise to a singular association of adventurers, who, from an obscure origin, gradually acquired great power, became famous for their courage, enterprise and crimes, and were for a long period the terror of those regions. These were the Buccaneers, or Brethren of the Coast, called by the French " *Flibustiers*." They first attract our notice in the island of St. Domingo. After the failure of the mines in that island, it was almost utterly neglected by the Spaniards; the greater part of its flourishing cities were abandoned by the inhabitants, and the few who remained were sunk into the most enervating indolence. A number of French wanderers who had been driven out of St. Christopher's by the Spaniards, took refuge here, and subsisted by hunting wild cattle. They met with no interruption from the Spaniards, and their numbers were augmented by adventurers from all quarters. They derived their name of Buccaneers from the Caribs, who taught the settlers in the West Indies a curious method of preserving meat, by smoking and drying. This meat was called *boucan*, and constituted the principal food of these adventurers.

As they had no wives nor children, they generally lived two and two together for mutual assistance; and when one died, the survivor inherited the property of his companion. Without government or laws, they had certain rules and customs adapted to their situation; nor do they seem to have had any great reason to lament the want of a more perfect policy. Differences seldom arose among them, and were easily adjusted. The dress of a Buccaneer consisted of a shirt dipped in the blood of an animal just slain; a pair of trowsers; a leather girdle, from which hung a short sabre and some Dutch knives; a hat without a rim, except a fragment before, to pull it on and off; and shoes of raw hide, without stockings. Each man had a heavy musket, and commonly a pack of twenty or thirty dogs. At daybreak, they usually set out in pursuit of wild cattle, and did not return till they had killed one apiece. The hides were sold to the Dutch and others, who resorted to the island for this trade, as soon as the Buccaneers began to be known. They possessed servants and slaves, consisting of those unfortunate persons who were decoyed to the West Indies, and sold, or who indented themselves for a certain number of years. These men were treated with great rigor. One of them telling his master that God had forbidden the practice of working on Sunday, by saying, " Six days shalt thou labor, and on the seventh thou shalt rest;" the Buccaneer replied, " And *I* say to thee, ' six days shalt thou kill cattle, and on the seventh shalt thou carry their hides to the shore.' "

The labor of each week was the same, till they had furnished the stipulated number of hides; for they had regular contracts with the traders. They drank nothing but water; and their *boucan* was seasoned with pimento and orange juice. After a time, they began to make inroads upon the Spanish settlements, and furnish themselves with other necessaries. The Spaniards, too indolent to make effectual defence, procured soldiers from the neighboring islands, who fell upon the scattered parties of the Buccaneers, and put many of them to the sword. Seeing themselves in danger of being totally exterminated, they adopted a new organization : and by acting in concert, they laid waste the Spanish settlements with fire and sword. The Spaniards saw no other means of getting rid of these ferocious enemies than the destruction of all the wild cattle by a general chase. This had the desired effect. The Buccaneers abandoned St. Domingo, and took refuge in the small island of Tortuga.

They now found themselves absolute lords of an island, eight leagues long and two broad, mountainous and woody. The northern coast was inaccessible ; the southern had an excellent harbor. So advantageous a situation soon brought to the spot a multitude of adventurers and desperadoes from every quarter ; and the Buccaneers from cattle-hunters became pirates. It was at this period that they assumed the name of the Brethren of the Coast. They made their cruises in open boats, exposed to all the inclemencies of the weather, and captured their prizes by boarding. They attacked the ships of every nation, but the Spaniards were the grand object of their hostilities ; they imagined that the cruelties exercised by them upon the natives of America, offered a sufficient apology for any violence that could be committed upon that nation. Accommodating their conscience to these principles of religion and equity, they never embarked upon an expedition without publicly offering up prayers for success; nor did they ever return laden with booty without solemnly thanking God for their good fortune.

In dividing their booty, they first provided a compensation for such as were maimed in the expedition. If any one had lost a right arm, he received six hundred dollars, or six slaves, and in proportion for other wounds.   After this, the remainder was divided equally.   The commander could claim but one share, although, when he had acquitted himself ably, they complimented him with several shares.   The spoil being   divided, the Buccaneers abandoned themselves to all kinds of rioting and licentiousness, till their wealth was expended, when they went to sea again.   They seldom attacked any except the homeward bound European ships, as these always carried gold and silver.   They commonly pursued the Spanish galeons and flota as far as the Bahama channel, and if by accident a ship separated from the rest, they instantly attacked her, and she seldom escaped.   Such a terror did their very name inspire, that the Spaniards generally surrendered the moment they came to close quarters.

The Buccaneers rapidly increased in numbers and strength.   They sailed in larger vessels, and carried on their enterprises with still greater audacity.   Miguel de Basco captured, under the guns of Porto Belo a Spanish galeon valued at a million of dollars. Lawrence, another Buccaneer, in a small vessel, with a few hands, was pursued and overtaken by two Spanish ships, carrying one hundred and twenty guns and seven hundred men, which he repelled. Montbars, a French gentleman, was induced to join the Buccaneers by an unconquerable antipathy to the Spaniards, which he had imbibed in his youth by reading the history of the cruelties which they had practised upon the native Americans. This antipathy rose even to frenzy. His heated imagination, which he loved to indulge, constantly presented to him innumerable multitudes of innocent people swept away by a set of ruthless adventurers nursed among the mountains of Castile. These unhappy victims seemed to call upon him for vengeance; he longed to imbrue his hands in Spanish blood; and no sooner had war broken out between France and Spain, toward the middle of the seventeenth century, than he embarked for America, where he became one of the most formidable of the Buccaneer commanders. His audacious courage was equalled only by the pleasure he took in avenging the slaughter of the Indians by shedding torrents of Spanish blood. Humanity in him became the source of the most unfeeling barbarity.

Two Buccaneers, Lolonois and Basco, sailed for the Spanish Main, with eight vessels and six hundred and sixty men. At the entrance of the Lake of Maracaybo, they attacked and captured the castle which defended the strait. Passing up the lake, they next captured the city of Maracaybo, where they spent a fortnight in rioting and debauchery. The inhabitants had carried their most precious effects to Gibraltar, at the further end of the lake, which the Buccaneers might have taken, had they proceeded directly thither. But by delaying, they gave the Spaniards time to erec.

fortifications, and they defended these long enough to enable the inhabitants to transport their wealth to another place for security. Exasperated by this disappointment, the Buccaneers set fire to Gibraltar, and Maracaybo would have shared the same fate, had it not been ransomed. Besides the money which they received for sparing the city, they carried off all the crosses, pictures and bells of the churches, intending, as they said, to build a chapel at Tortuga, and consecrate this part of their spoil to sacred purposes.

Henry Morgan, an English Buccaneer, sailed on an expedition against Porto Belo, in 1668. He captured the town before the Spaniards could take any measures for its defence. The citadel held out, and the chief citizens had retired into it with their most valuable effects, and all the plate of the churches. Morgan practised a stratagem to reduce the fortress without any loss. He compelled the priests, nuns and other women whom he had taken prisoners, to plant the scaling-ladders against the walls, from a persuasion that the gallantry and superstition of the Spaniards would not suffer them to fire upon the objects of their love and veneration. But the governor was a sturdy and resolute soldier, and ordered his men to repulse all assailants. Morgan, therefore, found himself compelled to storm the citadel. The garrison made an obstinate defence, and great numbers of them fell, sword in hand, by the side of their commander: but the place was carried. The Buccaneers obtained plunder and ransom amounting to two hundred and fifty thousand dollars, besides a vast quantity of valuable merchandise.

The following year, Morgan made an expedition to Maracaybo. He found the place deserted, but had the good fortune to discover the wealth of the citizens, which they had secreted in the neighboring woods. He then proceeded to Gibraltar, where for many weeks he practised the most cruel tortures upon the people to extort a discovery of their treasures. These, however, were unsuccessful; and when about to depart, he found himself blockaded by three Spanish men-of-war. These he attacked, burnt two of them with a fire-ship, and defeated the other. The next year he undertook an expedition on a still greater scale. With a fleet of thirty-seven vessels and two thousand men, he made a descent upon the island of St. Catharine, which was very strongly fortified, but which was easily taken in consequence of the cowardice of the governor, who concerted a pretended plan of defence to save his reputation, but made a secret bargain with Morgan, and allowed himself to be vanquished without bloodshed. The Buccaneers destroyed the fortifications, and took on board an immense quantity of warlike stores, which they found in the island. They now determined to attack Panama, on the opposite coast of the isthmus of Darien, and, with this view, sailed toward the river Chagres, which has its source near the Pacific.

On arriving at the mouth of this river, they found it defended by a strong fort built upon a steep rock, whose base was washed by the sea. It was garrisoned by a band of brave soldiers, under a commander of courage and abilities. They made a stout defence, and the Buccaneers would have been repulsed but for a very singular accident. Morgan, despairing of success, was about to give orders for a retreat, when an arrow shot by an Indian lodged in the eye of one of his men. Exasperated by the anguish of his wound, he drew out the arrow, wrapped the end of it in cotton, put it into his musket, and discharged it into the fort. The buildings were all of wood, with thatched roofs; and the arrow, ignited by the discharge, struck the roof of a house and set it on fire. The garrison were so intent on defending their walls, that they did not perceive the flames till they had made great progress. A sudden panic then seized them, as they saw the fire approaching the powder magazine. Terror and confusion prevailed; every man consulted his own safety, with the exception of fifteen or twenty, who continued fighting by the side of their commander till he fell, covered with wounds. The Buccaneers having renewed the attack with the utmost vigor, they were compelled to surrender.

The marauders pursued their voyage up the river in launches, leaving a part of their men on board the fleet which remained at anchor below. They proceeded as far as Cruces, where they landed, and marched for Panama. They defeated the Spaniards in several skirmishes, and captured the city, but found it almost deserted, the inhabitants having fled to the woods. They plundered Panama at their leisure; and their savage leader fell in love with one of his female captives. As neither his character nor person were such as to inspire her with any favorable sentiments towards him, he pleaded his passion in vain. He caused her to be thrown into a dungeon, and ordered that she should be supplied with food barely sufficient to sustain life.   Hoping to conquer her obstinacy by this cruel treatment, he made a long stay in Panama, till his men began to murmur at being kept inactive by such a caprice.   He therefore was compelled to depart, and agreed with the Spaniards for a considerable sum to evacuate the city without committing any further damage ; but after the money was paid, Panama was set on fire, whether by accident or design, is not known.   The Buccaneers returned to the mouth of the Chagres with an enormous booty.

In 1683, twelve hundred Buccaneers, in six ships, under the command of Van Horn, Grammort, Godfrey, Jonqué, and De Graff, attacked Vera Cruz. Under cover of a dark night, they landed at a distance, reached the town without being discovered, and obtained complete possession of it by daybreak.   The inhabitants fled to the churches, where the Buccaneers confined them, and placed barrels of gunpowder at the doors, with preparations to blow them up at the least appearance of resistance.   They then pillaged the city undisturbed during three days ; after which they offered to ransom their prisoners for two millions of dollars.   These unfortunate people, who had neither eaten nor drank for the whole period, gladly accepted the terms.   Half the money was paid, and the remainder expected from the interior, when a fleet of seventeen ships appeared off the harbor, and a considerable body of troops showed themselves on a neighboring eminence, marching toward the town. The Buccaneers quietly retreated to their vessels,

carrying off fifteen hundred slaves as an indemnity
for the half of the ansom which they had lost, and
compelling the inhabitants to sign a bond for the payment of it, with interest.   They boldly sailed through
the Spanish fleet, which let them pass without firing a
gun.

The following year, the Buccaneers made their
appearance in the South Sea, where they captured and
pillaged fifteen or twenty towns along the coast.   The
Spaniards never ventured to defend themselves unless
they greatly outnumbered them, and then they were
commonly routed.   They were so enervated by ease
and luxury that they had lost all military spirit and
skill, and had almost forgotten the use of arms.   They
were, if possible, more ignorant and cowardly than
the Indians whom they trampled upon.   This pusillanimity was augmented by the terrors which the
name of the Buccaneers inspired.   The monks had
represented them as devils, cannibals, and beings destitute of the human form.   As the Spaniards always
fled on the approach of the enemy, they knew no
other method of taking revenge than by burning or
cutting in pieces the bodies of the Buccaneers which
had been killed.   These corpses they dug up, mangled, and exposed to mimic tortures ; an exhibition
of impotent and childish rage which only stimulated
the ferocity of their enemies.   The towns which these
captured were set on fire, and the prisoners were
massacred without mercy, unless both were ransomed
with gold, silver or precious stones.   Silver was often
so common as to be despised, and they abandoned
heaps of it in every quarter.

These ravages almost totally annihilated the **Spanish** commerce in America. Hardly a ship ventured to sea, and all communication between the different provinces was cut off. Their richest and most populous territories were laid waste, and the people hardly dared to show themselves without the walls of their towns. Cultivation was neglected, to the great distress of the inhabitants, and the Indians saw themselves partially revenged on their tyrants, whose sufferings were drawn on them by that very gold which had stimulated them to bloodshed and oppression.

The last remarkable event in the history of the Buccaneers, is the capture of Carthagena, in **1697.** Twelve hundred of them, under Pointis, made themselves masters of this large, opulent and well-fortified city, where they obtained a booty of eleven millions of dollars. Had they been under the direction of an able leader, and had their object been conquest instead of plunder, they might have subjugated nearly all the West Indies, and erected an independent state. Morgan is said at one time to have entertained such a design. The war between Great Britain and France, which followed the accession of William III., was a severe blow to the Buccaneers, who were composed chiefly of the subjects of these two powers. They turned their arms against each other, and never confederated afterwards. The treaty of Ryswick, and the accession of a French prince to the throne of Spain, completed their dispersion. Many of them turned planters, or returned to their original occupation of sailors on board merchant ships. Others, who had fast-sailing vessels, escaped into remote seas, and practised piracy there. For nearly two centuries, the Buccaneers had been a people wholly distinct in history; they at last disappeared, and left not a trace of their existence behind.

MADAME GODIN.

A COMPANY of French astronomers and men of science, consisting of M. de la Condamine, Godin, Bouguer and others, were despatched to South America, in the year 1735, by the French government, to measure a degree of the meridian near the equator. The researches and adventures of these individuals, are among the most remarkable to be found in the narratives of modern travellers. Hardly anything in romance can surpass in interest the recital of suffering and peril exhibited in the history of Madame Godin, the wife of one of the members of the expedition.

After a residence of several years in Peru, M. Godin found himself under the necessity of returning home, in order to regulate some of his domestic affairs. He sailed down the river Amazon, and arrived at Cayenne, in 1750. His wife, being in a delicate situation, was left behind; and on his attempting to return to Peru by the same route, such was the incredible delay of the Portuguese government in furnishing his passports, that fifteen years passed away before he found himself ready to set out. Finally, in 1765, a Portuguese galliot was provided for him, with instructions to the commander to transport M. Godin up the Amazon as far as the first Spanish settlement. Unfortunately, just at this time

MADAME GODIN.

he fell sick; and being unable to proceed, he sent in stead a person named Tristan d' Orcasaval.

This man proved unfaithful to his trust. Instead of making the best of his way up the river, he passed a long time among the Portuguese settlements, trading on his own account, and spending the money which had been lodged in his hands for the purpose of bringing home M. Godin's wife and children. The letters addressed to that lady, he gave purposely to an individual who took care that they should never come to hand. By this piece of dishonesty, Madame Godin was for a long time kept in ignorance of the preparations that had been made for enabling her to join her husband; but at length, some vague rumors began to obtain circulation through the province of Quito, and soon reached her ears, that letters were on their way to her, and that a Portuguese vessel had arrived in the upper missions on the Amazon, to transport her to Cayenne. After the most diligent search, the letters could never be found. Madame Godin despatched a negro with several Indians down the river, to ascertain the fact respecting the Portuguese vessel. Encountering great obstacles, they were obliged to return; but more fortunate on a second trip, the negro reached Loreto, the most distant Spanish mission, where Tristan had arrived. On his return with this intelligence, Madame Godin determined immediately to set off for that place.

Accordingly, having made a hasty sale of a portion of her effects, she deposited the remainder in the care of her brother-in-law, and left her residence at Riobamba, forty leagues south of Quito, on the 1st of

VII.—10

October, 1769.   Her companions consisted of her two
brothers, a nephew nine or ten years of age, a French
physician designated as M. R., a negro, thirty Indians,
and three female mulatroes.   The first point on the
journey was the village of Canelos.   An avant-courier
which had preceded them a month before, to prepare
everything necessary on the road, found this place
well inhabited, and immediately moved onward.   In
the interval, however, between his departure and the
arrival of the expedition at Canelos, the small pox
made its appearance here, and utterly depopulated the
village.   The inhabitants first attacked by the disease
immediately died, and the remainder, panic-struck,
instantly dispersed among the woods.   The Indians
who carried the baggage had been paid in advance;
and, on arriving at the deserted village, they took
fright and all ran away.

Madame Godin, being thus suddenly deserted by
nearly all her attendants, at length discovered a couple
of Indians belonging to the neighborhood.   They had
no boat, but agreed to build one, and carry the travellers down the river Bobonaza to the mission of Andoas,
about twelve days' voyage.   She paid them beforehand, and, the canoe being finished, they embarked
and left Canelos.   At the end of two days, the Indians
ran off.   Without pilot or steersman, they continued
their voyage, and passed the day without accident.
The next day, at noon, they discovered a canoe in a
small creek adjoining a rude hut, in which was a
sick Indian, who was prevailed upon to pilot them.
On the third day after this, one of the party acci-
dentally dropped his hat overboard; the Indian, stoop-

ing over the gunwale to pick it up, fell into the river, and, not having strength to get back or reach the shore, was drowned. Behold this unfortunate crew again without a steersman, and totally unacquainted with the method of managing a boat, on a deep and rapid stream, full of whirls and eddies. It was not long before the canoe was overset; but they were so fortunate as to save themselves. They gained the shore, and finding it too dangerous to pursue their voyage, they built themselves a hut.

They were within five or six days' journey of Andoas, but the country was a howling wilderness. It was impossible for all the party to proceed, and M. R. offered to push onward with another Frenchman of the party, and Madame Godin's faithful negro. This was agreed to, and they embarked in the canoe, M. R. taking especial care to leave none of his effects behind. This individual behaved in the basest manner toward his unfortunate companions. He assured them that within a fortnight a canoe should be returned to them, fully manned and equipped to carry them onward; but, more careful of his own comfort than of their lives, no sooner had he reached Andoas, than he departed with his companion and baggage for Omaguas, without making any efforts to rescue from destruction those whom he had left behind. The negro, however, remained at Andoas.

The fortnight elapsed, and no one appeared with help for the party in the wilderness. They waited still longer, and at the end of twenty-five days they lost all hope of hearing from Andoas. They had no alternative but to starve in the woods or again attempt to sail down the river. A raft was constructed, and they embarked with their effects. As might have been expected, so unwieldy a craft soon proved dangerous to the navigators. Ere long, it struck against a snag, overset, and plunged the whole party and all their baggage into the water. Madame Godin twice sunk, but, by the great exertions of her brothers, she was saved, to endure new perils and sufferings. Owing to the narrowness of the stream at this spot, all the party gained the shore, but everything else was lost. Their situation was now truly alarming. With neither boat, raft, tool nor implement of any sort, with no clothing or means of shelter beside what they wore on their backs, and utterly destitute of provision, they found themselves in a desert solitude, surrounded by an almost impervious thicket of trees, underwood, herbage and tangled lianas.

Bending their course backward, however, and breaking their way through the thickets, they reached their hut, where, fortunately, they had left a part of their provisions. Taking these, they began their journey down the river. At first they kept along the banks of the stream, but finding its sinuosities greatly lengthened their journey, they struck off into the forest, and in a few days utterly lost themselves. Their condition was now truly appalling. Their provisions were exhausted ; no water was to be found ; so many days' journey through the woods had wasted their strength ; their feet were lacerated and torn with thorns and brambles. Occasionally a palm cabbage or some other wild fruit afforded them a little relief ; but at length these failed, and, overpowered with hunger, thirst, pain and weariness, they threw themselves on the ground, and quietly awaited their end.   One after another, they expired.   Madame Godin's two brothers, her nephew, three young women and a young man, seven in all, lay dead, by the side of each other, and this unfortunate lady remained the only human being in the midst of a frightful wilderness, abounding in wild beasts and venomous reptiles. A situation more utterly hopeless can hardly be conceived.   How justly has it been remarked, that " truth is stranger than fiction."

Stretched on the ground amid the bodies of her companions, stupefied, half delirious, and tormented with choking thirst, this heroic female determined not to abandon herself to her fate while a breath of life yet remained.   With great difficulty, she summoned strength enough at the end of two days to rise and drag herself forward.   She had no shoes, and her clothes were torn into shreds ; she cut the shoes off the feet of her dead brother, and made a pair of sandals of the soles.   Thus wretchedly equipped, she wandered up and down in the dreary solitude.   The spectacle she had witnessed in the melancholy death of her friends, leaving her alone in the wilderness ; the appalling darkness of the night in the desert ; the perpetual apprehension of death, which every hour served to augment, had so powerful an effect upon her spirits that her hair turned suddenly gray.   On her second day's march, she found water, and the following day met with some wild fruit and birds' eggs.   These, after great efforts, she was enabled to swallow, for, owing to her want of aliment, her throat had become so parched

H   10*

and stiffened as to be hardly able to perform its office. This food sufficed to support her emaciated frame, and she continued her course through the pathless woods. On the eighth or ninth day after she left the spot where her companions lay, she reached the banks of the Bobonasa. At daybreak, she was startled by a noise very near her, and in the momentary terror at the thought of a wild beast, she fled into the woods ; but, after a short reflection, satisfied that nothing worse could befall her than to remain in her present forlorn condition, she proceeded to the shore of the stream, and discovered two Indians launching a canoe. Her deliverance was now at hand. The Indians advanced toward her, and she learnt that they belonged to Canelos, but had abandoned that place on the appearance of the small pox, and had taken up their residence with their families in a hut in the woods. They received Madame Godin with a humanity and kindness truly affecting. Thus this heroic woman, at a moment when she least expected it, suddenly found herself snatched from the horrible death which had so long impended over her. Ten days had she been alone, in the woods, two awaiting death by the corpses of her companions, and eight more wandering up and down she knew not whither !

For the final preservation of her life, she was entirely indebted to this casual discovery of the two Indians. Her faithful negro had made every exertion at Andoas, and raised a company to go to her relief. This party reached the hut where the expedition had been left, but found no one there. They traced Madame Godin and her companions through the woods till they came to the spot where they found the seven bodies, so disfigured that no one of them could be identified. At this spectacle, they concluded that none of the party had survived, and, returning to the hut, where many valuable articles had been abandoned by the unfortunate sufferers, they took these and departed for Andoas, where they arrived before anything had been heard of Madame Godin. The negro thence repaired to M. R. at Omaguas, and delivered to him the property of his mistress.

The two Indians conducted Madame Godin safely to Andoas. She rewarded them for their fidelity with the only valuable articles which still remained in her possession, consisting of two massy gold chains. The simple natives could not have been more delighted and astonished had all paradise been opened to them. Alas for the poor Indians!—a Spaniard, who had just come into office, and officiated as a sort of lay missionary at Andoas, had the inconceivable baseness to rob them of these presents before the very face of Madame Godin, giving them in exchange three or four yards of coarse cotton cloth. Fired with indignation at this infamous conduct, she instantly demanded a canoe and men, and set out for Laguna. An Indian woman at Andoas made her a cotton skirt, for which she sent her a recompense after her arrival at Laguna. On reaching that place, she was kindly received by Dr. Romero, the chief of the mission, and during six weeks' stay there, her health and strength were partially restored. M. R. was still at Omaguas, and an express was despatched to that place, to inform him of her arrival. Upon this intelligence, he found himself compelled to restore to Madame Godin a portion of the property in his hands. He accordingly hastened to join her, bringing with him five silver dishes, and some trifling articles of clothing belonging to herself and others. He denied having possession of the other valuables, consisting of jewels of gold and precious stones. Madame Godin addressed him in the language of great indignation, charging him with robbing her of her property, and with having been the cause of all her misfortunes. She avowed her determination to have no further association with him. Yet, at the intercession of Dr. Romero, who represented that if she abandoned him there he would be without the means of returning to his country, she had the magnanimity to overlook his base conduct, and allow him to continue with her.

The remainder of Madame Godin's voyage down the Amazon, was comparatively safe and easy. After twenty years' separation, she had the happiness of again joining her husband, in the year 1770. The courage, fortitude and perseverance of this remarkable woman during her strange vicissitudes and sufferings in the American wilds, are, perhaps, without a parallel in the annals of adventure.

ALEXANDER SELKIRK.

THE island of Juan Fernandez, near the coast of Chili, has obtained an extraordinary reputation from the adventures of this individual; and the interest which every reader must feel for the spot is of so romantic a cast, that we shall sketch a short narrative of the circumstances which have gained it such notoriety, and given rise to one of the most ingenious and agreeable fictions in our language.

Alexander Selcraig, or Selkirk, as he called himself after he went to sea, was born at Largo, in the county of Fife, in Scotland, in 1676. He received a common school education, and was then put to his father's business of shoemaking. He was the seventh son of his parents, and soon became a spoiled child. His waywardness of temper gave them much uneasiness. A strong desire to go to sea rendered his employment irksome to him, and an occurrence at last afforded him an opportunity to indulge his predilection. His irregularities rose to such a pitch that he fell under the formal censure of the church, and was cited to appear before the session. He was at this time eighteen years of age, and too stubborn to submit to a rebuke for his behavior; accordingly he left home, and nothing was heard of him for six years. There are good reasons for believing that he was with the Buccaneers in the South Seas during this period.

ALEXANDER SELKIRK.

In 1701, we find him again at Largo, but with the same irascible and intractable temper, and involved in constant broils with his family. As his fondness for a maritime life was unabated, he did not remain long in Scotland, but proceeded to London in search of new adventures.

At the metropolis he fell in with Captain Dampier, who was then fitting out an expedition against the Spaniards in the South Sea. Selkirk shipped with him as sailing-master of the Cinque Ports galley, a consort of Dampier's ship, the St. George, and sailed from London in the spring of 1703. After various adventures, both vessels arrived at the island of Juan Fernandez, in February, 1704. Having remained here some time to refit, they continued their cruise, and made numerous captures. The two vessels separated, and after this a violent quarrel broke out between Selkirk and Stradling, the commander of the Cinque Ports. So bitter was this animosity, that Selkirk resolved to leave the vessel, whatever might be the consequence. In a short time, the want of provisions and the crazy state of the vessel compelled Stradling to put back to the island. Here he remained for some time, repairing and provisioning his vessel. When about to sail, Selkirk announced his determination to remain in the island, and was accordingly set on shore with all his effects. He leaped upon the land with a joyful feeling of liberty, shook hands with his comrades, and bade them a hearty adieu. But this joyous feeling was soon chilled. Scarcely had the sound of their oars as they pulled away from the land, fallen upon his ears, when his heart sunk within him, and the horrors of solitude and the loss of all human society, perhaps forever rushed into his mind. His resolution instantly abandoned him, and he called to his comrades to be taken on board; but Stradling was deaf to his entreaties, and took a pleasure in mocking his despair. The ship was soon out of sight, and Selkirk found himself the only human being in that lonely isle. This was near the end of September, 1704.

Juan Fernandez is about a dozen leagues in circuit. A great part of the island is mountainous and covered with wood, chiefly pimento, cotton and cabbage trees. The climate is delightful; wild goats run at large in the woods, and the shores are frequented by vast numbers of seals and sea-lions. It is a charming region, and might seem an agreeable residence, but the solitude in which Selkirk was placed, made it as dreary to him as a desert. For many days after the departure of the ship, his dejection of mind was so extreme, that he sat immovably fixed upon the shore, gazing at the spot where her sails had sunk beneath the horizon, vainly hoping to see her return and relieve him from his misery. He took no food until compelled by the sharpest hunger, nor indulged in sleep until overpowered by watchfulness. The season was now the beginning of spring in that hemisphere, and all nature was verdant, blooming and fragrant; but his forlorn condition caused the beauties of the scenery and the balminess of the air to be disregarded. What greatly added to the horror of his loneliness, was the dismal wail of the sea-lions at night; to this was added the frequent crashing of falling trees and rocks among the heights, which often broke the drear stillness of midnight with strange and appalling sounds that echoed from valley to valley. In an excess of terror and despair, he often meditated suicide; but, after several months, his melancholy began to wear away, and he cast about to see by what means he could improve his condition.

He had brought with him on shore, his clothes and bedding, a musket, some powder and shot, tobacco, a hatchet, a knife, a pewter pot, a flip-can, some mathematical instruments and books, and a Bible. The building of a hut was his first undertaking; this he constructed of pimento wood, and thatched the roof with long grass. At some distance he erected a smaller building for his kitchen. Both were lined with goatskins. He shot these animals as long as his powder lasted, which was but a pound; afterwards he caught them by running them down. At first, he could overtake only the kids, but afterwards, so much did his frugal habits, joined to air and exercise, improve his strength, that he could overtake the swiftest goat on the island in a few minutes, toss it over his shoulder, and carry it with ease to his hut. This agility on one occasion nearly cost him his life. While pursuing a goat, he made a snatch at it on the brink of a precipice, which he did not perceive, as it was hidden by bushes, and both fell from a great height. He was so stunned and bruised by the fall, that he lay senseless for some hours, and when he came to himself, he found the goat lying dead beneath him. This happened about a mile from his hut, and he lay twenty-four hours before he was able to move. After crawling home with ex reme difficulty, he remained ten days stretched upon his bed in great pain.   This, however, was the only accident of the kind that happened to him during his residence in the island.

After his powder was exhausted, he obtained fire by the Indian method of rubbing two pieces of wood together.   The cabbage-palm offered him a tolerable substitute for bread ; vegetables of various kinds grew spontaneously, and a bed of turnips had been sowed on the island by Dampier's men ; his meat he seasoned with pimento.   Thus having food in abundance, and finding the climate healthy and pleasant, in about a year and a half he became reconciled to his situation.   The time no longer hung heavy on his hands ; his constant devotion, and the study of the Bible, soothed his feelings, and elevated his thoughts ; undisturbed health, a temperate regimen, and the perpetual serenity of the sky, filled his mind with cheerfulness. He took delight in everything which lay around him, ornamented his hut with fragrant branches, and formed a verdant and delightful bower in which he tasted the sweets of repose after the toil of the chase.   Hunting was his chief amusement ; and he caught many more goats than he required for food ; it was his custom, after running them down, to mark their ears and let them escape.   The kids he carried to the green lawn in front of his hut, and employed his leisure in taming them.   They in time supplied him with milk, and even with something like social amusement, for he taught them to dance, and he often declared afterwards that he never danced with a lighter heart than he did to the sound of his own voice with his dumb companions.

At first, he suffered much annoyance from rats, which gnawed his feet during sleep; for a remedy, he caught some of the cats which ran wild in the woods, and tamed them. These put the rats to flight, and became his companions. He taught them to dance like his goats, and divert him by a variety of odd capers. The cats multiplied to such an extent, that he soon had a house full of them, and he was at times saddened by the thought of being eaten up by them after death.

His clothing soon wore out, and he made new dresses of goat-skins, in which he looked more wild than his brute companions. He always went barefoot, and neither shaved nor sheared his locks. After his knife was worn out, he chanced one day, in strolling along the beach, to find several iron hoops which had been left behind by some vessel. This was a discovery of more value to him than a mine of gold or diamonds would have been, and afforded him materials for making tools as long as he staid on the island. One of them, which he had used as a chopper, was afterwards carried to London, and for many years was exhibited as a curiosity at the Golden Head Coffee-house near Burlington Gate. He occasionally amused himself by carving his name upon the trees, with the date of his arrival in the island. Several times, during his stay, he saw vessels pass near Two of them came to anchor. Selkirk always concealed himself on the approach of a vessel; but on one occasion, being anxious to know whether the ship was

French or Spanish, he approached too near, and was discovered. A pursuit commenced, and several shot were fired at him. None of them took effect, and he hid himself by climbing up into a tree. His pursuers stopped under the tree and killed several goats near it, but not discerning Selkirk, they returned to the ship and sailed away. Had they been French, he would have given himself up, but as he saw that they were Spaniards, he chose to remain on the island and die alone, rather than run the risk of being shot, or linger out a life of misery in the mines of Peru or Mexico, which he supposed might be his fate if he should fall into their hands. It was a strict maxim of their policy never to allow an Englishman to return to Europe, who had gained any knowledge of the South Seas.

Selkirk had lived alone in the island upwards of four years, when, on the last day of January, 1709, he discovered two ships approaching ; and as they drew near, he ascertained that they were English. Great was the tumult of emotions that now stirred his breast ; but the love of society and of home overpowered every other desire. It was late in the afternoon when the ships came first in sight, and for fear they might sail by, without knowing there was a man on the island, he made a large fire to burn during the night. His hopes and fears banishing all thoughts of sleep, he employed the night in killing goats, and preparing an entertainment for his visitors. The ships were the Duke and Dutchess, two large cruisers, under the command of Woodes Rogers, with Dampier for pilot. The sight of the fire on shore caused great alarm, and they conjectured that some hostile ships of war lay at anchor under the island. The ships were cleared for action, and during the forenoon of the following day, they kept a sharp lookout for the enemy. No vessel appearing, about noon a boa was sent on shore. Selkirk ran down to the beach, and astonished the crew by the wildness of his appearance, which literally struck them dumb. He had at this time his last shirt upon his back; his feet and legs were bare, and the rest of his body was covered with rough and shaggy goat-skins; his beard was of above four years' growth. His long disuse of conversation had affected his power of speech, and he uttered his words by halves.

Selkirk was received on board, and engaged as mate of Rogers' ship, the Duke; he served in that capacity during the remainder of the expedition, and much to the satisfaction of the commander. After a long cruise, he arrived in England, in October, 1711, with eight hundred pounds of prize money, having been absent more than eight years. He no sooner had made his appearance in London, than his strange adventures attracted great attention, and he became an object of lively curiosity. Most of his visitors who have left any account of him, describe him as an unsociable person, of eccentric habits, and far from communicative. As he spoke in a broad Scotch dialect, it was with difficulty that he could be understood. Among his visitors was Sir Richard Steele, who collected from him such particulars as he could recollect of his life in the island, which he afterwards

11 *

published, with reflections of his own, in the twenty-sixth number of the Englishman.

The reader may wish to know the sequel of Selkirk's history. He returned to his native town, where his parents received him with joy; but his recluse habits induced him to shun society, and he constructed a cave in the garden, where he lived in solitude. He purchased a boat, amused himself with fishing, and took lonely walks among the roads and glens in the neighborhood. In these rambles, he often met a young girl, Sophia Bruce, seated alone, and tending a single cow, the property of her parents. Her lonely occupation and innocent looks made a deep impression upon him, and he watched her for hours unseen, as she gathered wild flowers or chanted her rural lays. At length, he joined her in conversation; their attachment became mutual, and they eloped to London. It is supposed that she died a few years afterwards, or that Selkirk deserted her, as he returned to Scotland alone, and became involved in broils which brought him under the discipline of the church. This drove him once more to England, and he entered the navy. He died some time in 1723. In a house at Craigie Well, strangers are yet gratified with the sight of the room in which he slept; they are also shown his sea-chest, and a cocoa-nut shell cup that belonged to him. But the most interesting relic, by far, is the flip-can which he had in the island, and which is now in the possession of his great grand nephew, John Selcraig.

Such is the story of the man whose adventures gave birth to the romance of Robinson Crusoe. Few persons have obtained so high, yet unsought renown. Selkirk never aimed at notoriety, yet immortality has been conferred upon him by one who knew him not. The story of Selkirk was first communicated to the world by Woodes Rogers, in the narrative of his voyage; after which the tale appeared in various shapes by other hands. Defoe adopted it for the groundwork of his romance of Robinson Crusoe; but there appears to be no evidence that Selkirk wrote a narrative himself, from which Defoe purloined his materials, as has been often suggested. The leading idea only was borrowed from Selkirk's adventures; but the whole arrangement and execution, all the filling up of incident, reflection and character in Robinson Crusoe, were truly and entirely created by the genius of Defoe.

THE JESUITS IN PARAGUAY.

THE establishment of the Jesuits in Paraguay, affords the most remarkable instance on record of full success in converting to Christianity and partial civilization the natives of the New World. The missionaries of this order went to South America, after the country had been devastated by the Spanish conquerors, who hunted the Indians like wild beasts. The Jesuits believed that these unfortunate natives were capable, by a milder course of treatment, of being redeemed from their degraded condition. They obtained from the court of Spain, about the beginning of the seventeenth century, a declaration that all their Indian proselytes should be considered free men, and that the Jesuits should have the government of the communities of converts which they should form in the interior of the country. This privilege became the foundation of the most flourishing missionary establishment which the New World has ever seen.

The Jesuits immediately entered upon the scene of action, and opened their campaign with the spiritual conquest of the Guaranies, a nation inhabiting the banks of the Uruguay and the Parana. Twelve thousand of these people were removed to Paraguay, in order to save them from the incursions of the Portuguese, who, regardless of the progress of Christianity among the natives, carried off the new converts to serve as slaves in the mines of Brazil. The same number of inhabitants were procured from other districts, and the colonial plan went immediately into successful operation. Large towns and villages were formed, and the establishment was rapidly augmented by the acquisition of new tribes from every quarter. Within little more than a century, they possessed thirty-eight towns in a high state of improvement; and fifty years afterward, the Jesuits are supposed to have had no less than three hundred thousand Indian families under their spiritual government.

The nature of that government, and the means by which such a multitude of wandering savages were collected, and brought to submit to civil regulations

I

and religious observances, require an attentive exam ination.   With no arms but those of persuasion, the Jesuits freely mingled with the most barbarous tribes, they learned their languages, and by all those arts of address and insinuation for which they have long been famous, they gained the confidence of these wild hordes.   They engaged to protect them from the aggressions of the Spaniards and Portuguese, as well as to secure them against those inconveniences to which they were exposed in their forests, provided they would agree to live in society and contribute to supply each other's wants, according to the instructions which should be given them.   As soon as they had drawn together a certain number of families, they provided for their comfort and instruction, taking care to render them tractable, reasonable and contented, before they began to unfold to them the mysteries of the gospel.   They did not attempt to make them Christians before they had made them men.   This seems to have been the true secret of their success. The Indians, having realized the promises of the Jesuits in regard to the comforts of this world, doubted not what was told them of the next.   At first they respected, but now they revered their teachers, and those shrewd propagandists did not fail to take the most certain steps for perpetuating the influence which they had acquired.   They reserved to themselves all civil and religious authority; and by having the absolute disposal of everything which belonged to the community, all property was nearly the same as their own.

The Indians entertained a firm conviction that whatever the Jesuit fathers recommended was good, and whatever they condemned was bad. With such impressions in the subjects, the administration of government was an easy thing. Over each of the missions, or districts, a Jesuit presided in chief. He was supreme in all cases, civil, military and ecclesiastical; and governed not only with the sway of a sovereign, but with the reputation of an oracle. The inferior magistrates in the towns were chosen by the Indians from among their own body, subject to a confirmation by the presiding Jesuit.

The Indian towns were all very neat, and well built. The churches were large, and admirably constructed; their decorations were scarcely inferior to the richest in Peru. The dwelling-houses of the Indians were built with symmetry and taste, and were so commodiously and elegantly furnished, as to excel those of the Spaniards in many populous cities of South America. Every church had its band of music, consisting of a great number of vocal and instrumental performers, and divine service was celebrated with all the pomp and solemnity of the European cathedrals. At public processions and religious festivals, the Indian magistrates paraded with great ceremony, and there was an imposing display of gold-laced uniforms and rich dresses, with skilful dancing. No town was without a school for instruction in reading, writing, dancing and music. Many of the Indians became proficients in Latin. In every considerable place were shops for painters, sculptors, gilders, silversmiths, locksmiths, carpenters, weavers, watch-makers, and other artisans. Every one worked for the benefit of the whole town, and the " co-operative system," which has often been attempted, but has as often failed in modern times, was here carried into full success.

Every town had an armory, in which were kept the muskets, swords and pikes used by the militia when they took the field, either to repel the insults of the Portuguese, or the heathen nations of the fron·tiers. The militia comprised all the men capable of bearing arms; and they were exercised on the evening of every holiday in the public squares. They manufactured their own gunpowder. All private distress was prevented by a charitable fund derived from the produce of a farm in each village, on which the inhabitants labored two days in every week. The surplus of this fund went to purchase ornaments for the churches, and to pay the royal revenues. That the Indians might never be in want of necessary arti cles, it was one part of the priest's duty to have always on hand a stock of different kinds of tools, clothing and miscellanies, which were sold to the Indians for their agricultural or manufactured produce. This barter was managed with the strictest integrity, that the Indians might have no reason to complain of oppression, and that the high character of the priests for justice and sanctity might be studiously preserved. By this means the Indians had no occasion to leave their own country for the purposes of trade, and were kept from the contagion of those vices which they would have contracted in such an intercourse with the people of other districts, where the morals of the inhabitants were not restrained by good examples and laws

The missionary fathers would not allow any of the inhabitants of Peru, whether Spaniards, mestizoes, or even Indians, to come within the limits of their establishment in Paraguay : not with a view of concealing their transactions from the world, but in order that their converts, being newly reclaimed from savageness and brutality, and initiated into morality and religion, might be kept steadfast in this state of innocence and simplicity. They adhered inflexibly to this system, and in this they were justified by the melancholy example of the missions of Peru, which were ruined by an open intercourse with the people around them. Acting upon their original views they formed an Utopia of their own, the first object of which was to remove from their people all temptations which are not inherent in human nature, and by establishing, as nearly as possible, a community of goods, to exclude a large portion of the crimes and miseries which embitter the life of civilized man. For this, they might plead the authority of sages and legislators.

Under this system, an Indian never knew, during his whole progress from the cradle to the grave, what it was to take thought for the morrow : all his duties were comprised in obedience. The strictest discipline soon becomes easy when it is certain and immutable : that of the Jesuits extended to everything, but it was neither capricious nor oppressive. The children were considered as belonging to the community : they lived with their parents, that the course of natural affection might not be interrupted ; but their education was a public duty. The Jesuits boast that years would sometimes pass away without the commission of a deadly sin, and that it was even rare to hear a confession which made absolution necessary. Few vices, indeed, could exist in such communities. Avarice and ambition were excluded; there was little room for envy, and little to excite hatred and malice. Drunkenness, the vice which most easily besets savage and half-civilized man, was effectually prevented by the prohibition of intoxicating liquors; and licentiousness was guarded against by the strictest rules of behavior.

Money was scarcely known in Paraguay; all payments were made in kind; everything had a fixed rate of barter, and he who wanted to purchase an article, gave another in payment for it. They exported cotton and tobacco, rosaries and little saints, articles which were in great demand in those quarters. Their staple export, however, was the *maté*, or Paraguay tea, which grows on a shrub resembling the orange tree, but much larger. The twigs of this tree are gathered and laid before a slow fire, when the leaves crackle like those of the laurel; after being toasted, the leaf and stalk are pulverized. The Guaranies prepared it more delicately by carefully picking off the leaves and bruising them slightly in a mortar. The use of this tea by the Spaniards of South America is almost universal, and great virtues are ascribed to it. Hunger and thirst are relieved by it. The Indians who have been laboring all day, feel immediately refreshed by a cup of this tea, made by simply mixing the leaf with rain water. In Chili and Peru, the people believe that they could not exist without rt, and many persons take it every hour in the day, intoxicating themselves with it as the Turks do with opium. The Spaniards learnt the use of it from the natives.

Never was there a more absolute despotism than the government of the Jesuits in Paraguay; but never has there existed any other society in which the welfare of the subjects, temporal and eternal, has been the sole object of the government. The rulers, indeed, erred grossly in the standard of both, but erroneous as they were, the sanctity of the end proposed, and the heroism and perseverance with which it was pursued, deserve the highest admiration. The Jesuits were accused, among other things, of living in all the luxury of princes in their empire of Paraguay; but this charge is groundless, and they appear to have been guided mainly by a sense of duty towards God and man. The life of a missionary, after he began his labors in seeking out the wild Indians, was spent in the most arduous toils, the severest privations, and the greatest dangers; these being often terminated by untimely death.

Incredible were the exertions which the first missionaries made—the difficulties which they encountered, and the risks they ran, in seeking out and reclaiming the wild tribes. The itinerant set forth with his breviary, and a cross, six feet high, which served him for a staff. About thirty converted Indians attended him as guides, interpreters and servants, or fellow-laborers; they were armed, but not with firelocks, and carried axes and bills to open a way through the woods, a stock of maize for their supply in case of need, and materials for striking fire. Hammocks might easily have been added, but the missionaries seldom indulged themselves with anything that could possibly be dispensed with. The danger from wild beasts is not great in Paraguay and the adjoining provinces, but there are few parts of the world where the traveller has so many plagues to molest him. The first business upon halting for the night, or even for a meal in the daytime, is to beat the ground and trample the grass for a safe distance round, in order to drive away the serpents, which are very numerous, and are attracted by fire. The torment from insects s also insufferable. Where there is fine grass, where there are thickets or marshes on the borders of lakes or rivers, or where there are thick woods, if you are to pass the night you must not dream of sleeping. The open country swarms with that wingless tribe, so famous for their agility ; and he who lies down on what he supposes to be clean turf, where there is no vestige of man or beast, will rise up black with these vermin. Breeze-flies and wasps torment the horses and mules ; but the common fly is the most dreadful annoyer both to man and beast in this country, and is considered equal to all the other insects and all the venomous reptiles in this part of the world. It gets into the ears and noses of those who are asleep, deposits its eggs, and unless timely relief be applied, the maggots eat their way into the head, and cause the most excruciating pain, and even death. In addition to these evils, the missionaries were compelled to endure the extremes of fatigue and hunger when making their way through swamps and woodlands ;

and when, having persevered through all these obstacles, they found the savages of whom they were in quest, they and their companions sometimes fell victims to the ferocity or the suspicion of the very persons for whose benefit they had endured so much.

Among the South American Indians, were tribes of cannibals, who considered human flesh as the most exquisite of all dainties. A Jesuit one day found a Brazilian woman in extreme old age, and almost at the point of death. Having catechized her, instructed her, as he conceived, in the nature of Christianity, and completely taken care of her soul, he began to inquire whether there was any kind of food which she could take. "Grandam," said he, that being the word of courtesy by which it was usual to address old women, "if I were to get you a little sugar now, or a mouthful of some of our nice things which we get from beyond sea, do you think you could eat it?" "Ah, my grandson," she replied, "my stomach goes against anything. There is but one thing which I think I could touch. If I had the little hand of a tender little Tapuya boy, I think I could pick the little bones. But woe is me! there is nobody to go out and shoot one for me!"

One of the most eminent of the Jesuit missionaries was Cypriano Baraza, who may be considered the most enlightened member of that order that ever labored in Spanish America. The scene of his labors comprised a tract of a hundred and twenty square leagues, in the wildest part of the country. He plunged into the wilderness, with a few Indian guides, and spent many years learning the language of the sav-

12*

ages and conciliating their good will.   They assured
him that toward the east there was a nation of women
who killed all their male infants and bred up the girls
in warlike habits.   Baraza was a man whose veracity
might be relied on, and it is worthy of notice that in
this same direction other travellers have heard of the
Amazons.   Baraza collected about two thousand of
these wild people; other missionaries were then sent
to his assistance, and leaving them in charge of his
converts, he advanced further into the country.   He
had now acquired a sufficient command of their languages, had accustomed himself to their manners in
all lawful things, and gained at once their good will
and respect by kind offices, unwearied benignity,
and superior knowledge.   He dressed the wounds of
the Indians, he administered medicine to the sick; he
taught them weaving, carpentry and agriculture, and
procured cattle for them from the Spanish settlements.
Having heard that there was a pass across the mountains which would materially shorten the road to
Peru, from which this distant mission was supplied,
he employed three years in exploring it, and at length
gained the summit of the Andes, and saw before him
the low country toward the Pacific Ocean.   He fell
upon the ground and returned thanks to God for the
successful termination of his search.

But Baraza was now near the close of his merito-
rious career.   He proceeded to the Baures, a people
east of the Moxos, and the most improved of all these
numerous tribes.   Their villages were built on hills
with some regularity; each was a fortification, so
palisadoed as to be secure against any sudden attack,

and having loop-holes for their own archers; as a further precaution, pitfalls were concealed in the paths. Their shields were made of platted cane covered with cotton and feathers, and arrow-proof. The chief of one of these tribes was supposed to be the Great Moxo, whom the early conquerors of Peru believed to have succeeded to the Inca's treasures, and to have founded a richer empire in the centre of the continent than that which Pizarro overthrew. The more improved customs of these people were in reality the wrecks of Peruvian civilization.

In many of these towns, Baraza was well received, and listened to with apparent complacency. But being lodged in a place which he had not visited before, his companions were alarmed during the night by a loud sound of drums; and as they knew the manners of the people, they were instantly aware that their destruction was intended. Without a moment's delay, they urged Baraza to fly. He had scarcely attempted to leave the place, before the savages rushed out. A shower of arrows was poured upon him, which in a moment checked his flight, and he was then murdered with a hatchet. Thus he died, in the sixty-fifth year of his age, after having labored upwards of twenty-seven years in civilizing and instructing the Indians. It is worthy of remark, that the Jesuits seem never to have adorned his history with miracles, as if they felt that no fables were required to exalt his character, or exaggerate the success of his labors.

The Jesuit missions continued to flourish till the middle of the last century. But in 1750, Spain, by a treaty with Portugal, thought proper to give up seven districts in Paraguay, to the latter power, in exchange for other territory in South America. The Spanish government ordered the Jesuits and their Indian pupils to abandon their homes, and remove to some other part of the Spanish territory. The fathers in vain remonstrated against the injustice and cruelty of expelling men from the fields which they had by their own industry reclaimed from the wilderness; the harsh mandate was repeated, and the Jesuits were forced to obey. But the natives refused to submit, and resisted the Spanish and Portuguese forces which were sent against them. A subsequent change in the diplomatic relations of the two countries, left the Indians in possession of their territory; yet the Jesuits were falsely accused of having encouraged what was styled a rebellion. The Spanish government, after mature investigation, acquitted them; but the Portuguese minister, Pombal, a harsh and unprincipled man, believed, or affected to believe. in the rebellious spirit of the fathers, whom he wished to expel from Portugal. An attempt by some noblemen to murder the king, was charged upon the Jesuits, because Father Malagrida, one of the society, was confessor to some of the guilty accessories. No proof could be obtained against him, but he was condemned by the Inquisition, on a charge of heresy, and executed. In September, 1759, orders were given for the expulsion of the Jesuits from the Portuguese territories, and the confiscation of their property. The order was executed with the greatest severity; the fathers were shipped off with indecent haste like so many cattle, in vessels bound for Italy, where they were landed in a state of utter destitution. Such was the end of the most promising missionary enterprise ever undertaken among the savages of the western continent.

BOLIVAR.

BOLIVAR.

THE Spanish colonies of South America remained for three centuries in quiet submission to the mother country, if we except the desperate attempt of the Peruvian Indians, under Tupac Amaru, to throw off the yoke of their oppressors. Never were despotism, avarice and slavish obsequiousness to power, more thoroughly displayed than in Spanish America, under the government of the viceroys and captains-general, who, with all the principal officers of the viceroyal court, were sent to America from Madrid, and who, without being under any efficient responsibility, administered their authority with every species of tyranny and venality. Justice was bought and sold, and the most important legal decisions were made in favor of the highest bidder. The mercantile policy of the parent country was equally despotic and rapacious. The establishment of manufactures was not permitted, while cargoes of Spanish commodities, the refuse of the shops, were forced, in barter for silver and gold, upon a half civilized people, who neither wanted nor could possibly use them. Foreign commerce was interdicted on pain of death; all social improvement was suppressed; and to prevent the inhabitants from knowing the extent of their degradation, all intercourse whatever was strictly forbidden with any country or people, besides Spain and Spaniards, and allowed even with them only under many restrictions. Superstition and ignorance were upheld as the surest support of the colonial system; so that, previous to 1810, the whole continent, from Lima to Monte Video, contained but one wretched printing press, and that in the hands of the monks, who consigned to the dungeons of the Inquisition every man who possessed a prohibited book.

The example of the revolt of the British North American colonies, had a slow effect in propagating revolutionary ideas in the south; and the usurpation of the crown of Spain by Napoleon, precipitated those movements which resulted, after a bloody struggle, in wresting from the dominion of Spain the whole of her continental possessions in America. In this momentous contest, Simon Bolivar bore the most conspicuous part, and his life comprises the substance of the history of the country in which his military exploits were performed during its most eventful period.

This celebrated man was born in the city of Caraccas, in July, 1783. He belonged to a family of distinction, and was one of the few natives of the Spanish colonies who were permitted to visit Europe. After finishing his studies at Madrid, he went to France, and during his stay at Paris rendered himself an acceptable guest in its social circles, by the amenity of his manners and his other personal recommendations. In the midst, however, of all the seductions of that gay capital, his sanguine temper and ardent imagination anticipated the task which the future fortunes of his country might impose upon him, and even in his twenty-third year he is said to have contemplated the establishment of her independence. While at Paris, his favorite occupation was the study of those branches of science which contribute to the formation of the character of a warrior and statesman. Humboldt and Bonpland were his intimate friends, and accompanied him in his excursions in France; nor did he think his travels finished till he had visited England, Italy, and a part of Germany. On his return to Madrid, he was married, and shortly afterwards returned to America, where he arrived in 1810, at the very moment when his countrymen were about to unfurl the standard of independence. On his passage homeward, he visited the United States, where he gathered some political knowledge, which subsequent events rendered highly useful to him.

The revolution began in Venezuela on Good Friday, April 19th, 1810, when, by a popular movement, the captain-general of Caraccas was arrested and deposed, and a congress convened to organize a new government. The talents and acquirements of Bolivar pointed him out as the best qualified person to be placed at the helm; but he disapproved of the system adopted by the congress, and refused a diplomatic mission to England. He even declined any connection with the government, though he continued a staunch friend to the cause of independence. But at length, he consented to proceed to England, where he solicited the British cabinet in vain to espouse the cause of the revolution. Finding them resolved to maintain a strict neutrality, he returned to Caraccas after a short stay. In the mean time, the declaration of independence was boldly maintained by military force. Miranda was appointed commander-in-chief. Bolivar took the post of colonel in the army, and governor of Puerto Cabello, the strongest place in Venezuela.

Success attended the arms of the patriots till 1812, when a remarkable event caused them the most serious reverses. In March of that year, a violent earthquake devastated the whole province, and among other places totally destroyed the city of Caraccas, with all its magazines and munitions of war. This dreadful calamity, in which twenty thousand persons perished, happened, by a most remarkable coincidence, on the anniversary of the very day in which the revolution had broken out, two years before. The priesthood, who, as a body, were devoted to the royal interest, eagerly seized upon this circumstance. In their hands, the earthquake became the token of the Divine wrath against the revolutionary party. The superstitious multitude was easily deluded and terrified with such representations and denunciations. Priests, monks, and friars were stationed in the streets, vociferating in the midst of credulous throngs of people trembling with fear, while the royalist commanders improved the occasion by overrunning one district after another. Bolivar was compelled to evacuate Puerto Cabello. Miranda's conduct having become suspicious, he was arrested by the patriot leaders and delivered up to the Spanish commander, who sent him to Spain, where he died in a dungeon. Bolivar is supposed to have had a share in this transaction, in consequence of which he has been severely censured.

There were some circumstances, however, which appeared to justify a suspicion that Miranda was engaged in a hostile plot with the British cabinet.

Bolivar was now entrusted with the command of an army of six thousand men, which he led across the mountains to the farther extremity of New Granada. In the hostilities of this period, deeds of the most revolting ferocity were perpetrated by the royalist troops, and the whole country was reduced to a frightful state of misery. On the most trivial pretexts, old men, women and children were arrested and massacred as rebels. Friars and military butchers reigned triumphant. One of the Spanish officers, named Suasola, cut off the ears of a great number of patriots, and had them stuck in the caps of his soldiers for cockades. Bolivar, who had hitherto conducted the war with great forbearance, was inflamed with indignation at these cruelties; he swore to avenge his countrymen, and declared that every royalist who fell into his hands should be consigned to the vengeance of his soldiery. But this spirit of inexorable justice and retaliation ill accorded with Bolivar's character, and it was exercised only on one occasion, when eight hundred Spaniards were shot. Afterwards it was formally announced by Bolivar, that " no Spaniard shall be put to death except in battle. The war of death shall cease."

The royalists, who, by the practice of the most bloody and ferocious atrocities, had gained possession of nearly the whole country, now began to give way before the arms of Bolivar. Passing from one victory to another, he drove the enemy from every post, and

on the 4th of August, 1814, made his triumphant
entry into the renovated city of Caraccas.   The enthusiasm and joy of the people exceeded all bounds, and
this was certainly the most brilliant day in his whole
career.   Greeted by the acclamations of thousands of
the inhabitants, artillery, bells and music, the Libera
tor was drawn into the city in a triumphal car by
twelve beautiful young ladies of the first families of the
capital, dressed in white, and adorned with the patriot
colors, while others crowned him with laurel, and
strewed his way with flowers.   All the prisons were
thrown open, and hundreds who had been suffering for
political opinions came forth, pale and emaciated, to
thank him for their liberation.   The royalists through
out the province capitulated, and the triumph of the
patriots was complete.

Bolivar was now constituted dictator, and entrusted
with unlimited power.   This measure was prompted
by the sentiments of enthusiasm and gratitude during
the first moments of exultation in the people ; but, as
is the case in all infant republics, they soon began to
give manifestations of a jealousy for that liberty which
had cost them such sacrifices.   The power of the
dictator, who delegated his authority to his inferior
officers, by whom it was frequently abused, redoubled
their apprehensions.   Suspicions arose, that the pri-
mary object of Bolivar was his own aggrandizement.
In consequence of this, on the 2d of January, 1814,
he made a formal tender of his resignation.   This
ulled the suspicions of the people, and the royalists
having begun to rally and arm their negro slaves, he
was solicited to retain the dictatorship.   The wa· was

now renewed, and many battles were fought. On the 14th of June, 1814, Bolivar was defeated at La Puerta, with the loss of fifteen hundred men; and again on the 17th of August, near his own estate of San Mateo, where the negro leader Boves, with a squadron of cavalry named the "infernal division," with black crape on their lances, rushing with hideous shouts from an ambush, scattered his remaining forces, and would have made him prisoner but for the fleetness of his horse. His cousin, Ribas, was taken and shot, and his head set upon the wall of Caraccas. Bolivar's beautiful family mansion was burnt to the ground, and he was compelled, in September, to leave the royalists again in complete possession of all Venezuela, while thousands of the patriot army deserted to their ranks.

In spite of these reverses, we find him, in December of the same year, at the head of two thousand men, marching upon the city of Bogota, which he stormed and captured. But other circumstances having caused him to despair of any permanent success against the Spaniards at that time, he left the country in May, 1815, and retired to Jamaica. The war in Europe being brought to a close, the Spanish government were enabled to send an army of twelve thousand men, under General Morillo, to Venezuela and New Granada. This commander overran both provinces, and executed two thousand of the inhabitants. While Bolivar resided at Kingston, in Jamaica, he employed himself in writing a defence of his conduct in the civil war of New Granada, and issued several spirited exhortations to the patriots, for which his assassination

13*

was attempted by the royalist party. A Spaniard, stimulated by a bribe of fifty thousand dollars and a promise of perfect absolution by the church, ventured upon this undertaking. He obtained admission into Bolivar's apartment, and stabbed to the heart his secretary, who, by chance, was lying in the general's hammock.

From Jamaica, Bolivar proceeded to Hayti, where he raised a force of blacks and patriot emigrants, with which he landed in Cumana, in July, 1816. But, at Ocumare, he was surrounded by the royalists, defeated with great slaughter, and again expelled from the country. A few months afterwards, he landed once more upon the continent, and, after a battle of three days, completely routed the army-of Morillo. This success re-instated him in his office of captain-general and supreme head, and he followed up this advantage by other victories over the royalists. On the 15th of February, 1819, the congress of the Venezuelan republic was installed at Angostura, when Bolivar submitted the plan of a republican constitution, and formally laid down his authority. A strong representation of the exigencies of the times was again pressed upon him, and became his inducement to resume it. In the following summer he undertook an expedition across the Cordilleras. Fatigue and privations of every kind were endured with exemplary fortitude in the advance of the army through this wild, precipitous and barren region, where they lost their artillery and most of their equipments. On the heights of Tunja, they found a Spanish army of three thousand five hundred men, whom they instantly attacked and defeated.

This, and a subsequent victory at Boyaca, compelled the Spanish commander-in-chief, Barreyro, to surrender the remnant of his army. Samano, the Spanish viceroy, fled from Bogota, leaving in the treasury a million of dollars behind him; and the deliverance of New Granada was complete.

The immediate consequence of this success was the union of the two provinces of Venezuela and New Granada, under the title of the Republic of Colombia, and Bolivar was appointed president, in 1819. It would much exceed our limits to relate all the military events which followed till the final expulsion of the Spanish armies from the country. Peru had now revolted, and solicited the aid of the Colombians. Bolivar marched an army into that country in 1822, drove the royalists from Lima, and was appointed dictator by the Peruvian congress. On the 6th of August, 1824, he gained the important victory of Junin, and the Peruvian congress shortly after tendered him a present of a million of dollars, which he refused. The royalists being again defeated at Ayacucho, by General Sucre, on the 9th of December, 1824, the war of Spanish American independence was finally closed, after one hundred thousand lives had been sacrificed. Bolivar resigned the dictatorship of Peru in the following February, and in his tour through the country, witnessed one uninterrupted scene of triumph and extravagant exultation,—of dinners, balls, bull-fights, illuminations, triumphal arches and processions. A sumptuous banquet was given on the summit of the famous mountain of Potosi, and the Liberator, in the enthusiasm excited by the

excessive adulation which he received, exclaim..d on
that occasion, " The value of all the riches that are
buried in the Andes beneath my feet is nothing compared to the glory of having borne the standard of
independence from the sultry banks of the Orinoco,
to fix it on the frozen peak of this mountain, whose
wealth has excited the envy and astonishment of the
world."

A new republic, formed out of the conquered provinces, was now constituted, and named, from the Liberator, *Bolivia*.   From this republic he received a gift
of a million of dollars, on condition that the money
should be appropriated to the liberation of negro slaves
in that territory.   At the request of the congress, he
framed a scheme of government, known as the " Bol-
ivian code."   This was adopted both in Bolivia, and
by the congress of Lima, where Bolivar was made
president.   On the 22d of June, 1826, a scheme projected by him for a grand congress of the Spanish
American republics, was carried into effect, and this
meeting, consisting of deputies from Colombia, Mexico, Guatimala, Peru and Bolivia, was convened at
Panama.   The main object of this congress was to
establish an annual convention of state representatives,
to discuss diplomatic affairs, decide international disputes, promote liberal principles, and ensure a union
of strength in repelling any foreigr. attack.   This
was a noble idea, but too vast an undertaking for the
means of performance which actually existed within
the control of the Liberator, and it led to no great
practical results.

On the return of Bolivar to Colombia, he found

two thirds of the republic in a state of insurrection. Great dissatisfaction existed in Venezuela with the central government, and the inhabitants, headed by Paez, a mulatto general, rose and dec..ared themselves in favor of a federal system. Bolivar, having reached Bogota, the capital, assumed extraordinary powers, being authorized to take that step by the constitution, .n its provisions for cases of rebellion. He then proceeded to Venezuela ; but, instead of punishing the ˙nsurgents, he announced a general amnesty, and confirmed Paez in the command which he had assumed. This led to strong suspicions that the insurrection had been instigated by Bolivar, in order to afford a pretext for assuming the dictatorship, and that he and Paez had acted with a collusive understanding. The truth, on this subject, has never yet been clearly revealed. The presence of Bolivar quieted the commotion, as, in spite of the suspicions which rested upon him, his popularity was still very great. He addressed a letter to the senate of Colombia, disclaiming all ambitious designs, and offering his resignation. This proposal caused violent debates in the congress, and many members voted to accept it ; but a majority were in favor of continuing him in office.

At a congress held at Ocana, in March, 1828, Bolivar assumed more of an anti-republican tone, and recommended strengthening the executive power. Many of his adherents, in which the soldiery were included, seconded his views, and declared that the people were not prepared to appreciate the excellence of institutions purely republican, a fact of which there can be little doubt. They carried this doctrine, however, to an unwarrantable extreme, by insisting that the president should be intrusted with absolute discretionary power. This proposition was indignantly rejected by a majority of the congress, and the partisans of Bolivar vacated their seats; in consequence of which, that body was left without a quorum, and dissolved. The city of Bogota then took the matter into its own hands, and conferred upon Bolivar the title of Supreme Chief of Colombia, with absolute power to regulate all the affairs of government. His immediate concurrence in this illegal and revolutionary measure has been deemed a sufficient proof that it was brought about by his instigation. On the 20th of June, 1829, he entered that city in magnificent state, and assumed his authority. These proceedings could not but lead to violent measures. An attempt was soon made to assassinate the dictator. Several persons broke into his chamber at midnight, and shot two officers of the staff, who were with him; Bolivar himself only escaped by leaping out of the window and lying concealed under a bridge. Santander, the vice-president, and several officers of the army, were tried and convicted of being implicated in this conspiracy. The former was sentenced to death, but Bolivar was satisfied with banishing him from Colombia.

The whole country became rent with factions, commotions and rebellion. The popularity of the Liberator was gone, and his authority was disclaimed in almost every quarter. The events which ensued do not require to be specified here, as they are nothing more than a repetition of what had been acted over many times before. At length Bolivar, finding his influence at an end, and his health and spirits broken, determined to withdraw from public life, take leave of the country, and retire to Europe. At a general convention at Bogota, in January, 1830, he resigned his authority for the last time, and rejected many entreaties to resume it. He withdrew to the neighborhood of Carthagena, where he spent nearly two years in retirement, when, finding his end approaching, he issued his farewell address to the people of Colombia, in the following words :—

" Colombians,—I have unceasingly and disinterestedly exerted my energies for your welfare. I have abandoned my fortune and my personal tranquillity in your cause. I am the victim of my persecutors, who have now conducted me to my grave : but I pardon them. Colombians, I leave you. My last prayers are offered up for the tranquillity of my country ; and if my death will contribute to this desirable end by extinguishing your factions, I shall descend with feelings of contentment into the tomb that is soon to receive me." A week afterwards, he breathed his last, at San Pedro, near Carthagena, on the 17th of December, 1831, at the age of forty-eight.

His death appears to have afflicted his countrymen with the deepest sorrow and remorse. In an instant, they forgot the jealousies and suspicions which had filled their breasts with regard to their great chief, and, by a sudden revulsion of feeling they indulged in the most bitter self-reproach at the reflection, that the man who had devoted his fortune and his life to

the liberation and welfare of his country, had sunk
under their ungenerous reproaches, and died of a
broken heart, the victim of national ingratitude.
Almost every town in Colombia paid honors to his
memory by orations, funeral processions, and other
demonstrations of grief and respect.

The fortunes of this eminent man were most singular.   During one period, he was regarded as one of the
greatest characters of modern times.   At the present
moment, he is almost forgotten ; and another generation may witness a revival of his fame.   In the early
part of his career, he was believed to be a disinterested
patriot ; at the close, he had totally lost the confidence
of his countrymen, and he died tainted with the suspicion of intriguing with the French government to
subjugate the country by European arms and establish
a monarchy.   There are some acts of his life which
have an equivocal character ; but, judging of his whole
conduct from such evidence as is within our reach,
we are compelled to pronounce his acquittal of the
charge of entertaining designs hostile to the liberties
of his country.   Bolivar is not to be judged by the
standard which we apply to the character and merits
of Washington.   The cool-tempered, orderly, intelligent, and well educated North Americans, who
achieved their independence with a moderation, sobri-
ety and self-restraint which drew forth the applause
and admiration of the world, were a very different
race from the heterogeneous population of Colombia,
ignorant, insubordinate, superstitious, fanatical, ferocious, little advanced in civilization, and subject to all
the sudden impulses of a rash and fiery southern

temper. It was impossible to govern such men, amid the turbulence of jealous factions, by the weak instrument of a written constitution.

The proofs of Bolivar's disinterestedness are very strong. He sacrificed a large fortune in the cause of his country; and had many opportunities of acquiring enormous wealth, all of which he neglected. As a military commander, he is entitled to high praise. Though often defeated, his perseverance and fortitude in rising superior to every obstacle, are everywhere conspicuous. The difficulties of marshaling, disciplining and leading an army to battle during the revolution of Colombia, are hardly to be conceived. Bolivar's troops often consisted chiefly of desperate adventurers, eager only for pay and plunder; ragged creoles, Indians, naked negroes, and cavalry of half-savage *Llaneros* mounted on wild horses. Whole regiments often deserted from one side to the other, and back again, according to the chance of success.

The fatigues, cares and anxieties to which he was constantly exposed during a most eventful career of nearly twenty years, were strongly marked in his countenance, and at forty-five he had the appearance of a man of sixty. He was capable of enduring the most severe labor; was a remarkably bold horseman, and was fond of dancing in his spurs. He was abstemious in personal matters, but hospitable and highly munificent in giving entertainments. His manners were easy and dignified, and he was gifted with an extraordinary faculty of prompt repartee in conversation. In one instance, he was known to give seventeen unpremeditated answers in succession, each of which, if prepared by deliberate study, would have been admired for its happy adaptation to the subject and the occasion. In proposing a toast, in returning thanks, or in speaking impromptu on any casual subject, he never was surpassed.

THE DICTATOR FRANCIA.

SPANISH AMERICA, which, in its revolutionary career, has offered to our view examples of the wildest excesses of popular violence and unbridled democracy, has also shown an instance of the sternest and most unmitigated despotism. This example is presented to us in the case of Doctor Francia, of Paraguay, who, from an obscure origin, raised himself to power more absolute than that of Napoleon, and, after reigning twenty-six years the sole authority in the state, and the supreme arbiter of the life and death of every inhabitant of the country, died peaceably in his bed, sincerely bewailed and regretted by the people. So extraordinary a man is without a parallel in modern times, and it were to be wished that we possessed more abundant materials for writing his history and analyzing his character. A strange man himself, he lived in a strange country, and most accounts of him have been composed under circumstances liable to suspicion.

José Gaspar Rodriguez Francia was born near Assumpcion, in Paraguay, in the year 1757. His father was either a Frenchman or a Portuguese, and his mother a Paraguay creole. He was one of several children. At the University of Cordova, in Tucuman, he received such an education as a classical seminary in the interior of South America could furnish. Being

THE DICTATOR FRANCIA.

a person of shrewd, saturnine disposition, and retired, studious habits, he contrived, by close application, to acquire a degree of knowledge seldom placed within the reach of a student whose pursuits were watched by the jealous ecclesiastics of that region. In addition to the branches of education common in the university, he contrived to acquire some knowledge of algebra, geometry and Greek. Having prosecuted his studies through the ordinary term, he returned to Paraguay, and entered into practice as a lawyer.* His professional reputation, in that country where justice was regularly bought and sold, was not only unsullied by venality, but conspicuous for rectitude. The following anecdote of his uprightness has been related by a writer no way disposed to be unduly partial to the subject of it.

Francia had an acquaintance in Assumpcion, of the name of Domingo Rodriguez. This man had cast a longing eye upon a certain Naboth's vineyard; and this Naboth, named Estanislao Machain, was Francia's open enemy. Rodriguez, never doubting that the young advocate, like other lawyers, would undertake an unrighteous cause for a suitable reward, went to him, offered a liberal retaining fee, and directed him to institute a suit in law for the recovery of the estate in question. Francia saw at once that the pretensions were founded in injustice and fraud; and he not only refused to act as his counsel, but plainly told Rodriguez, that, much as he disliked his antago-

* As he also studied medicine, it is supposed that the title of Dr. was derived from that circumstance; though it seems that he never practised in the medical profession.

K   14*

nist, Machain, yet, if he persisted in his iniquitous suit, he would himself undertake the cause of the injured party.   Covetousness, however, is not so easily driven from its purpose.   Rodriguez persisted, and as he was a man of great fortune, the suit appeared to be going against Machain and his estate.   At this critical stage of the affair, the slave who attended the door of the luckless Machain, was astonished one evening to see Francia present himself before it, wrapped up in his cloak.   Knowing that the doctor and his master, like Montague and Capulet, were " smoke in each other's eyes," he refused him admittance, and ran to inform his master of this strange and unexpected visit.   Machain, no less struck by the circumstance than his slave, for some time hesitated, but at length determined to admit his old enemy.   In walked the silent visiter to Machain's chamber, and spread the papers connected with the law case upon the table.

" Machain," said Francia, " you know I am your enemy.   But I know that my friend Rodriguez meditates, and will certainly, unless I interfere, carry on against you an act of gross and lawless aggression. I have come to offer my services in your defence." The astonished man could scarcely credit his senses ; but he poured forth his expressions of gratitude in terms of thankful acquiescence.

Pleas, it would appear, are made in that country by writing.   The first paper sent into court, confounded the adverse counsel, and staggered the judge, who was in their interest.   " My friend," said that functionary to the leading advocate for the plaintiff. " I cannot proceed in this matter, unless you bribe Dr. Francia to be silent."   " I will try," was the answer.

and the advocate went to him with a hundred doubloons. He offered them as a bribe to Francia, to let the matter slip ; and more surely to gain his consent, he advised him that this was done at the suggestion of the judge himself.

" Leave my house with your vile proposals and contemptible gold !" was the indignant answer ; and the menial tool of the unjust judge waited for no further dismissal. Francia, putting on his capote, hurried at once to the residence of that magistrate. " Sir," said he, after mentioning the attempt to bribe him, " you are a disgrace to law, and a blot upon justice. You are, moreover, completely in my power ; and unless to-morrow you pronounce a decision in favor of my client, I will make your seat upon the bench too hot for you ; and the insignia of your judicial office shall become the emblems of your shame." The morrow did not fail to bring a decision in favor of Francia's client. The judge lost his character, and the young doctor's fame resounded far and wide.

His uncommon reputation for integrity, a more than common acuteness and learning in his profession, profound knowledge of the foibles and peculiarities of his countrymen, together with his fame for a mysterious familiarity with the occult sciences, soon caused Dr. Francia to be regarded as a most remarkable personage. In the deplorable state of ignorance then existing in South America, it was a wonderful faculty that enabled a man to multiply and subtract the letters of the alphabet ; to read a language written in strange characters ; to measure an angle and ascertain the height of a mountain with a theodolite.   Francia, celebrated for universal knowledge, stood upon high vantage-ground, and in a great public exigence could not fail to be looked upon as one of the individuals destined to take the lead in public affairs.

When the province of La Plata revolted from Spain, the people of Paraguay refused to acknowledge the authority of the former government; in consequence of which an army was sent from Buenos Ayres, in 1810, under General Belgrano, to reduce Paraguay. He was defeated and driven back.   The next year a revolutionary government was established, and Francia, who had previously been in public office as a member of the municipal council and mayor of the capital, Assumpcion, was appointed secretary of the congress.   Everything was in confusion; the army, as is usual on such occasions, seemed inclined to take the lead, and for some time, faction and terror alone prevailed; but Francia, at this critical moment, obtained an ascendency which he never afterwards lost. His superior talents, address and information were continually in requisition, and made him indispensable on all occasions.   Nothing of any importance could be transacted without him.   The members of the congress were entirely inexperienced in political matters, and grossly illiterate.   Such a body attempted to found a republic, and we are told that their consti tution was compiled from passages in Rollin's Ancient History.

The business proceeded with small success under such auspices.   Intrigues, cabals and factions disgusted Francia to such a degree that he resigned his office, and retired to his country seat. The reader may wish for a picture of so remarkable a man as this Dionysius of the western world, and we will copy the following description of him at the period of his retirement. It is drawn by an English merchant, who resided in Paraguay at that time.

"On one of those lovely evenings in Paraguay, after the south-west wind has both cleared and cooled the air, I was drawn, in my pursuit of game, into a peaceful valley, remarkable for its combination of all the striking features of the scenery of the country. Suddenly I came upon a neat and unpretending cottage. Up rose a partridge; I fired, and the bird came to the ground. A voice from behind called out, "*Buen tiro*,"—" a good shot." I turned round, and beheld a gentleman of about fifty years of age, dressed in a suit of black, with a large scarlet *capote*, or cloak, thrown over his shoulders. He had a *maté* cup in one hand, a cigar in the other; and a little urchin of a negro, with his arms crossed, was in attendance by the gentleman's side. The stranger's countenance was dark, and his black eyes were very penetrating; while his jet hair, combed back from a bold forehead, and hanging in natural ringlets over his shoulders, gave him a dignified and striking air. He wore on his shoes large golden buckles, and at the knees of his breeches the same.

"In exercise of the primitive and simple hospitality common in the country, I was invited to sit down under the corridor, and to take a cigar and *maté*, or cup of Paraguay tea. A celestial globe, a large telescope, and a theodolite were under the little portico; and I immediately inferred that the personage before me was no other than Doctor Francia. He introduced me to his library, in a confined room, with a very small window, and that so shaded by the roof of the corridor as to admit the least portion of light necessary for study. The library was arranged on three rows of shelves extending across the room, and might have consisted of three hundred volumes. There were many ponderous books on law ; a few on the inductive sciences ; some in French and some in Latin upon subjects of general literature, with Euclid's Elements, and some schoolboy treatises on algebra. On a large table were several heaps of law papers and processes. Several folios, bound in vellum, were outspread upon it. A lighted candle, though placed there solely to light cigars, lent its feeble aid to illumine the room ; while a *maté* cup and inkstand, both of silver, stood on another part of the table. There was neither carpet nor mat on the brick floor ; and the chairs were of such ancient fashion, size and weight, that it required a considerable effort to move them from one spot to another."

Francia's withdrawal left the government without an efficient adviser. Embarrassments multiplied, and a second congress was convened ; " such a congress," as we are told, " as never met before in the world : a congress which knew not its right hand from *its* left ; which drank infinite rum in the taverns, and had one wish,—that of getting on horseback home to its field-husbandry and partridge-shooting." Such men, and we need not wonder, could not govern Paraguay. Francia was called from his retirement, and a new constitution was formed, with two chief magistrates, called consuls. Francia and a colleague were appointed to these offices for one year, each in supreme command for four months at a time ; but as the former took the precedence, he had two thirds of the year for his own term of authority. Two carved chairs were prepared for the use of the consuls, one inscribed with the name of *Cæsar*, and the other with that of *Pompey*. It is needless to say which of the consuls took possession of the former. By consummate address and management, and by the influence which he had obtained over the troops, Francia got rid of his colleague at the close of the year, in 1814, and was proclaimed dictator for three years. At the end of that time, he found no difficulty in assuming the dictatorship for life. From the moment that he felt his footing firm, and his authority quietly submitted to, his whole character appeared to undergo a remarkable change. Without faltering or hesitation, without a pause of human weakness, he proceeded to frame the boldest and most extraordinary system of despotism that was ever the work of a single individual. He assumed the whole power, legislative and executive ; the people had but one privilege, and one duty— that of obedience. All was done rapidly, boldly, unreservedly, and powerfully ; he well knew the character of the people at whose head he had placed himself, and who, strange to say, once thought themselves possessed of energy and virtue enough for a republic.

The army, of course, was his chief instrument of power. It consisted of five thousand regular troops, and twenty thousand militia. He took care to secure their most devoted attachment, and it does not appear that during his whole career of despotism the smallest symptom of disaffection was ever manifested in their ranks.   Francia, at the time of his accession to the supreme authority, was past the age when any dormant vice, save that of avarice, is likely to spring up in the character.   He was not dazzled with the pomp and circumstance of exalted rank, nor even by that nobler weakness, the desire of fame ; for he took no pains to make an ostentatious display of his power, or spread his reputation among foreign nations, or hand his name down to posterity.   On the contrary, he carefully shrouded himself, and, as far as possible, his dominions, in haughty seclusion.   His ruling, or rather absorbing passion, was a love of power, and of power for itself alone.   It was with him a pure, abstracted principle, free from desire of the splendor which usually surrounds it, of the wealth which usually supports it, and of the fame which usually succeeds it.

The most remarkable feature in his administration, was the perfect isolation in which he placed the country.   Intercourse with foreign nations was absolutely interdicted.   Commerce was at an end : the ships lay high and dry, their pitchless seams yawning, on the banks of the rivers, and no man could trade but by the Dictator's license.   No man could leave Paraguay on any pretext whatever, and it became as hermetically sealed against the escape of its inhabitants as the " Happy Valley " of Abyssinia.   In this restrictive policy, he was assisted by the peculiar geographical features of the country.   Paraguay, in the midst of an immense and thinly-peopled continent, stood alone and impenetrable; its large rivers, wide forests and morasses render travelling difficult and hazardous. Any one attempting to cross the frontiers, must encounter the danger of losing himself in the wilderness, of being destroyed by those immense and terrible conflagrations to which the thick woods are subject, of excessive fatigue and exposure, of starvation, and of attacks from venomous reptiles, wild beasts and savages. The only possibility of escape is during the time that the river Paraguay overflows the surrounding plains; it is then barely practicable. A Frenchman, with five negroes, made the attempt in 1823. One of them died of fatigue, another by the bite of a snake. At one time they were surrounded by the burning woods; and at another were involved in an immense glade in the midst of a forest, where they wandered about for fifteen days in search of an outlet, and were finally obliged to return by the opening through which they entered. Being at last so reduced by fatigue and famine that they were unable to resist a single man, they were recaptured by a ser-geant of militia.

But Francia's tyranny was not without signal ben efits to the country. The land had peace, while all the rest of Spanish America was plunged into frightful anarchy, raging and ravening like a huge dog-kennel gone mad. Paraguay was domineered over by a tyrant, but Peru and Mexico, Chili and Guatimala, suffered the oppression of forty tyrants. Francia's soldiers were kept well drilled, and in strict subordination, always ready to march where the wild Indians

or other enemies made their appearance. Guard-
houses were established at short distances along the
rivers and around the dangerous frontiers; and wher-
ever an Indian cavalry horde showed itself, an alarm
cannon announced the danger; the military hastened
to the spot, and the savage marauders vanished into
the heart of the deserts. A great improvement, too,
was visible in other quarters. The finances were
accurately and frugally administered. There were
no sinecures in the government; every official person
was compelled to do his work. Strict justice between
man and man was enforced in the courts of law.
The affair of Naboth's vineyard could not have
occurred under the Dictator's rule. He himself would
accept no gift, not even the smallest trifle. He introduced schools of various sorts, promoted education by
all the means in his power, and repressed superstition
as far as it could be done among such a people. He
promoted agriculture in a singular manner, not merely
making two blades of grass grow where one grew
before, but two crops of corn in a season. In the year
1820, a cloud of locusts devastated the whole country,
and the prospect of universal famine threatened the
land. The summer was at an end, and there was
no foreign commerce by which supplies might be
obtained from abroad. Francia hit upon an expedient,
such as had never entered into the contemplation of
any man in Paraguay before. He issued a peremp-
tory command, ordering, under a severe penalty, that
the farmers throughout the country should sow their
lands anew. The result was, that a second crop was
produced, and the people were amazed with the im-

portant discovery that two harvests were, every year, possible in Paraguay. Agriculture made immense progress; the cultivation of many articles, before unknown in the country, was now successfully introduced, and among others rice and cotton. Manufactures kept pace with agriculture, and the clothing of the people, which had previously, for the most part, been imported ready made, at a great expense, was now entirely produced at home.

The city of Assumpcion was an assemblage of narrow, crooked, irregular streets, interspersed with trees, gardens and clumps of tropical vegetation. It had no pavements, and, standing on a slope of ground, the sandy thoroughfare was torn by the rain into gullies impassable except by taking long leaps. Numerous springs issued from the soil in every part of the city, and formed streams or stagnated into pools, where every species of filth became deposited. Francia determined on having it remodeled, paved and straightened. The inhabitants were ordered to pull down their houses and build them anew. The cost to private purses was great, and caused infinite grumbling; but Assumpcion is now an improved, paved city, and possesses convenient thoroughfares.

Francia's method of dealing with his subjects is well illustrated by the following anecdote. One afternoon a shoemaker brought him a couple of grenadier's belts, which he had been ordered to make. The Dictator did not like the work—" Sentinel ! " cried he ; and in came the sentinel, when the subjoined conversation took place.

Dictator. Take this lazy whelp to the gallows over

the way, and march him under it half a dozen times. Now (turning to the trembling shoemaker) bring me such another pair of belts, and instead of walking *under* the gallows, we shall try how you can *swing* upon it.

Shoemaker. Please your Excellency, I have done my best.

Dictator. Well, lazybones, if this be *your* best, I shall do *my* best to see that you never again spoil any more of the state's leather. The belts are good for nothing but to hang you up on that little machine which the grenadier will show you.

Shoemaker. God bless your Excellency! The Lord forbid! I am your vassal, your slave. Day and night have I served and will continue to serve my lord. Only give me two more days to prepare the belts, and, by the soul of a sorrowful cobbler, I will make them to your Excellency's liking.

Dictator. Off with him, sentinel!

Sentinel. March, lazybones!

Shoemaker. Most excellent sir, *this very night* I will make the belts according to your Excellency's pattern.

Dictator. Well, I will give you till morning; but you must pass under the gallows; it is a salutary process, and may at once quicken the work and improve the workmanship.

Sentinel. March, you lazy dog! the Supreme commands it.

The poor cobbler was marched off, and, after being compelled to take half a dozen turns under the gibbet, he fell to work with all his might. On the following morning, he had produced a pair of belts without a parallel in South America ; and he is now if still alive, belt-maker general of Paraguay, a most thriving and driving man, who must thank the gallows for putting him at the top of his profession.

The stern temper and arbitrary political system of Francia led him to acts which could not fail of being denounced as the wanton excesses of a sanguinary disposition. He put to death upwards of forty persons, as we are assured by a traveller, who utters the bitterest denunciations against him. He had frightful prisons, and banished disorderly persons to a desolate spot in the wilderness. How far his executions were wanton and unjustifiable, we have not sufficient means of judging. In the early part of his career, a plot was formed for the purpose of taking his life ; it was discovered, and executions followed ; after this we hear nothing more of these sanguinary deeds. His enemy, the bandit chieftain Artigas, had done a great deal of injury to Paraguay, and had incensed him further by fomenting revolts among his Indians. Yet, when one of this chieftain's lieutenants rebelled against him, and forced him to retreat with the wreck of his army, Artigas threw himself on the mercy of the Dictator, and was treated with clemency. He suffered him to reside in Paraguay, assigned him a house and lands, with a pension, and ordered the governor of the district to furnish him besides with whatever accommodations he desired, and to treat him with respect.

The Dictator's treatment of the foreigners who found their way into his dominions, was most rigorous and unjust, and has contributed more than any other cause to blacken his character among strangers. Paraguay was a sort of mousetrap, easy enough to get into, but very difficult to get out of.　M. Bonpland, the fellow-traveller of Humboldt, and two Swiss naturalists, wandering into Francia's domains, were detained there many years.　Sometimes, by special permission, an individual was allowed to leave the country, but these instances were rare.　The foreigners detained were informed that they might pursue what avocations they pleased, provided they did not interfere with the government.

The father of Francia was a man of very eccentric habits; his brothers and one of his sisters were lunatics, and the Dictator himself was subject to fits of hypochondria, which seem occasionally to have affected his intellect.　When under such influence, he would shut himself up for several days.　On one of these occasions, being offended at the idle crowds gazing about the government house, he gave the following order to a sentinel.　" If any person presumes to stop and stare at my house, fire at him.　If you miss him, *this* is for a second shot, (handing him another musket loaded with ball.)　If you miss again, I shall take care not to miss *you!*　"　This order being quickly made known throughout the city, the inhabitants carefully avoided passing near the house, or, if their business led them that way, they hurried on with their eyes fixed on the ground.　After some weeks, an Indian, who knew nothing of the Spanish language, stopped to gaze at the house, and was ordered to move on, but still continued to loiter.　The sentinel fired, and missed him.　Francia, hearing the report, was alarmed, and summoned the sentinel. " What news friend ? " On being told the cause, he declared that he did not recollect having given such an order, and immediately revoked it.

The domestic establishment of the Dictator of Paraguay consisted of four slaves, three of them mulattoes and the fourth a negro, whom he treated with great mildness. He led a very regular life, and commonly rose with the sun. As soon as he was dressed, the negro bought him a chafing-dish, a kettle, and a pitcher of water. The Dictator made his own tea, and after drinking it, he took a walk under the colonnade fronting upon the court, smoking a cigar, which he always took care previously to unroll, in order to ascertain that it contained no poison ; although his cigars were always made by his sister. At six o'clock came the barber, an unwashed, ragged mulatto, given to drink, but the Dictator's only confidential menial. If his excellency happened to be in good humor, he chatted over the soapdish, and the shaver was often intrusted with important commissions in preparing the public for the Dictator's projects ; so that he might be said to be the official gazette of Paraguay. He then stepped out, in his dressing gown of printed calico, to the outer colonnade, an open space which ranged all round the building ; here he walked about, receiving, at the same time, such persons as he admitted to an audience. About seven, he withdrew to his room, where he remained till nine. The officers then came to make their reports and receive orders. At eleven, his chief secretary brough the papers which required inspection by him, and wrote from his dictation till noon. He then sat down to table and ate a frugal dinner. After this he took a siesta, drank a cup of *maté*, and smoked a cigar. Till four or five in the afternoon, he again attended to business; the escort then arrived to attend him, and he rode out to inspect the public works. While on this duty, he was armed with a sabre and a pair of double-barrelled pocket-pistols. He returned home about nightfall, and sat down to study till nine, when he took his supper, consisting of a roast pigeon and a glass of wine. In fine weather, he took an evening walk in the outer colonnade. At ten, he gave the watchword, and returning into the house, he fastened all the doors with his own hands.

Though possessing unlimited sway over the finances of the state, he made no attempt to enrich himself, and his small salary was always in arrears to him. His two nephews, who were officers in the army, were dismissed, lest they should presume upon their relationship. He banished his sister from his house because she had employed a grenadier, one of the soldiers of the state, on some errand of her own. He was a devoted admirer of Napoleon, whose downfall he always deplored. The Swiss traveller, Rengger, who, after a long detention, was permitted to depart, left behind him a print of the French emperor. Francia sent an express after him, inquiring the price of it. Rengger sent him for answer, that the print was at his excellency's service—he did not sell such trifles. The Dictator immediately despatched the print after him; he would receive no gifts. There seems to have existed originally in him somewhat of that simple and severe virtue, which is more characteristic of a stern republican than of a sanguinary tyrant. He has left one witticism upon record, which we will subjoin, as it is much in character. Rengger, who was a surgeon, was about to dissect a body. "Doctor," said the Dictator, "examine the neck, and see whether the Paraguayans have not an extra bone there, which hinders them from holding up their heads and speaking out."

In the accounts which were written of this extraordinary man during his lifetime, he has been represented as an arbitrary and cruel oppressor, universally detested, and whose death, inasmuch as he had made no provision for the continuance of the government, would plunge the state into anarchy and ruin. Both these representations have been completely falsified by the event. Francia died peaceably, on the 20th day of September, 1840, aged eighty-three; the people crowding round his house with much emotion, and even, as we are assured, with tears of anxiety and sympathy. The funeral discourse pronounced on the occasion, surprised the world; it was filled with praises of the deceased Dictator, whom it represented as the real father of his country.

Enough is known of Dr. Francia to assure us that he was a most remarkable individual; but it would be both difficult and unsafe to draw his character with confidence and minuteness, from the meagre and questionable materials which we possess respecting him. That he was a man of iron integrity in a country where corruption and venality were almost matters of course with public men; that he spent thirty years

L

of his life in toilsome devotion to his country; that he was above the vulgar love of money, and disdained to take advantage of his unlimited power for enriching himself,—are all incontrovertible facts; that his government was also, on the whole, advantageous to his country, is not to be denied. But what were the motives which guided his conduct? Was it patriotism, or a simple love of power? Why adopt so strange a system of policy—that of interdicting all intercourse with other nations? Was it from a conviction that this was best adapted to the condition of the people, or that it was indispensable to the preservation of his despotic sway? Why enshroud himself in such mysterious isolation, holding as little commerce of affection and sympathy with his fellow-men as of trade with foreign nations? These are questions which we cannot easily answer. If we may rely upon the scattered glimpses of his career that have been presented to us, we should venture to decide that the main elements of his character consisted of stern integrity and devoted patriotism; blended, however, with natural sternness of temper, a love of power, and a conviction that a despotic government was best suited to the condition of the people. His singular habits were probably the result of native eccentricity; his exclusive policy was doubtless adopted for the double motive of perpetuating his authority, and ensuring tranquillity to the country. Of the vigor of his mind and energy of his character, there can be no doubt. That he should have created and sustained, for thirty years, the sternest despotism that the world ever witnessed, in the heart of a continent where everything besides was tending to the dissolution of tyrannical power and the establishment of popular institutions, is a phenomenon that may well excite the curiosity and astonishment of the world. We may indeed suppose that his government was modelled after that of the Jesuits, the effects of which were still visible in his time; but that he should have been able to assume to himself, and exercise for so long a period, the unlimited power wielded by these sagacious priests, must still excite our surprise. If we suppose that his interdiction of intercourse with other nations, was designed as a means of keeping his people from the infection of those new political notions which were teeming around him, we must still admire .the energy and success with which this feature of his policy was maintained.

TOUSSAINT L'OUVERTURE.

TOUSSAINT L'OUVERTURE.

HISPANIOLA, or St. Domingo, was at one period the most fertile and valuable of all the West India Islands. In the richness and variety of its productions, and its local beauties, it surpassed every island in the western hemisphere. Its plains and valleys presented the most inviting scenes of rich and perpetual verdure. The extreme salubrity of the climate, and the abundance of its delicious fruits, rendered it one of the most delightful abodes in the world. Divided between France and Spain, it was a source of great revenue to both of those powers, from the flourishing commerce carried on in the exportation of the numerous products of its luxuriant and well-cultivated soil. The French division, although comprising less than a third part of the island, was considered the most valuable spot of its dimensions in the western world. The exports to France of sugar, coffee, cotton, indigo, cocoa, and other articles, exceeded thirty millions of dollars annually.

When the French revolution broke out, the planters of St. Domingo did not look on in silence; and the National Assembly, in requiring a more equal representation of the people, tacitly acknowledged that the colonies ought to have a voice in the legislature. The colonists, perceiving this, determined to seize the advantages which it offered. They selected their deputies, formed their colonial assemblies, and proceeded to establish a new constitution for the internal government of the island. This constitution, when published, sufficiently showed that nothing short of their independence of the mother country was the object at which they remotely aimed. Among the motives which led them to form this resolution, was the decree of the National Assembly, which declared that "all men are born free and equal as to their rights." This declaration they interpreted as tacitly recommending the emancipation of their slaves. The island was soon distracted by commotions; the royalists and revolutionists were arrayed against each other in all the heat of faction; violent measures were pursued by both parties, and the utmost ferment prevailed throughout the colony, in which all classes, the slaves not excepted, took an active interest.

A society had been formed in France, called the *Amis des Noirs*, composed partly of men who afterwards became leaders in the revolution, and partly of mulattoes, resident in Paris. Their avowed object was to procure the emancipation of the slaves; but their measures for its accomplishment were violent and injudicious. They demanded immediate emancipation; forgetting, in the heat of their zeal, that the negroes were unfit at that period to value and improve the advantages of freedom. They were equally rash in the methods by which they made their designs known to the slaves. Inflammatory addresses were dispersed among them, and various other arts were practised to induce them to rise against their masters. The colonists, at the same time, acted with equal 'ndiscretion. They took no measures to quiet the murmurs of their slaves, and would listen to none of their demands, however reasonable. The slaves, finding that, notwithstanding the decrees of the National Assembly, their privileges were still withheld, determined to secure them by force of arms. Accommodation soon became impossible; the French would offer no terms, and shut their eyes to the tremendous dangers that were impending over them. The slaves rose in insurrection, and St. Domingo became the scene of as fearful ravages as the world has ever witnessed. Conflagration, pillage, and massacre spread over the island, and the mind recoils in horror from the details of this fearful period.

Toussaint L'Ouverture, who distinguished himself early in this war, and subsequently became the leader of the blacks, was one of the most extraordinary characters of modern times, and exhibited proofs of genius and elevation of character which give him a high rank in the annals of great men. He was born a slave, of African parents, at Breda, near Cape François, in 1743. After he became the chief man in the island, one of his flatterers compiled a genealogy, declaring his descent from an African king. We do not know this to be false, but, although Toussaint was willing to have it believed, it is, probably, without foundation. In his youth, he was employed as a cattle-driver on the estate of the Count de Noé, to whom he belonged; he was taught reading and writing by another negro. In due time, he rose to the dignity of coachman to the manager of the estate; and when the revolution broke out, he held the office of over-seer, and possessed the confidence of his owner.

At the commencement of the struggle, many of the slaves adhered to the cause of their masters. Toussaint was one of these. From the beginning of the massacres of 1791, to the appearance of the procla-mation of the 4th of February, 1794, which declared all slaves free, he continued loyal, and made himself conspicuous by his zeal for the Catholic religion and royalty. At first he bore the title of " Physician of the Royal Armies," though we are not told what knowledge of medicine he possessed. He then be-came aid-de-camp to the negro leader, Jean François. His influence with the negroes increased, and the Spanish president, Garcia, honored him with his full confidence. When the negroes rejected the first overtures of the French commissioners, Toussaint assigned as a reason, that they had always been gov-erned by a king; could be governed only by a king; and having lost the king of France, had betaken them-selves to the protection of the king of Spain. But the proclamation of the French, emancipating the slaves, opened new views to him, and he negotiated with their general for a return to his old associates. Being promised a commission of brigadier-general, he went over to the French. His abandonment of the Spaniards caused the surrender of many of their most important posts.

Laveaux, the French governor, treated Toussaint, at first, with reserve and coolness, which compelled him to withdraw into retirement. He was now past his fiftieth year, and looked upon his days of activity and his public career as ended. But in 1795, he was sudden y called forth by a conspiracy of the mulattoes, who arrested and imprisoned the governor at Cape François. Toussaint raised an army of negroes, and being supported by the partisans of the French, found himself at the head of ten thousand men. With this force, he marched to the capital and set the governor at liberty. Laveaux, in his gratitude for this deed, proclaimed his deliverer the protector of the whites, the avenger of the constituted authorities, and the "black Spartacus," who, according to the prediction of the Abbe Raynal, was destined to arise and avenge his race. Toussaint's importance now rapidly augmented. He was made a general of division, and his influence was so predominant, that he was, in fact, the supreme arbiter of the fortunes of the colony. He reduced the whole north of the island, with a trifling exception, to the dominion of the French, and was the first that succeeded in establishing discipline among the armed negroes.

He was now commander-in-chief of the armies of St. Domingo. The island appeared to be firmly re-established under the French government, but the distrust of their commissioner, Hedouville, caused a renewal of the troubles. He attempted to thwart all the plans of Toussaint for the welfare of the colony. The latter persuaded the negroes to return to their agricultural labors, and thought it advisable that they should work five years for their former masters, reserving one fourth of their earnings, before they assumed the full extent of their freedom. At length, Hedouville, who had become odious to the inhabitants,

16 *

from his supposed hostility to the interests of the colony was dismayed by an insurrection at Cape François and fled, with all his adherents, comprising twelve or fifteen hundred men, to France. A strong animosity had subsisted from the beginning between the blacks and the mulattoes. The departure of the commissioner caused this feud to break out again in all its violence. Rigaud, the mulatto chief, led his ferocious partisans on to rapine and massacre. Toussaint used his utmost exertions to check the sanguinary deeds of his own men; and he carried on the war with such success, that he captured all the strong-holds of the mulattoes except Aux Cayes, where he besieged Rigaud, in 1799, and finally compelled him to abandon the island.

In the mean time, Bonaparte had become First Consul of France, and one of his first measures was to send a deputation to St. Domingo, who informed Toussaint that he was confirmed in his authority. This chief was now at the summit of his prosperity. Early in 1801, he subdued the whole Spanish portion of the island, and planned a scheme of a colonial constitution, in which he was appointed governor for life, with power to name his successor and appoint all the officers under the government. He exercised this authority to the full extent. He quelled an insurrection of the negroes, and did not hesitate to punish with death his own nephew, who had placed himself at the head of it. Under his strict but equitable sway, the agriculture and commerce of St. Domingo were soon in a flourishing state. Slavery was abolished, and the blacks were placed on an equality with the whites. Many of the plantations remained in the hands of the original proprietors. The negroes gave every proof of industry, subordination and content. They diligently cultivated the plantations, and received the wages of their labor. They submitted cheerfully to all those regulations which it was thought necessary to establish, and, living in possession of their freedom, seemed perfectly happy.

Toussaint, whose ability, integrity, and mildness had established this favorable order of things, assumed a good deal of state, and affected to cast a shade of mystery around the circumstances of his early life. He took pride in proclaiming himself the negro deliverer foretold by Raynal. He observed great simplicity in respect to his own person, but surrounded himself with a brilliant staff. His popularity was unbounded, and he appears to have been as solicitous for the maintenance of the French interest as for any part of his scheme of government. The colony had seldom been more productive, or the revenue which it afforded to the mother country more abundant. The island seemed to enjoy a fair prospect of advancing in prosperity; the inhabitants were improving in the arts of peace and civilization; the produce of the soil was yielding increased wealth both to the proprietors and the cultivators; and the distinctions of color, and the prejudices founded on them, might at last have been forgotten, had not the restless ambition of the ruler of France, and the foolish discontent of the ex-colonists, disturbed the tranquillity of the island, and suddenly brought back the troubles which had been so happily quieted.

The conduct of Bonaparte towards Toussaint had now become such as to cause serious anxiety in the mind of the latter.   He had sent two of his children to France to receive their education, but the First Consul preserved an ominous silence towards all his overtures for friendship.   After the treaty of Amiens, Bonaparte issued a proclamation, announcing that slavery was to continue in Martinique and Cayenne, and that St. Domingo was to be " restored to order." This caused a well-grounded alarm, and Toussaint met it by a counter proclamation, on the 18th of December, 1801, in which he professed obedience to the French Republic, but at the same time appealed to the soldiery in language which left no doubt of his determination to take up arms in case any attempt should be made to take away the civil right as recognized by the existing governments.   The policy of Napoleon appears to be thus explained.   Wanting employment for his armies during the truce of Amiens, and instigated by the fugitive colonists who had been expelled at the beginning of the revolution, and who were anxiously longing for their lost possessions, he determined on subjugating the island by force, re-establishing slavery, and re-instating the ex-colonists in their original possessions.   He despatched a fleet of fifty-four sail, with an army of twenty-five thousand men, under his brother-in-law. General Leclerc, to effect this purpose.

The expedition reached St. Domingo in January, 1802.   Toussaint was filled with apprehensions at the sight of this formidable force, and his followers were intimidated and divided.   Leclerc brought with him a proclamation of the First Consul, couched in his usual ambiguous style, and intended, no doubt, to deceive the colored population, by seeming to confirm their rights as freemen, while the real object of the expedition was to reduce them to slavery. This proclamation was received among the wavering as one of perfect sincerity, and their apprehensions were quieted. Many of them, in consequence, went over to the French. But Toussaint was not to be deceived. His two sons had been brought out by Leclerc, to be held as hostages in his hands, and as such to check any opposition which their father might be disposed to make to the measures of the French. Leclerc attempted to inveigle him by means of an interview with his sons, in the course of which every appeal was made to his paternal feelings to induce him to submit to the invaders; but Toussaint resisted this attempt with the stern inflexibility of a Roman. " Take back my children," said he; " since it must be so, I will be faithful to my brethren and my God."

War now commenced between the French and the natives, who, under the conduct of Toussaint, Christophe and Dessalines, carried on their enterprises with various success. Leclerc, in February, 1802, proclaimed Toussaint an outlaw, and the blacks sustained serious reverses. Toussaint, however, continued to defend himself, and laid the country waste around him, to obstruct the approach of the enemy. At last, the defection of Christophe and Dessalines obliged him to listen to terms, and his sentence of outlawry was reversed. But, on placing himself in the power of the French, he was treacherously arrested and sent to France where he was at first lodged in the prison of the Temple at Paris, and afterwards in the castle of Joux, near Besançon, where he was subjected to a rigorous confinement, which, as was probably foreseen and intended, speedily terminated his existence. He died on the 27th of April, 1803. His family were confined at Brienne en Agen, where one of his sons died; and the survivors were not set at liberty till the restoration of the Bourbons.

The perfidy and cruelty exercised to vard Toussaint L'Ouverture, was one of the blackest deeds of Napoleon's reign. He did not fail to reflect upon it during his imprisonment at St. Helena. "I have to reproach myself," said he, "for the expedition to St. Domingo. It was a great fault to try to subject the island by force. I ought to have been content with the inter-mediate government of Toussaint. Peace was not then sufficiently established with England; and the territorial wealth to which I looked in trying to subject it, would only have enriched our enemies. It was undertaken against my opinion, in conformity to the wishes of the council of state, who were carried away by the cries of the colonists."

Toussaint, from the united te imony of his friends and enemies, deserves to be classed among great men. His plans were devised with great skill, and produced the happiest results. His agricultural improvements excited the surprise and astonishment of all those who had an opportunity to observe them. He sought to replenish the wasted population by every possible means. He held out to those who had emigrated during the contest, every encouragement to re urn, pledging himself to re-instate them in their property and assuring them that their agricultural undertakings should receive all the support which it was possible for him to afford. This had a most beneficial effect, and many returned, and brought with them the slaves who had accompanied them in their flight, but who, of course, became free on their arrival. His reserved and yet energetic character commanded the respect of the negroes, enabled him to restrain them from excesses, and keep them steady to labor, he thus restored confidence to the whites. He had strong devotional feelings, and a nice sense of domestic morality. Under these influences, he made constant efforts to suppress licentiousness of manners by promoting marriage throughout the colony. He was aware of the evil effects of the system of polygamy which prevailed among his brethren, and his endeavors to abolish it resulted not only in an improved state of morals, but in an increased population. Toussaint was sometimes harsh in his judgments, and rigid in exacting obedience to his authority, but he was always grateful, and never left an obligation unrequited. If there was one trait in his character more conspicuous than the rest, it was his unsullied integrity. That he never violated his faith, was a proverbial expression in the mouths of the white inhabitants of the island, and of the English officers who were employed in hostilities against him. Upon a fair view of his life, if we consider the nature of his early training, his defective education, and the oppressive influences which surrounded him, we cannot but look with admiration upon his career. Possessing force and eleva tion of character which triumphed over all obstacles, he became an able general, a wise statesman, a sound patriot, a great and good man, an honor not merely to " the African race," but to human nature.

LA SALLE AND HENNEPIN.

The French were early competitors of the English in making discoveries in the western world. While the latter were founding along the coast the most flourishing and prosperous colonies in North America, their rivals were actively pursuing a different career. They were penetrating into the interior of the continent, ascending and descending those mighty rivers, and coasting along the shores of those vast lakes, which seem to convey to the most inland depths of North America the character and benefits of a maritime region. The leaders of the French expeditions, both political and religious, displayed great enterprise and address, and effected extensive discoveries with much less disaster than might have been expected in these novel undertakings, beset with great and singular perils.

The valley of the St. Lawrence and the more northern portions of the continent formed the quarter to which the French directed their special attention. Considerable establishments were formed in Canada as early as the middle of the seventeenth century, and they had already penetrated to the great lakes, where they learned from the Indian tribes who came from the boundless regions beyond the Alleghany mountains, that far along the western plains there rolled a river, so mighty that even the hitherto unequalled

LA SALLE.

stream of the St. Lawrence could not be compared with it. They were informed that this vast body of waters flowed in a direction different from that of all the American streams yet discovered, and sought some distant ocean far to the south and west. In the prevailing ignorance as to the boundaries and extent of the continent, it was concluded that this could only be the *Vermilion Sea*, a name then given to the gulf of California, by which it was hoped that the long-sought-for passage might be found to the golden regions of India.

M. Joliet and Father Marquette, a Jesuit missionary who had been a long time in Canada, undertook, in 1673, to explore this great and unknown region. The Indians warned them that the most formidable and supernatural dangers would attend them should they embark upon this mighty river. Monsters of a strange form and huge dimensions would open their jaws and swallow as a single morsel a canoe and all its crew. If they escaped this peril, they would come to a place where a mighty demon bestrode the stream, who by a single blow would strike into the depths of the waves any bark so adventurous as to approach near him. The French, however, disregarded these bugbear stories, and set out upon the expedition ; they had only two little Indian canoes, with three men in each. They proceeded through Lakes Erie and Michigan to Green Bay, being well received by the natives along the route, and from the head of Fox River crossed by a portage to the Wisconsin, a branch of the Mississippi. On this stream, they found wild rice growing so thickly amid the waters that they appeared to be sailing among cornfields.

Their voyage down the Wisconsin was easy and prosperous, and they saw it, with great exultation, opening into that grand stream, of which they were in search. On the broad Mississippi they pursued their voyage for more than two hundred miles, through majestic solitudes in which they did not discover a human being. At length, they discovered the print of human feet upon the shore, and followed the track till they saw Indian villages, upon which they set up a loud shout. The natives came toward them, and presented the pipe of peace. They conducted the French to the cabin of their chief, entertained them with a feast, and cautioned them against going further down the river. These were the Illinois Indians, a tribe which Marquette considers the most civilized of all he had seen in America. The French took leave of their kind hosts, and proceeded down the Mississippi. Steep and lofty rocks rose along the banks, one of which had monsters painted in very brilliant colors on its perpendicular sides; this was probably the origin of some of the Indian tales of terror. Soon after this, they heard on the right hand a mighty roar of waters, and saw trees and floating islands rushing down the channel. This was the mouth of the great Missouri; and the current, which was before clear and gentle, now became rough, muddy and rapid.

Presently they saw, hovering in the centre of the rushing waters, the *demon*, of which they had been so solemnly forewarned. This was a range of cliffs, crossing nearly the whole stream, and against which the waves dashed with great noise and fury. Great

=kill and caution were required to guide the canoes through this dangerous strait. After passing the mouth of the Ohio, they suffered severely from moschetoes, and they were obliged, in imitation of the natives, to build a hut over their canoe, and kindle a fire beneath it, the smoke of which drove away their tormentors. They came to several villages, where the Indians at first assumed a hostile appearance; but on presenting their calumet of peace, a friendly intercourse was always established. When they reached the Arkansas, they were informed that they were within five days' sail of the sea, on which they became convinced that the Mississippi emptied into the Gulf of Mexico, and not into the Sea of California. They considered that by proceeding downward, they might fall into the hands of the Spaniards, from whose jealous enmity they might suffer death or imprisonment; they therefore returned to Canada by the route they had already traced.

A young Frenchman named La Salle, who happened to be at Quebec when they returned, was struck with the accounts which they gave of this vast river, which seemed to afford a key to the whole interior of the continent. He set sail for France, and engaged a party of thirty men to accompany him thither on an expedition of discovery. Their preparations in Canada lasted two years, and after many adventures, La Salle found himself on the Miami, with forty-seven companions. They ascended that stream, and sailed down the Illinois to the Mississippi. The banks of the Illinois were beautiful, fertile, and contained many large Indian villages. The first they saw was com-

17 *

posed of five hundred wooden cabins, but the inhabitants had left it.   In descending the river, they found themselves suddenly between two large bodies of Indians, encamped on the opposite banks.   These were the Illinois, who, alarmed at the appearance of the strangers, ranged themselves in order of battle; as did also the French.   They did not, however, come to blows; the French declared that they were sent by their king, to instruct the Indians, and do them all the good in their power, on which the calumet of peace was offered, and a grand festival of three days followed.

La Salle now began to experience great trouble from the mutinous spirit of his men.   This, with the loss of his principal bark, caused him such anxiety, that in building a small fort to secure his encampment, he gave it the name of *Crevecœur*, or Heartbreak. His followers did much to justify this appellation, although they had no sufficient cause of complaint against their leader.   They spread jealousies among the Indians, by representing him as a spy of the Iroquois, their ancient enemies.   Not satisfied with this, they attempted to poison him and all his friends, at a Christmas dinner.   The poison, however, did not prove mortal; and the villains, finding all their schemes frustrated, fled into the wilderness.

By this desertion, La Salle's force was so much weakened, that it was necessary to return to Canada for a fresh supply of arms and ammunition.   Six of his followers, among whom was Father Hennepin, were ordered to proceed to the Mississippi, and ascend that river to its source.   La Salle left the remainder

of his men at Fort Crevecœur; but after his departure
these soon became involved in trouble with the Indians, and were forced to retreat likewise to Canada.
Even under this accumulation of disasters, La Salle
did not lose courage. He collected twenty men, with
the requisite provisions and stores, and set out again
early the next season. The rivers being frozen, he
proceeded at first by land, but at length embarked on
the Illinois, and sailed down to the Mississippi. He
soon reached the Missouri, on which he conferred the
name of the Osage; the Ohio he called the Wabash.
Descending the Mississippi sixty leagues, he came to
the settlements of the Chickasaws, whose pride it
was to flatten the faces of their children, by applying
wooden tablets, strongly girt with bands, to their fore-
heads. The Indians were numerous, the country was
productive, and they were supplied with abundance of
everything they wanted. Fifty leagues further down,
they came to the Cappas, where they were at first
alarmed by the sound of a drum; but, on joining the
natives, they found them quite friendly and partially
civilized. They next reached the Arkansas tribe;
and, an account of them having preceded their arrival,
great crowds assembled to see them and witness the
discharge of their fire-arms. Here they procured
guides to the Taencas, where they found a state of
society decidedly superior to anything they had yet
seen in America. 'The streets of the village were
straight and regular; a palace and a temple exhibited
a considerable degree of magnificence. The women
wore dresses of woven cloth, and necklaces and ear-
rings of pearl; they had deep brown complexions.

and black, sparkling eyes, which seemed to have enchanted the gallant leader of the expedition.   Seeing one of the princesses cast a longing eye on a case of scissors which had been presented to the king, he slipped a pair into her hand, and received a cordial squeeze in return.   As another lady cast a rather rueful glance at the thorns with which her train was rudely fastened, he delighted her by a present of a quantity of pins.

Taking leave of this hospitable tribe, they proceeded farther down the river, and were met by a canoe containing a hundred Indians, armed with bows and arrows.   The French ranged their canoes in line of battle; but on presenting the calumet of peace, the Indians saluted them cordially.   These were the Natchez tribe, and La Salle was invited to their town, which presented, on a greater scale, a similar spectacle to that they had witnessed among the Taencas. Another tribe, the Quinipissas, received them in a different manner, and, lining the shore with their warriors, answered the hailing of the French with a shower of arrows.   The adventurers wisely sailed on; and at Tangibao beheld a terrible picture of savage warfare.   The village had just been surprised by enemies and sacked; the dead bodies of the inhabitants were lying piled in heaps upon each other. Two leagues lower down, the river began to assume a new character; it expanded to a breadth so immense, that one bank could not be seen from the opposite one; the taste of the water became more and more salt, and the shore was strewed with large and beautiful shells. They had now reached the mouth of the Mississippi.

The great object of the expedition was now accomplished, and La Salle celebrated this event with extraordinary rejoicings. *Te Deum* was sung, a cross and the arms of France were set up, and formal possession was taken of the country. The return of the party up the river was much more difficult and perilous than the descent had been. Many of the savages were hostile, and in their conflicts, the French killed several of them. They were some months in proceeding up the Mississippi and Illinois, but finally reached Quebec without the loss of any of their number.

In the mean time, Hennepin was pursuing his expedition up the Mississippi. Eight leagues above the Falls of St. Anthony, he and his companions were made prisoners by a large party of Sioux Indians, who were at war with the Miamies, and treated the French as enemies, because they came from that tribe. The prisoners were told to prepare for death; but on producing from their stores some hatchets, knives and tobacco, they appeased the savages to a certain degree, and their execution was deferred. The French were carried along with them on their return home, and Hennepin caused great astonishment among the Indians by performing the Catholic service before them. They imagined he was exorcising the devil. The Indians were divided in opinion on the subject of killing their prisoners, and in this state of things their life was spared. Besides this constant prospect of death, the captives endured unspeakable hardships in their journey. The savages marched at an almost incredible speed, regardless of the obstacles presented by rocks, swamps and tangled forests.   The French, in their soundest condition, were very unequal to such efforts, and being soon overcome with fatigue and the pain from their wounded limbs, could with difficulty walk at all. No allowance was made for this; the Indians, enraged that their progress should be impeded, used the most cruel methods of urging them forward.   When everything else failed, they set the dry grass behind them on fire; the flames spread rapidly, and they must run or be destroyed by the devouring element. After nineteen days of terrible suffering, they reached a spot in the midst of almost impassable swamps, where the tribe had their head quarters.

They here divided their captives and spoil.   Hennepin fell to the share of a chief who had been one of the most unrelenting of that party which insisted on putting the prisoners to death.   He now considered it time to prepare for his last hour on earth; but, to his great astonishment, the chief offered him the calumet of peace, informing him that the national custom allowed him the alternative either to kill him or adopt him as a son, and that he had chosen the latter. Hennepin was then introduced to his kindred, consisting of six mothers and a proportionable number of brothers and sisters.   He was suffering under a severe rheumatism, caused by the fatigues and exposures of the last nineteen days, and was unable to rise without assistance.   The Indians laid him on a bearskin and rubbed him with the grease of wild-cats; they then shut him up for several hours in a vapor-bath, while his father and three brothers partly sung and partly wept, straining their voices to the highest pitch.

Hennepin thought this remedy would speedily send him to the other world; but a few applications of it entirely restored him to health.

Hennepin now set about learning their language, in doing which, he wrote down the words on paper, an operation so strange and unintelligible to these Indians, as to pass for a kind of sorcery. The paper, or *white*, as they called it, was imagined to be a spirit, with whom he conversed. They amused themselves with repeating to him long catalogues of names, always adding, " Spirit, tell that to *white*." During the winter they suffered from a scarcity of provisions, and Hennepin was nearly starved; but this famine was, fortunately, the means of deliverance of the Frenchmen from their captivity. The Indians now allowed them to depart; they sailed down the Mississippi, meeting with a variety of adventures, and returned in safety to Canada.

We must add to these narrations an account of the melancholy fate of the intrepid La Salle. He projected a scheme for planting a colony at the mouth of the Mississippi, which was approved by the French government; he was also furnished with a fleet of four vessels, and a commission of governor of all that great region in the interior of America, extending from the lakes to the Gulf of Mexico. He arrived on the coast of Florida in 1684; but here an unforeseen perplexity awaited him. He had no means of finding the Mississippi, for, although he had descended that river to its mouth, he could not know what appearance it presented from the sea. No observation of longitude had been made, and he inquired fruitlessly of all the pilots and navigators in that quarter, on the subject. What little information he obtained only misled him, and he passed the main opening of the Mississippi without knowing it. He coasted along more than two hundred miles further westward, and discovered a bay, afterwards named St. Bernard. The inviting appearance of the country tempted him to form an establishment here, and he proceeded to erect a fort.

Serious misfortunes now began to press upon him. His store-ship sunk in the river, and but a small part of her lading was saved; the greater portion being stolen by the Indians. La Salle took violent measures for compelling them to restore the property, and war was the consequence. The health of the French now began to sink under a tropical climate; one of the officers was bitten by a rattlesnake and died; and a flat-bottomed vessel, which had been brought out for the purpose of surveying the coast, was lost. In the mean time, no intelligence was received of an expedition from Canada which was to join them by the route of the Mississippi. This party, commanded by the Chevalier de Tonti, had safely reached the mouth of that river, and had despatched boats along the coast, east and west, for twenty leagues, without finding a trace of La Salle. He then abandoned the search in despair, and returned up the Mississippi.

La Salle struggled with great energy against the difficulties of his situation. He had become convinced that he was not upon the shores of the Mississippi, and determined to penetrate inland, and explore the country. He took with him his nephew, a young man of talent, but somewhat haughty, and an object of hatred to some fierce and turbulent mutineers in the party. These formed a plot for his murder, and on one occasion, having gone a few miles with him on a hunting excursion, they suddenly fell upon him and his servant, and put them to death. None of the party making the.r appearance the next morning, La Salle felt an ominous foreboding, and set out in search of the missing people. It was not long before he was shocked by the sight of his kinsman, weltering in his blood. As he looked round for the assassins with every expression of grief and rage, two of them, who were concealed in the grass, started up and fired at him. He was shot through the head, and fell lifeless to the earth. Thus perished, in the lonely wilderness, one of the bravest and most distinguished of those daring leaders to whom the world is indebted for its earliest knowledge of the interior of the American continent.

THE PILGRIMS.

IT was on the sixth day of September, 1620, that the Puritans sailed from England, to seek a new home in the Western World. Religious persecution had driven them first to Holland, but believing that their liberty of conscience and the purity of their faith would be safer in the wi.ds of America, they resolved to establish a colony there. A settlement had already been made by the English in Virginia, but the other parts of the country were imperfectly known. The attempt of the Puritans was perilous.

and the issue uncertain. They had no warran for their undertaking from the king, nor any charter from the companies who claimed the country toward which they were directing their attention. They embarked, after many delays and mischances, in the Mayflower, a vessel of one hundred and eighty tons, commanded by an individual who, it seems, had received a bribe to thwart their purposes. Their number was one hundred and one persons. The winter was approaching, and the severities of that season, in the region to which they were proceeding, were greater than they had ever experienced. Such was the unpromising commencement of an enterprise, which the courage, fortitude, and energy of a handful of men achieved with the most triumphant success, and caused it to stand in history as the most memorable and important event of the seventeenth century.

Their original purpose was to establish themselves on the Hudson, but the Dutch, having designs of their own in that quarter, had bribed the captain of the Mayflower to mislead them, and, after a passage of sixty-three days, they made the land at Cape Cod, on the ninth of November. But " what could they see," says Morton in his Memorial, " but a hideous and desolate wilderness, full of wild beasts and wild men? and what multitudes there might be of them, they know not. Neither could they, as it were, go up to the top of Pisgah, to view from this wilderness a more goodly country, to feed their hopes. For which way soever they turned their eyes, save upward to the heavens, they could have little solace or content in respect of any outward objects. For summer being gone, all things stood for them to look upon with a weather-beaten face; and the whole country, being full of woods and thickets, represented a wild and savage hue. If they looked behind them, there was the mighty ocean which they had passed, and which was now as a main bar and gulf to separate them from all the civil parts of the world."

After two days, lying off and on, they cast anchor in the harbor of Provincetown, where they were greeted by the sight of " the greatest store of sea-fowl they ever saw." Here they framed a social compact, the first democratical constitution of modern times. This memorable document, which may be regarded as the beginning of American liberty, was drawn up as follows:

" In the name of God, Amen. We, whose names are underwritten, the loyal subjects of our dread sovereign lord, King James, by the grace of God, of Great Britain, France and Ireland, king, defender of the faith, &c.——having undertaken, for the glory of God, and advancement of the Christian faith, and honor of our king and country, a voyage to plant the first colony in the northern parts of Virginia, do, by these presents, solemnly and mutually, in the presence of God and of one another, covenant and combine ourselves together into a civil body politic for our better ordering and preservation, and furtherance of the ends aforesaid; and by virtue hereof to enact, constitute and frame such just and equal laws, ordinances, acts, constitutions and offices, from time to time, as shall be thought most meet and convenient for the general good of the colony; unto which we promise

all due submission and obed'ence. In witness whereof, we have hereunder subscribed our names, at Cape
Cod, on the 11th of November, in the year of the
reign of our sovereign lord, King James, of England,
France and Ireland, the eighteenth, and of Scotland
the fifty-fourth, Anno Domini 1620."

No Indians were seen, and the land was completely
covered with a forest of oaks, pines, junipers, sassafras,
" and other sweet wood."   A party of sixteen men,
under Captain Miles Standish, each individual equipped with a match-lock, sword and corslet, set out to
explore the country. They marched in single file
along the shore, and at the end of a mile discovered
five or six Indians with a dog, who, on espying the
English, ran into the woods.   Standish and his men
tracked them through the forest for ten miles, and got
sight of them running up a hill as night was approaching.   They encamped in the woods, and recommenced
their pursuit of the Indians the next morning, hoping
to discover their dwellings.   The thick wood shattered their armor, and they were distressed with thirst.
About the middle of the forenoon they came to a deep
valley, full of bushes and long grass, where they saw
a deer, and found springs of fresh water, " of which
they were heartily glad, and sat down and drank their
first New England water with as much delight as
ever they drunk drink in all their lives." Further
onward, they saw signs of cultivation, and, digging
into a heap of sand, they found a basket of Indian corn
containing three or four bushels, " with some six and
thirty ears, some yellow and some red, and others
mixed with blue, which was a very goodly sight."

Near this spot were the remains of an old fort, which appeared to have been built by Europeans. On the banks of a creek were two canoes; but nothing else was discovered, except some Indian utensils.

They made a great fire, and kept watch with three sentinels all night. It rained hard, and it was with much difficulty that they were able to put their muskets in an effective condition. They now bent their course toward the ship, but soon got lost in the woods. One of the party was caught in a snare, made by bending a strong sapling downward, and was jerked up by the leg, and held dangling in the air. "It was a very pretty device," says the narrator, who probably was not the individual caught in it. They saw partridges, geese, ducks and deer, but shot nothing. At length they found their way back to the vessel, bringing a portion of the corn which they had discovered. meaning to pay the owners for it when they should meet with them.

They now felled timber, and built a shallop. Nearly all the men were afflicted with coughs and colds, by wading in the water, in raw and stormy weather; many died shortly after, from the consequences of this exposure. At length thirty-four persons embarked in the shallop and long-boat, to explore the coast. The cold increased, and they were much incommoded by ice and snow. On the second day of their expedition they shot three fat geese and six ducks, and the next day two more geese, which proved a seasonable supply. They then bent their course to the spot where they had obtained the corn. They dug up what they had left the first time, and found more, amounting to ten bushels, besides a bag of beans and some " Indian wheat." This they sent back to the ship with some of the feeblest of their party; eighteen of them remained. The next morning they came to a broad, beaten path, which seemed to be the road to an Indian village. They lighted all their matches, and prepared for an encounter, but the path turned out to be only an approach to a deer-trap.

On the same day, they made a discovery somewhat curious. We shall transcribe the narrative of one of the party. " When we had marched five or six miles into the woods, and could find no signs of people, we returned another way; and as we came into the plain ground, we found a place like a grave, but it was much bigger and longer than any we had yet seen. It was also covered with boards, so as we mused what it might be, and resolved to dig it up. We found first a mat, and under that a fair bow, and under that another mat, and under that a board about three quarters [of a yard] long, finely carved and painted, with three tines or broaches on the top, like a crown. Also, between the mats we found bowls, trays, dishes, and such like trinkets. At length we came to a fair new mat, and under that two bundles, the one bigger, and the other less. We opened the greater, and found in it a great quantity of fine and perfect red powder, and in it the bones and skull of a man. The skull had fine yellow hair still on it, and some of the flesh unconsumed. There were bound up with it a knife, a packneedle, and two or three old iron things. It was bound up in a sailor's canvass cassock and a pair of cloth breeches. The red powder was a kind of embalmment, and yielded a strong, but not offensive smell; it was as fine as any flour. We opened the less bundle likewise, and found of the same powder in it, and the bones and head of a little child. About the legs and other parts of it were bound strings and bracelets of fine white beads. There was also by it a little bow, about three quarters long, and some other odd knacks. We brought sundry of the prettiest things away with us, and covered the corpse up again. There was a variety of opinions amongst us about the embalmed person. Some thought it was an Indian lord and king. Others said the Indians have all black hair, and never any was seen with brown or yellow hair. Some thought it was a Christian of some special note who had died amongst them, and they thus buried him to honor him. Others thought they had killed him, and did it in triumph over him."*

Not far from this place, they discovered two Indian wigwams, containing furniture and provisions; but none of the natives were seen. They now held a consultation as to their future course. The lateness

---

* The particulars of this account have induced the belief that this was the body of one of the Northmen, who, as we have seen, landed on Cape Cod, and were involved in hostilities with the natives. The mode of burial with mats, planks, and domestic utensils, is precisely that of the Scandinavians. The same is the case with embalmment, a practice unknown to the Indians of New England. Yellow hair is the characteristic of the Danes; and no Indian has any other than black hair. The piece of wood finely carved and painted, with three tines or broaches on the top like a crown, is as exact a description as could be given of the *rymstocke*, or Runic staff, which is still in use among the Scandinavian nations.

of the season made it indispensable that they should fix upon some spot convenient for passing the winter. Cape Cod did not please them, and some proposed going to Agawam, which they understood to be about twenty leagues to the north, with a good harbor and fishery, and a better soil than they found at the Cape. There were some inducements, however, to remain. Great numbers of whales came daily playing about their ship, " of the best kind for oil and bone," and tempted them with the hopes of a profitable fishery. One of them, when the sun shone warm, came, and ay above water as if she had been dead for a considerable time, within half musket shot of the vessel. Two of the men fired their muskets at her. The first one exploded, splitting barrel and stock into fragments, yet nobody was hurt. " But when the whale saw her time, she gave a snuff, and away ! "

At length, by the persuasion of the pilot, who informed them of a great navigable river and a good harbor opposite the cape, not more then eight leagues distant, they sent off another exploring party, under the direction of Standish, Carver, Bradford, Winslow, and others. These departed on the 6th of December, and coasted along the cape in their boat. The cold was intense ; the water froze on their clothes, and ' made them many times like coats of iron." They discovered a dozen Indians, who ran away at the sight of them. A portion of them went on shore and barricaded themselves to pass the night. They saw the light of the Indian encampment, four or five miles distant. All the next day, they ranged up and down, following the tracks of the Indians. They were struck with the appearance of a great cemetery, "one part whereof was encompassed with a large palisado like a church-yard, with young spires four or five yards long, set as close by one another as they could, two or three feet in the ground." This enclosure contained a great number of graves, some surrounded by palings, and others housed in. At sunset, the party on land discovered the boat, from which they had been separated all the day, and their whole company passed the night together. About midnight they were alarmed by a hideous cry, and all ran to their arms; but on firing a couple of muskets, the noise ceased. They supposed it to proceed from a horde of wolves or foxes.

Early the next morning, they carried their arms on board the boat, and sat down to breakfast, at some distance from the water. Suddenly, they heard a terrible war-whoop, and a cry from one of their own men, of "Indians! Indians!" The next moment, a cloud of arrows fell about them. They ran with all speed to recover their arms, and had the good fortune to reach them before the savages came up. A battle now ensued, and many shots were exchanged. The Indians showed great bravery. One of them, supposed to be their leader, stationed himself behind a tree within half a musket shot of the English, and let fly his arrows at them. He stood three shots of a musket, but at length was apparently wounded, for one of the English, taking full aim at him, fired, on which he "gave an extraordinary cry, and away they went all." This conflict took place in the morning twilight, and the English had but an indistinct view of their enemies, who fought under cover of the woods. They picked up eighteen of their arrows, some of which were headed with brass, others with deer's horns, and others with eagles' claws. The English suffered no loss. They named this place *The First Encounter*.

All that day, they sailed along the coast, without finding harbor or creek to put into. It rained and snowed, and the sea was rough. Towards night, the pilot said he saw the harbor, and they kept before the wind, crowding all sail. The sea rose high, and the gale increased, and as they approached the shore, their mast snapped into three pieces. They were now on the verge of destruction, for at this critical moment the pilot, discovering that he had mistaken the spot, exclaimed, "Lord be merciful! My eyes never saw this place before!" They were about to run the boat ashore, in a cove full of breakers, where they would all have perished, but a steersman called to the rowers, "About with her if you be men, or we are cast away!" They put about and stood off. Presently they discovered the opening of a harbor, into which they made their way, and found a safe anchorage under the lee of a small island.

They were now in the harbor of Plymouth, where they remained the two following days, Saturday and Sunday. On Monday, the twelfth day of December, Old Style, they landed on that memorable spot, now famous in history as *Forefathers' Rock*. No Indians were seen; they found cornfields, running brooks, and a good situation for a settlement; they also sounded the harbor, and found it a good haven for their shipping. All things invited them to establish them-

selves in this spot, and they returned to the ship
" with good news to the rest of their people, which did
much comfort their hearts." The Mayflower weighed
anchor and proceeded to the place. A spot was
selected for a town, and the name of Plymouth was
bestowed upon it, in commemoration of the hospital-
ities which the Pilgrims had received at the port from
which they last sailed, on leaving England. Amidst
the snows and storms of winter, they built their
houses, and fortunately were not molested by the Indians. Traces of these were apparent at Plymouth,
and they sometimes discovered the smoke of their
fires at a distance ; but the neighborhood had been
depopulated by a pestilence, and none of the original
occupants were alive to lay claim to the territory.

Sickness, want and hardship prevailed during the
winter, and great numbers of them died. One day,
in March, 1621, an Indian suddenly made his appearance among them, and exclaimed, " Welcome, English-
men ! " This was Samoset, a Wampanoag, who had
learnt a little of their language by intercourse with
the fishermen who frequented the coast of Maine.
He proved a very useful mediator, in bringing about
an intercourse between the English and the neighboring tribes. In a short time, Massasoit, the greatest
sachem in that part of the country, the chief of the
Massachusetts Indians, made a visit to Plymouth,
which at this time contained not above fifty inhabitants, so severe had been the mortality among the settlers. They received the sachem with feelings of
friendship, and all the ceremony which their reduced
condition allowed. A treaty of peace was entered

into, both parties agreeing to abstain from injuries and encroachments upon each other, and to deliver up all offenders. The English were to receive assistance from Massasoit, if they were attacked by enemies, and to assist him, if he should be unjustly assailed. This treaty included the confederates of the sachem, and is the most ancient act of diplomacy recorded in the history of New England. It was concluded in a single day, and, being founded on reciprocal interests, was sacredly kept for more than half a century.

Such was the beginning of the first permanent settlement in New England. These Puritans were soon followed by others, and, though the infant colonies were subjected to every species of hardship which could spring from famine and a rigorous climate, they were borne with a patience and resignation, which the firmest faith alone could have supplied. With an energy and perseverance that could not be baffled, a wisdom far superior to the age, and a piety which never wavered, these settlers pursued their object, and laid the foundations of those blessings which are now enjoyed by more than two millions of people, and which are extending their influence over the whole Union.

SALEM WITCHCRAFT.

THERE are few portions of either ancient or modern story which exhibit stranger or more tragical and affecting scenes than that known by the title of Salem Witchcraft, and few occurrences that are matter of authentic history remain so deeply shrouded in mystery at the present day. This delusion, notwithstanding the intense curiosity it has always excited, has never yet been satisfactorily explained ; time has rather obscured than thrown light upon the subject, and a prominent place may be assigned to it among that large class of historical facts, for which succeeding generations find it impossible to account. That it was attended by fraud and imposture, and that the people labored under a frenzy in their treatment of it, admits of no doubt. But it was not all fraud and imposture, and there were certain phenomena exhibited during its career which it is impossible to explain upon any principles of natural philosophy which were known to that age or the present.

The belief in witchcraft at that time was general throughout Christendom, and the existence and criminality of the practice were recognized in the penal code of every state. Persons suspected of being witches and wizards, were tried, condemned and put to death by the authority of the most enlightened tribunals in Europe Only a few years before the occurrences in New England, Sir Matthew Hale, a judge highly and justly renowned for the strength of his understanding, the variety of his knowledge, and the eminent Christian graces which adorned his character, had, after a long and anxious investigation, adjudged a number of men and women to die for this offence. The reality of witchcraft had never yet been questioned, nor were there any persons to whom that reality appeared unimportant or incredible except those who regarded the spiritual world as altogether a mere speculation, vague, visionary and delusive. Among other believers in the practice, were some of the accused themselves who suffered for the crime. Instigated by fraud, folly or cruelty, or possessed by demoniacal frenzy, some of these unhappy beings professed, more or less openly, to hold communication with the powers of darkness ; and by the administration of subtile poisons, by disturbing the imagination of their victims, or by mysterious powers which have baffled the ingenuity of modern times to explain, they committed crimes and inflicted injuries, which were punished, perhaps, under an erroneous name.

The colonists of New England could by no means have been expected to be free from a belief which was general throughout Christendom ; on the contrary, it was natural that they should regard witchcraft with a degree of abhorrence and indignation corresponding to those strong religious feelings, for which they were so remarkably distinguished. Their experience in America tended to strengthen the sentiments on this subject which they brought with them from Europe ; for they found the belief of witchcraft firmly rooted among the aboriginal tribes, and the practice of it, or what was so esteemed, prevalent among those people, whom, as heathens, they regarded in the light of worshippers of demons.   Moreover, the persecution to which the Pilgrims had been exposed in their own country, and the sufferings which they endured in the early years of their residence here, acting upon them in co-operation with the political and ecclesiastical occurrences which marked the commencement of the seventeenth century, had imparted a gloomy, severe and romantic turn to their dispositions, which was transmitted in full strength to their children.   It was the triumphant age of superstition.   The imagination had been expanded by credulity, till it had reached a wild and monstrous growth.   The Puritans were always prone to subject themselves to its influence, and New England was, at this time, a most fit and congenial theatre upon which to display its power.   Cultivation and civilization had made but a partial encroachment upon the wilderness. Wide, deep and gloomy forests covered the hills, hung over the unfrequented roads, and frowned upon the scattered settlements.   The woods were still the abode of wild beasts and wild Indians.   A strongly-rooted sentiment of hostility and horror became associated in the minds of the colonists with the name of Indian.   The tomahawk, scalping-knife and firebrand had laid waste the frontier, the seacoast was infested with hostile privateers, and ruthless pirates were continually prowling along the shores.   It was the darkest and most desponding period in the istory of this portion of our country.

The colonists, moreover, had been accustomed from an early period to "dream dreams and see visions." Sights and sounds esteemed supernatural often threw them into amazement and terror. Indian powows were seen upon the hill-tops at midnight, and demons were imagined to be flitting in the air above them; unearthly voices issued from the dark forests, and cannon were heard in the depth of the sea; strange apparitions in the sky struck all men with awe and wonder. One incident of this nature is detailed in the following narrative, which is supported by such unquestionable evidence, that there can be no doubt of its substantial truth. In January, 1646, a new ship, containing a valuable cargo, and having several distinguished persons on board as passengers, sailed from New Haven for England. The vessels which arrived in the colony during the ensuing season brought no accounts of her arrival. The pious colonists put up earnest and constant prayers that they might be favored with intelligence from the missing vessel. More than two years after, in June, 1648, as the narrative states, " a great thunder-storm arose out of the northwest; after which, the hemisphere being serene, about an hour before sunset, a ship of like dimensions with the aforesaid, with her canvass and colors abroad, although the wind was northerly, appeared in the air, coming up from the harbor's mouth, which lies southward from the town, seemingly with her sails filled under a fresh gale, holding her course north, and continuing under observation, sailing against the wind, for the space of half an hour." This phantom ship was borne along until, to the excited

19*

imaginations of the spectators, she seemed to h ⌐
approached so near that they could throw a stone on
board of her. The main-topmast then disappeared;
next all her masts faded away; and finally her hull
fell off and vanished from the view, leaving a dull and
smoke-colored cloud, which soon dissolved, and the
whole atmosphere became clear. All the inhabitants
were convinced that this airy vision was a precise
copy and image of the missing vessel, and that it was
sent to announce and describe her fate. They considered it the spectre of the lost ship, and the Rev.
Mr. Davenport, of New Haven, declared in public that
" God had condescended, for the quieting of their
afflicted spirits, this extraordinary account of his sovereign disposal of those for whom so many fervent
prayers were made continually." As these particulars are undoubted, the reader will have no difficulty
in explaining this phenomenon, by referring it to a
mirage, in which, under the influence of a peculiar
state of the atmosphere, distant objects are raised
above the horizon, and brought into the view of spectators far distant. It was no doubt the picture of a
Dutch ship sailing towards New York.*

The first trials for witchcraft in New England
occurred in 1645, when four persons charged with
this crime were put to death in Massachusetts. Goffe,
the regicide, in his diary, records the conviction of
three others at Hartford, in Connecticut, in 1662, and
remarks that after one of them was hanged, a young
woman who had been bewitched was restored to

---

* This anecdote has been dressed up into an amusing fiction
by Mr. Irving. See his tale of the " Storm Ship."

health. For more than twenty years after this, few instances occurred, and little notice has been preserved of similar prosecutions. But in 1688, a case happened in Boston which led to an execution, conducted with a degree of solemnity that made a deep impression on the minds of the people. Four of the children of one John Goodwin, a grave and steady man, were generally believed to be bewitched. The children were all remarkable for frankness of character, and had been religiously educated; the eldest was a girl of thirteen or fourteen years. She had charged a laundress with purloining some of the family linen. The mother of the laundress was a low Irish woman, of bad character, and gave the girl harsh language; soon after which the girl fell into fits, which were said to have something diabolical in them. One of her sisters and two brothers followed her example, and were tormented in the same part of their bodies at the same time, although kept in separate apartments, and ignorant of each other's complaints. One or two things excited special attention : all these phenomena happened in the daytime, yet they slept comfortably at night. They were struck dumb at the sight of the Assembly's Catechism, Cotton's Milk for Babes, and some other good books of the same stamp; but they could read without difficulty the Oxford jests, popish and Quaker books, the common prayer, and other works not in good odor among the Puritans. Sometimes they would be deaf, then dumb, then blind, and sometimes all these calamities would come upon them together. Their tongues would be drawn down their throats; their joints would appear to be dislocated;

they would make the most piteous outcries of burn-
ings, of being cut with knives, beaten, &c., and the
marks of wounds and bruises would afterwards be seen.
These things excited a general wonder and alarm.
The ministers of Boston and Charlestown kept a day
of fasting and prayer at the troubled house, after
which the youngest child made no more complaints.
The others continuing to be afflicted, the magistrates
interposed, and the old woman was apprehended; but
upon examination she would neither confess nor deny,
and appeared to be disordered in her senses. Upon
the report of physicians that she was *compos mentis*,
she was executed, declaring at her death that the children should not be relieved. It seems pretty evident
that this woman was persuaded by the circumstances
into something like a belief that she had exercised a
supernatural power over them. An account of this
transaction was published and circulated in England;
and so generally and firmly were the wise and good
of that age persuaded of the justice of the execution
that Richard Baxter, the celebrated nonconformist
divine, wrote a preface to the narrative, in which he
declared that any one who refused to believe it must
be no better than an obdurate Sadducee. The afflicted children returned to their ordinary behavior, and
ever afterward led sober and religious lives. One of
them was intimately known to the historian Hutchinson, who states that she was a sober and virtuous
woman, and never made any acknowledgment of
fraud in this transaction.

This was sufficiently strange, and no doubt it had
its effect in leading to that awful tragedy which ren-

dered New England for many months a scene of terror, madness and bloodshed. The commencement of what is called the "Salem Witchcraft," was in the family of Samuel Parris, minister of Salem village, now Danvers, in February, 1692. A quarrel had arisen between this clergyman and his people, which had grown in extent and exasperation, till it had spread animosities and malignant passions throughout the town; it finally became of such moment, that it was carried up to the General Court, and was a topic of discussion and altercation there. One writer states that the country was visited about this time with an epidemic disease, which bore some resemblance to epilepsy, but which the physicians, unable to explain or cure, readily ascribed to a supernatural cause. It appears not to have become epidemic till it was believed to be witchcraft. About the end of February, a young daughter of Parris, his niece, and two other young girls, began to make complaints similar to those which were made by the young Goodwins. The physicians, not understanding the disorder, pronounced the children bewitched. An Indian woman, who had been brought into the country from Mexico, and then lived in the house, tried some experiments of her own to discover the witch. The children, hearing this, cried out upon the poor Indian, affirmed she was pinching, pricking, and tormenting them, and fell into fits. Tituba, the Indian, acknowledged that she was a witch-finder, but denied that she was a witch herself.

It was not ong before the disorder spread; and this is not difficult to be explained without resorting to any

o

supernatural cause.   The love of notoriety, which is
one of the most mischievous evils of the present day,
and which we hourly behold leading multitudes of
both sexes into every sort of monstrous extravagance,
being a constituent part of the human character, must
have existed in a greater or less degree in those times.
The operation of it in this case is evident.   Several
private fasts were kept at the house of Parris, several
public ones by the whole village, and then a general
fast throughout the colony, " to seek to God to rebuke
Satan."   The great notice which these circumstances
directed toward the children so strangely affected,
together with the compassion and sympathy of the
multitudes who visited them, not only tended to confirm their course of conduct, but to induce others,
either through design, sympathy, or delusion, to follow
their example. .Accordingly, the number of the sufferers soon increased ; and among them were two or
three old women, and some girls of sufficient age to
be credible witnesses.   These charged as a witch
not only Tituba, but Sarah Osborn, a melancholy, distracted old woman, and Sarah Good, a bed-ridden
invalid.   At length, the Indian woman, having been
severely chastised by her master, confessed herself a
witch, and declared that the two old women were her
confederates.   They were in consequence committed
to prison ; and Tituba was found, on examination, to
have what they deemed " the devil's mark " upon her
back.

   About three weeks afterwards, two other women, re
ligious and of good character, named Corey and Nurse
were complained of as witches. and brought to an

examination; they were then sent to prison, although they denied the charge. Such was the infatuation, that a child of Sarah Good, not more than four or five years old, was also committed as a witch, being accused of biting some of the afflicted, who showed the print of small teeth on their arms. Grown people now began to show a desire to participate in the notoriety enjoyed by the afflicted children; and the wife of Thomas Putnam complained of Nurse, as tormenting her. On the third of April, Mr. Parris, who took up the matter with the most fiery zeal, preached a sermon from the text, "Have I not chosen you twelve, and one of you is a devil?" At these words, Sarah Cloyse, supposing the allusion to be made to Nurse, who was her sister, left the meeting; she was therefore complained of as a witch, examined, and committed. Elizabeth Procter was accused about the same time. Her husband accompanied her to the examination; for this he was charged with witchcraft, and subsequently lost his life.

The matter had now acquired a fearful interest. Danforth, the deputy governor, and five other magistrates, came to Salem. It was a great day; several ministers were present. Parris officiated, and it is plain, by his own record, that he elicited and brought forward every accusation in his power. This man was evidently not wholly guided by a blind zeal for the performance of what he considered his duty, but also actuated by a vindictive spirit against some of the individuals with whom he had quarrelled.

He may have been to some extent self-duped; for a man whose mind is ill regulated, easily persuades

himself that his enemies are allies of the devil.
There are few, perhaps, who ever make so gross a
display of their prejudices; yet there are thousands,
even at the present day, who, in condemning those
they hate, manifest the same kind of hallucination as
that which affected this great mover in the delusion at
Salem.   The credulity of the magistrates, who had
assembled for the trial of the accused, passed all
bounds; and their singular method of making the
investigations, led to the most deplorable results.
Instead of proceeding with caution and impartiality,
entertaining a prudent distrust of the witnesses, sift-
ing their testimony, and putting them upon cross-
examination, they made use of leading questions, put
words into their mouths, and suffered others to do the
same.   The following is a specimen of the proceedings at a trial involving questions of life and death:

Q. John, who hurt you?

A. Goody Procter first, and then Goody Cloyse.

Q. What did she do to you?

A. She brought the book to me.

Q. John, tell the truth; who hurts you? have you
been hurt?

A. The first was a gentlewoman I saw.

Q. But who hurt you next?

A. Goody Procter.   She choked me and brought
the book.

Q. Where did she take hold of you?

A. Upon my throat to stop my breath.

Q. What did this Goody Cloyse do?

A. She pinched me till the blood came.

[*Here one of the afflicted fell into a fit.*]

Q. Abigail Williams! Did you see a company at Mr. Parris' house eat and drink?

A. Yes, sir; that was their sacrament.

Q. How many were there?

A. About forty; and Goody Cloyse and Goody Good were their deacons.

Q. What was it?

A. They said it was our blood, and they had i twice that day.

Q. Mary Walcot—have you seen a white man?

A. Yes, sir, a great many times.

Q. What sort of a man was he?

A. A fine, grave man; and when he came, he made all the witches to tremble. [Abigail Williams confirmed the same, and said they had such a sight at Deacon Ingersoll's.]

Q. Who was at Deacon Ingersoll's then?

A. Goody Cloyse, Goody Corey, Goody Nurse and Goody Good. [Then Sarah Cloyse asked for water and " sat down as one seized with a dying fainting fit." Several of the afflicted fell into fits, and some of them cried out, " Oh! her spirit is gone to prison to her sister Nurse."]

Q. What do you say, Goody Procter, to these things?

A. I take God to be my witness that I know nothing of it, no more than the child unborn.

During the examination of Elizabeth Procter " Abigail Williams and Ann Putnam both made offer to strike at said Procter: but when Abigail's hand came near, it opened, whereas it was made up into a fist before, and came down exceeding lightly as it drew near to said Procter, and at length, with open, extended fingers, touched Procter's hood very lightly. Immediately Abigail cried out, ' her fingers ! her fingers ! her fingers burned !' and Ann Putnam took on most grievously, of her head, and sunk down."

No wonder, as Hutchinson remarks, the whole country was thrown into consternation, when persons of sober lives and unblemished characters were committed to prison upon evidence like this. Nobody was safe. The most effectual way to prevent an accusation was to become an accuser: accordingly, the number of afflicted increased every day, and the number of accused in proportion, who in general persisted in declaring their innocence, but being strongly urged to give glory to God by confession, and it being represented to them, by their friends, that this was the only way to save their lives, some were brought to own their guilt. The confessions multiplied the witches : new companions were always mentioned, who were immediately sent for and examined.   A monstrous doctrine now obtained currency ; " the gallows was to be set up, not for those who professed themselves witches, but for those who rebuked the delusion :" not so much for the guilty as for the unbelieving.   The whole community was now in a state of terror and alarm, which it is impossible adequately to describe.

Examinations and commitments were of daily occurrence. The purest life, the strictest integrity, the most solemn asseverations of innocence, were of no avail : husband was torn from wife, parents from children, brother from sister ; in some cases the unhappy victims saw in their accusers their nearest and dearest friends, sometimes even a wife, or a daughter, who took these steps with the hope of saving themselves. The jails were crowded, and more than a hundred women, most of them of fair characters and of the most reputable families in Salem, Beverly, Andover, Billerica and other towns, were apprehended and committed to prison.

At the trial of Bridget Bishop, John Cook testified that "about five or six years before, one morning about sunrise, he was in his chamber, and was assaulted by the shape of the prisoner, who looked on him, grinned at him, and very much hurt him with a blow on the side of the head; and that on the same day about noon, the same shape walked into the room where he was, and an apple strangely flew out of his hand into the lap of his mother." "Samuel Gray testified that about fourteen years before, he waked in the night, and saw the room full of light, and presently discovered a woman between the cradle and the bedside, who looked upon him. He rose, and she vanished, though he found all the doors fast. Looking out at the entry door, he saw the same woman again, and said, 'In God's name, what do you come for?' He went to bed, and had the same woman again assaulting him. The child in the cradle gave a great screech, and the phantom disappeared. It was long before the child could be quieted, and, although it was a very likely, thriving child, yet from this time it pined away and died, in a sad condition. He knew not Bishop, but when he saw her, after this, he was sure that the above was her spectre." John Bly and his wife testified that he bought a swine of the prisoner's husband, and paid the price to a creditor of his. The prisoner, being angry at being thus prevented from fingering the money, quarrelled with Bly, after which the animal was taken with strange fits, jumping and knocking its head against the fence. Whereupon a neighbor said she believed the creature was " overlooked," and sundry other circumstances concurred which made the deponents believe that Bishop had bewitched the animal.

John Lander testified that upon some little controversy with Bishop about her fowls, going well to bed, he awaked in the night by moonlight, and clearly saw the likeness of this woman grievously oppressing him. After this, being at home on a Lord's day, with the doors shut about him, he saw a black pig approach him : he attempted to give it a kick, on which it vanished away. Immediately after, sitting down, he saw a black thing jump in at the window, and come and stand before him. The body was like that of a monkey, the feet like a cock's, and the face much like a man's. He being so extremely affrighted that he could not speak, this monster addressed him thus : " I am a messenger sent unto you for I understand that you are in some trouble of mind and if you will be ruled by me, you shall want for nothing in this world." Whereupon he endeavored to clap his hands upon it, but could feel no substance, and it jumped out of the window again, but immediately came in at the porch, though the doors were shut, and said, " You had better take my counsel." He then struck at it with a stick, but hit only the

groun lsel, and broke the stick. The arm with which
he struck was presently disabled, and the spectre vanished away. He then went out the back door, and
spied this Bishop in her orchard, but he had not power
to advance one step toward her. He returned intc
his house, and was again accosted by the monster,
which was now going to fly at him ; but he cried out,
" The whole armor of God be between me and you ! "
on which the goblin sprang back and flew over the
apple tree, shaking down many apples, and flinging
dirt against the deponent, who was struck dumb, and
so remained for three days. Other persons testified
to many supernatural things, in which the prisoner had
borne a part ; and the members of the court themselves
appear to have been witnesses against her, for we are
positively informed that as she was passing, attended
by a guard, near the great meeting-house of Salem,
she gave a look toward the house, and immediately a
demon, invisibly entering the meeting-house, tore down
a part of it. Thus the monstrous fictions given as evidence, were mixed up with the most frivolous trifles.
One man testified to the witchcraft of another, because,
having received money from him, presently it was
gone. The learned court never thought of inquiring
whether this wiseacre had not a hole in his pocket.

The trial of George Burroughs affords one of the
clearest indications that individual malignity had a
share in these horrible persecutions. The accused
was a man of ability and education, and had formerly
been a minister in Salem village. There was a quarrel between him and Parris, the original instigator of
the delusion, and moreover Burroughs openly denied

the existence of witchcraft. There can be no doubt that these circumstances had a predominant influence in procuring his condemnation. The evidence against him was of a very loose and general nature, consisting, in a great measure, of things alleged to have been said or done by his shape or apparition; and attempts were made in this way to prove that he had murdered two wives and other persons. It was considered strong proof of witchcraft, that, being a small man, he possessed such strength as to be able to lift a barrel of molasses, and to hold a musket of seven feet barrel at arm's length. On his trial, he utterly denied that there was any truth in the popular notions of witchcraft, which alone was sufficient to condemn him. At his execution, Cotton Mather attended on horseback, and viewed the spectacle with great exultation. Many of the spectators were affected to tears, and it seemed as if they would hinder the execution; but Mather addressed the crowd, abused the victim, and asserted that the devil had often been transformed into an angel of light. Twenty others shared the fate of Burroughs; a hundred and fifty more were in prison awaiting trial; two hundred more were under accusation; and above a hundred and fifty had been tortured or terrified into confession.

Where was this to end? This question seems at last to have suggested itself to reflecting persons as the frenzy mounted to its utmost height, and the evil wrought its own cure by the extravagant length to which it had run. A madness so wild could not but spend itself in a short time. After raging for fifteen months, these atrocities began to appear in their true light, and the delusion abated. The minds of men were sobered down to cool reason, the spell was broken, and witchcraft was no more. People gazed at each other in astonishment, as if they had just waked from a horrible nightmare; universal shame and remorse succeeded to this storm of fanaticism. Thus terminated a scene of epidemic madness and delusion, which excited the astonishment of the civilized world, and exhibited a fearful picture of the weakness of human nature.

Most of the actors in this terrible drama atoned by the bitterest remorse and the most contrite repentance for their deplorable delusion. Parris, the minister, was driven from among his people; the humblest confession could not save him. Noyes, a minister of Salem, another chief agent, but less guilty than Parris, made a full and sincere confession, asked pardon of his people, and was forgiven. Sewall, one of the judges, made a confession of his error in the face of a public congregation. Cotton Mather, one of the most culpable of all the abettors of this persecution, was one of the last to repent, if indeed he ever repented. This selfish and intolerant bigot resisted all the endeavors of wiser men to dispel the delusion, and declared his determination to "box it about among his neighbors till it came he knew not where at last." He attempted to get up a case of witchcraft in his own parish; but the people of Boston were saved from the evils which his fanaticism might have induced, by the good sense and courage of several citizens of the town, among whom was a merchant named Robert Calef, who published a volume, exposing the imposture and wickedness of the whole business.

One of the most unaccountable of the circumstances attending these extraordinary events, is the fact
that none of the witnesses who had so unscrupulously
sworn away the lives of innocent persons were ever
brought to punishment.   Perhaps this arose from the
feeling that the past could not be repaired, that the
dead were beyond recall, and none wished to awaken a
recollection of such horrors.   Hutchinson affirms that
for many years afterward, the opinion maintained its
ground that there was something preternatural in this
strange affair, and that an epidemic disorder, inexpli-
cable in its nature, really affected both the bodies and
imagination of the afflicted persons.   This is, perhaps,
as charitable and rational a method as we can devise
for solving this strange mystery.

GENERAL PUTNAM.

OF the character of a New Englander " of the old school," we can hardly give a better illustration than in the history of this well-known individual, or " Old Put," as he was familiarly termed, from his intrepid temper, homely manners, and somewhat eccentric disposition. He was born in that part of Salem, in Massachusetts, which now constitutes the town of Danvers, January 7th, 1718. He showed early indications of a strong mind; but he enjoyed only such scanty means of school education as at that early period lay within the reach of the humblest class of our citizens.

While a boy, he was remarkable for strength of body, agility, and skill in athletic sports. He was brought up to the plough; and having married a wife during his minority, he removed from Salem to Pomfret, in Connecticut, in 1739, where he purchased a tract of land, and undertook the clearing and cultivation of a farm. A century ago, this territory, now the heart of the populous and thriving state of Connecticut, was exposed to constant depredation from hordes of wolves, which issued from the thick forest that overspread the country, and laid waste the fields and cattle-yards of the settlers. The following adventure of the hero of our story has become one of the classic legends of our land; it is so well related by

GENERAL PUTNAM.

Humphreys, in his biography, that we shall give it in his own words.

"In a single night, one of the inhabitants of Pomfret had seventy fine sheep and goats killed, besides many lambs and kids wounded. This havoc was committed by a she-wolf, which, with her annual troop of whelps, had for several years infested the vicinity. The young were commonly destroyed by the vigilance of the hunter, but the old one was too sagacious to come within the reach of gun shot. Upon being closely pursued, she would generally fly to the western woods, and return the next winter with another litter of whelps. This wolf at length became such an intolerable nuisance, that Mr. Putnam entered into a combination with five of his neighbors, to hunt alternately until they could destroy her. Two, by rotation, were to be constantly in pursuit. It was known that, having lost the toes from one foot by a steel trap, she made one track shorter than the other. By this vestige the pursuers recognized in a light snow the route of this pernicious animal. Having followed her to the Connecticut river, and found she had turned in a direct course towards Pomfret, they immediately returned, and by ten o'clock the next morning the bloodhounds had driven her into a den, about ten miles distant from the house of Mr. Putnam.

"The people soon collected with dogs, guns, straw, fire and sulphur, to attack the common enemy. With this apparatus, several unsuccessful efforts were made to force her from the den. The hounds came back badly wounded, and refused to return; the smoke of blazing straw had no effect, nor did the fumes of burnt brimstone, with which the cavern was filled compel her to quit her retirement. Wearied with such fruitless attempts, which had brought the time to ten o'clock at night, Mr. Putnam tried once more to make his dog enter, but in vain; he proposed to his negro man to go down into the cavern and shoot the wolf—the negro declined the hazardous service. Then it was that the master, angry at the disappointment, and declaring that he was ashamed to have a coward in his family, resolved himself to destroy this ferocious beast, lest she should escape through some unknown fissure of the rock. His neighbors strongly remonstrated against the perilous enterprise; but he, knowing that wild animals are intimidated by fire, and having provided several strips of birch bark, the only combustible material which he could obtain that would afford light in this deep and darksome cave, prepared for the descent.

"Having accordingly divested himself of his coat and waistcoat, and having a long rope fastened round his legs, by which he might be pulled back at a concerted signal, he entered, head foremost, with the blazing torch in his hand. The aperture of the den, on the east side of a high ledge of rocks, is about two feet square; from thence it descends obliquely fifteen feet; then running horizontally about ten more, it ascends gradually sixteen feet towards its termination. The sides of this subterraneous cavity are composed of smooth and solid rocks, which seem to have been divided from each other by some former earthquake. The top and bottom are also of stone, and the entrance in winter, being covered with ice, is exceedingly slippery. It is in no place high enough for a man to raise himself upright, nor in any part more than three feet in width. Having groped his passage to the horizontal part of the den, the most terrifying darkness appeared in front of the dim circle of light afforded by his torch; it was silent as the house of death; none but monsters of the desert had ever before explored this solitary mansion of horror. Cautiously proceeding onward, he came to the ascent, which he slowly mounted on his hands and knees, until he discovered the glaring eyeballs of the wolf, who was sitting at the extremity of the cavern. Startled at the sight of fire, she gnashed her teeth and gave a sullen growl. As soon as he had made the necessary discovery, he kicked the rope as a signal for pulling him out.

" The people at the mouth of the den, who had listened with painful anxiety, hearing the growling of the wolf, and supposing their friend to be in the most imminent danger, drew him forth with such celerity, that his shirt was stripped over his head, and his skin severely lacerated. After he had adjusted his clothes and loaded his gun with nine buck-shot, holding a torch in one hand and a musket in the other, he descended the second time. When he drew nearer than before, the wolf, assuming a still more fierce and terrible appearance, howling, rolling her eyes, snapping her teeth, and dropping her head between her legs, was evidently on the point of springing at him. At this critical instant, he levelled and fired at her head. Stunned with the shock, and suffocated with the smoke, he immediately found himself drawn out of the cave. But having refreshed himself, and permitted the smoke to dissipate, he went down the third time. Once more he came within sight of the wolf, who appearing very passive, he applied the torch to her nose, and perceiving her dead, he took hold of her ears, and then kicking the rope, the people above, with no small exultation, dragged them both out together."

The hostilities commonly known as the " old French war," brought Putnam into public service. In 1755, he was appointed to the command of a company of troops raised in Connecticut, and joined the army on its march to Crown Point, then occupied by the French. In this campaign, Putnam encountered numerous adventures, in which his courage, ingenuity, and presence of mind were highly conspicuous. The dangers to which he was exposed may be conjectured from the fact, that, on one occasion, after making his way into the midst of the enemy's camp in the darkness of the night, and escaping through a shower of random shots, he discovered, the next morning, fourteen bullet-holes in his blanket, and another through his canteen. At Sabbath-day Point, on Lake Champlain, Putnam and Captain Rogers, with a hundred men, defeated a body of three hundred of the enemy, with great slaughter. One day, General Webb, wishing for intelligence of the enemy, sent out Putnam, with five men, for the purpose of capturing some one who could give the desired information. They concealed themselves in the tall grass near a road, and in a short time saw a Frenchman and an Indian pass. Putnam sprang up and gave chase, ordering his men to follow. He overtook and seized the Frenchman, who was compelled to surrender; but on looking round, none of Putnam's men were seen, and the Frenchman began to resist. The former, finding himself betrayed, and two to one against him, let go his hold, stepped back, and snapped his gun at the Frenchman, but the piece missing fire, he was compelled to take to his heels. The Frenchman chased him back to his men, who suddenly started up from the grass, and the pursuer was forced to retreat in his turn. Putnam, indignant at the behavior of his followers, discharged them from his company immediately. It appears that they had taken offence at a reprimand which he had bestowed upon them a short time previous, and had adopted this method of wreaking their vengeance upon him.

His services during the campaign gained him the rank of a major; and in the following year he distinguished himself by a brilliant and dashing achievement at Fort Edward. A most barbarous massacre had been perpetrated by the enemy at Fort William Henry. That place had been surrounded by a strong force of French and savages, under the Marquis de Montcalm, and surrendered upon terms. But the savages, disregarding the capitulation, tomahawked every man and woman they met, nor could all the efforts of the French commander prevent the butchery of the greater part of the garrison, and above a hundred women. General Lyman, who commanded at Fort Edward, deemed it necessary o strengthen his position, and ordered out a hundred and fifty pioneers to cut timber. Captain Little, with fifty British regulars, was detached to cover them, and took post at the skirt of a thick swamp not far from the fort. For some days the men pursued their work unmolested, and no signs of the enemy were perceived. One morning, at daybreak, a sentinel had his attention attracted by what he imagined to be a number of birds which darted with amazing swiftness out of the swamp and disappeared in the air over his head. The singular shape, and most extraordinary celerity of these birds, excited his curiosity, and he watched their flight with great attention. All at once, he was startled to see one of these winged messengers strike the limb of a tree and stick fast. It was an Indian arrow! The sentinel gave the alarm, and a cloud of savages burst from their cover in the swamp, and fell with their tomahawks upon the wood-cutters. The covering party flew to their relief, and, by pouring in a prompt and well-directed fire, checked the savages in their onset, and enabled the unarmed laborers to retire to the fort.

Captain Little, finding his small party almost overpowered by numbers, sent to General Lyman for assistance; but that officer, believing that the main body of the enemy was in the neighborhood, ready for a general assault, ordered in the outposts and closed the gates of the fort. Putnam, with his company of Rangers, was stationed on an island near the garrison. Hearing the musketry, and being informed that his friend Captain Little was in the greatest danger, he plunged into the river at the head of his men, and waded through the water toward the spot where he heard the firing. His route passed so near the fort, that the soldiers espied him, and Lyman, imag-ming that these brave men were marching to certain destruction, mounted the parapet, and ordered Putnam to halt. Instead of complying, the major replied with a hasty apology, and marched onward with all haste. He soon arrived at the scene of action, and found the regulars obstinately maintaining their ground against a vast superiority of assailants. His timely arrival and prompt action saved this gallant band. Putnam immediately gave orders to his men to rush impetuously with loud shouts upon the enemy. This order was gallantly obeyed, and the savages instantly took to flight, and were pursued during the whole day with great loss. It does not appear that Putnam was ever brought to account for disobeying the orders of his general. The success atoned for the offence, and Lyman perhaps was sensible that his inferior in command was the better soldier of the two.

During the same year, Putnam defeated a large body of savages, who attacked him in his intrenchment on Lake George. In the winter which followed, he was in garrison at Fort Edward, when a fire broke out in the barracks at that place. Three hundred barrels of powder were in the magazine, which was built of wood, and stood only twelve feet distant from the building. The fire had made great progress when first discovered, and Colonel Haviland, the commander of the fort, endeavored in vain to demolish the barracks by discharging several pieces of heavy artillery against them. Putnam, who was stationed on an island in the river, hastened to the fort, and arrived at the moment when the fire reached the extremity of the barracks adjoining the magazine. Mounting a ladder to the eaves he endeavored to extinguish the flames by throwing upon them buckets of water. He stood enveloped in smoke, so near the fire that a pair of blanket mittens were burnt entirely off his hands. He was supplied with another, dipped in water, and maintained his post till the commander, fearing he would perish in the flames, ordered him to descend; but he entreated that he might be allowed to continue his exertions, since destruction must inevitably ensue should they allow the fire to continue its progress. The colonel, struck with his undaunted resolution and perseverance, consented, and although the flames continued to advance, he forbade any more effects to be carried out of the fort, and exhorted the men to redoubled exertions, exclaiming, " If we must be blown up, we will all go together!" Putnam remained on the ladder till the building began to fall, when he descended, and occupied himself in throwing water upon the magazine, the outer planks of which were now burnt away, leaving only a single thickness of timber between the fire and the powder. The universal trepidation at this extreme danger may easily be conceived, but Putnam, still undaunted and self-possessed, applied himself to the work of checking the flames for the space of an hour and a half, until the danger was over. The clothes were burnt from his body; he was blistered from head to foot, and the skin was entirely taken from his hands. It was a month before he recovered.

Putnam's intrepidity was soon after displayed in an incident of a different character. Being one day in a boat with five men on the Hudson, just above the rapids, he was surprised by a large Indian force. His only alternative was to remain and be cut to pieces, or to go down the falls with an almost absolute certainty of being drowned. He did not hesitate a moment to push off. The Indians were upon him so quickly, that they killed one of his men who had strayed a short distance from the rest on shore, and before the boat could be got under way, a shower of bullets whistled round her. The rapid current of the river soon carried her beyond the reach of the enemy's shot, but the crew speedily found themselves in the midst of dangers equally great. The rapids were a quarter of a mile in length, full of shelving rocks and whirling eddies, among which it seemed impossible to pass without a miracle. Putnam took the helm, and with the utmost coolness guided the boat as she shot swiftly along in the midst of these dangers. Every moment it was necessary to vary the course to avoid the shelves and whirlpools. The savages with amazement beheld the boat now mounting the billows, and now plunging abruptly downward, and now turning round and round, skilfully veering to the right and left among sharp points of rock, and shooting like an arrow through the contracted strait that afforded a chance of escape into the smooth stream below. The awe-struck and superstitious sons of the forest now believed that the daring leader whom they had endeavored to capture, bore a " charmed life," and imagined that it would be an offence to the Great Spirit should they attempt to kill him with powder and ball.

From the repeated and desperate hazards of these campaigns, i was hardly possible that a man of Put nam's bold and impetuous temper could long escape In August, 1758, he fell into an ambush of French and Indians, and was obliged to fight at a great disadvantage. Having discharged his musket several times, it at length missed fire, while he was aiming at a brawny savage only a yard or two distant. The warrior sprang forward, and, with his lifted tomahawk and a tremendous war-whoop, compelled him to surrender, and then bound him to a tree. Here he continued during the remainder of the action, in the course of which the movements of the hostile parties brought him between their two fires, and, for upwards of an hour, he was exposed to the bullets of both friends and foes, which continually whistled by him, often hitting the tree to which he was bound, and sometimes passing through the sleeves and skirts of his coat. At one time, when the enemy had nearly obtained the victory, a young savage began to divert himself by exciting the terrors of the captive. He threw his tomahawk a number of times at his head, taking care that it should not hit him, but strike the tree a hair's breadth from the mark. When he was tired of this savage amusement, a French officer, discovering Putnam in his defenceless state, levelled his musket at his breast, within the distance of a foot, and attempted to shoot him, but the piece missed fire. Putnam in vain expostulated with him on his cowardly behavior toward a prisoner of war; but the Frenchman, unable to fire his gun, beat him cruelly with the butt end of it, and then left him.

The Americans finally obtained the advantage, and drove their enemies from the field of battle; but Put-m was carried off a prisoner. He was mangled with a tomahawk and otherwise abused by his captors, insomuch that he begged they would put an end to his misery by knocking him on the head. When they encamped at night, the savages made preparations for burning him at the stake. He was stripped naked and bound to a tree; heaps of fagots and other inflammable materials were piled round him, dismal howls and screams were set up as his funeral dirge, and the piles were lighted. But at the moment when he had resigned himself to his fate, a sudden shower arose and extinguished the flames. The savages rekindled the piles, and the flames again threatened his destruction, when a French officer burst through the savage crowd, scattered the burning brands, and unbound the victim. After this, the prisoner was strictly guarded by the French, to prevent the Indians from glutting their diabolical revenge, which they still cherished in all its virulence against him. He was transported to Ticonderoga, and from thence to Montreal, where he was treated with humanity. After the capture of Frontenac, by General Bradstreet, an opportunity was offered for an exchange of prisoners, and Putnam obtained his liberty.

The campaign of 1760 again brought him into the field, and we find him in the army of General Amherst, in the expedition which ascended the Mohawk to Lake Ontario, and proceeded toward Montreal, by the route of the St. Lawrence. At Oswegatchie, two armed vessels obstructed the passage. Putnam, with a fleet of boats, undertook to board them: he put himself at the head with a chosen crew and a beetle and wedges, intending to fasten the rudders so as to prevent the manœuvring of the vessels. The boldness of the attack struck the enemy with a panic: they ran one vessel ashore, and surrendered the other, although they were well manned and equipped for fighting. This advantage was followed up by the capture of the fort at Oswegatchie, which was taken by a device of Putnam, who invented a new method of scaling the defences. Montreal was taken, and the conquest of Canada was effected without farther loss.

In the war which broke out between Great Britain and Spain, in 1762, Putnam served as lieutenant-colonel, in a regiment raised in Connecticut, which joined the expedition of Lord Albemarle against Havana. He sailed from New York, in a transport with five hundred men. On the coast of Cuba they were overtaken by a furious storm, and wrecked on a reef not far from the shore, but, by great exertions in constructing a raft, the whole crew were conveyed safely to land, and received on board the other ships. Havana was taken; but the provincial troops suffered so severely by sickness, that very few of them ever saw their homes again. In the Indian war of 1764, Putnam was again in command; after which he returned to private life, till called forth by public exigencies more critical and momentous than any we have yet described.

He was ploughing in his field when the news reached him of the battle of Lexington: he left his plough in the furrow, unyoked his oxen and, without changing his dress, set out for Boston. Finding the British blockaded in that town by a sufficient force, he returned to Connecticut, raised a regiment, under the authority of the legislature, and proceeded to Cambridge. He was now promoted to the rank of major-general in the provincial army, and his reputation stood so high that secret proposals were made to him by the British to abandon the American cause, in which case he might rely on being rewarded with a major-general's commission in the royal army, and a liberal sum of money. It is unnecessary to say that this offer was spurned with contempt and indignation. Shortly after this, the battle of Bunker Hill took place. The reader will find a description of this engagement in another chapter. The accounts of the movements of General Putnam on that day, and the share which he had in the battle, are so contradictory, that it is impossible to reconcile them, and it is now a controverted point whether he was in the action at all. There is no question as to the fact of his being near the battle-ground at the time, and as his bravery is undoubted, it is not probable that he was idle on that occasion. After the retreat, he intrenched himself on Prospect Hill.

From this period till the close of the year **1779,** he was actively engaged in military operations, during which he maintained his high reputation for bravery, enterprise and skill. But to recapitulate all the actions in which he fought, would be to write the history of these campaigns ; we can only subjoin a few anecdotes. While he was stationed at Peekskill, on the Hudson. a lieutenant in a newly levied company of tories was detected in his camp. Preparations were instantly made to hang him as a spy. Governor Tryon, who commanded the tory regiments, claimed him as a British officer, and threatened vengeance against Putnam, should he dare to execute a man bearing h s Majesty's commission. Putnam immediately wrote him the following letter :

SIR,—Nathan Palmer, a lieutenant in your king's service, was taken in my camp as a spy ; he was tried as a spy ; he was condemned as a spy ; and you may rest assured, sir, he shall be hanged as a spy.

I have the honor to be, &c.

ISRAEL PUTNAM.

His Excellency Governor Tryon.

P. S.——Afternoon. He is hanged.

In January, 1777, Putnam was directed to take post at Princeton, where he remained till spring. At this place, a sick prisoner, a captain, requested that a friend in the British army at Brunswick might be sent for, to assist him in making his will. Putnam was much embarrassed ; he had but fifty men under his command, and to disclose his weakness would infallibly occasion the loss of his post ; yet he was unwilling to deny the last request of a dying man. At length, he thought of a stratagem. He despatched a flag of truce, and directed the visiter to be brought in the night. Lights were placed in all the windows of the college, and in the apartments of the vacant houses in the town. The officer, on his return to the British camp, reported that Putnam's force could not be less than four or five thousand men.——While on a visit to his outpost at Horse Neck, in Connecticut, he found Tryon advancing upon him with a body of fifteen hundred men. Putnam had only a picket guard of one hundred and fifty soldiers, and two iron field-pieces, without horses or drag-ropes. He planted his cannon on an eminence near the meeting-house, and by firing several shots kept the enemy at bay for some time. At length, perceiving their cavalry about to charge, he ordered his men to retreat to a swamp inaccessible to cavalry, and provided for his own safety by plunging headlong down a steep descent, consisting of nearly a hundred stone steps. The British dragoons, who were within a sword's length of him, at this daring movement stopped short ; not one had the courage to follow him. Putnam gained the bottom in safety, and escaped amid a shower of bullets, one of which passed through his hat. Before the dragoons could ride round the brow of the hill, he was far out of their reach.

The year 1779 closed the military career of General Putnam. A paralytic affection impaired his physical powers, and he was compelled to retire from the army. He passed the remainder of his life in seclusion, retaining unabated his cheerfulness of temper, love of pleasantry, strength of memory, and all his mental faculties. His death took place on the 17th of May, 1790.

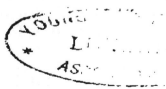

LEXINGTON AND BUNKER HILL

General Warren.

THE first attempt of the British government to tax the American colonies without their consent, was resisted and foiled with a promptness and resolution characteristic of a people jealous of their rights, and sharp-sighted in discovering the slightest encroachment upon them. The stamp act of 1765 was received with such an indignant show of opposition, that the officers of the crown found it impossible to carry it into effect, and the British parliament was reduced to the necessity of repealing it the following year. A more indirect and insidious attempt was next made to establish the principle of taxation, by imposing a duty on tea but this was met by a combination on the part of the colonists, who determined neither to import nor consume the taxed article. In order to circumvent them in this patriotic resolution, the British ministry, by a particular agreement, bargained with the East India Company to send a number of ships laden with tea to America; feeling confident that if the cargoes were once landed, their purpose would be accomplished, and the principle of taxation settled by a precedent. The colonists, however, were on their guard against these artful manœuvres; and the people of Boston were so determined to resist the landing of the taxed commodity, that, on the arrival of the tea-ships in their harbor, a party of disguised individuals immediately boarded them and threw the tea overboard.

Boston had, from the beginning, distinguished itself by the most resolute, bold and uncompromising measures against British encroachment, insomuch that the revolutionary party, in the early period of the contest, became known both in America and Europe by the name of the "Bostonians." The wrath of the British cabinet was raised to the highest pitch at this last act of resistance to their arbitrary measures; and they resolved to inflict signal vengeance on this devoted town, by utterly ruining its commerce. An act of parliament, in March, 1774, called the Boston Port Bill, shut up the harbor, removed the custom house, and put a complete stop to commerce, and every species of traffic and labor dependent upon it. A strong army had been quartered in the town, to enforce the measures of government; and the ministry enjoyed in anticipation the pleasure of seeing the Bostonians starved into compliance with their mandates. To their great astonishment, the spirit of resistance to their encroachments was rather strengthened than quelled. The citizens of the town manifested not the slightest disposition to recede from the ground they had taken in defence of their rights; and their distresses were alleviated by supplies of all kinds from the neighboring towns. Meantime, the petitions of the general congress to the king, for redress of the grievances of the colonists, had been received with contemptuous neglect; and the measures of the ministry for subjecting America to their arbitrary authority, grew more and more insulting. A reasonable attempt at conciliation, on the part of the mother country, would doubtless have dispelled all animosities, and restored the colonies to quiet and confidence; but the British ministry were urged on by a blind infatuation, and took no steps but such as were calculated to exasperate the irritated Americans. It was soon evident that the colonists must resign their ancient political rights, or prepare to maintain them by force of arms. At length, in the spring of 1775, all hopes of accommodation were dispelled by the arrival in America of the king's speech at the opening of parliament, in which the people of Massachusetts were declared to be rebels. The indignation and resentment of the colonists were wrought up to the highest pitch, and a single spark was only required to set the country in a flame.

The rashness of General Gage, the British commander in Boston, precipitated this event, and plunged at once the two countries into a war the most disastrous to Great Britain that she ever experienced. That officer, having learned that the provincials had collected a quantity of provisions and military stores at Concord, fourteen miles from Boston, resolved upon sending a party of troops to destroy them. He hoped also to seize John Hancock and Samuel Adams, two persons of high distinction and great influence in the colony, who had ardently espoused the cause of liberty. He made his preparations with the utmost secrecy and caution. On the 18th of April, a number of British officers were sent to dine at Cambridge; after which, towards evening, they scattered themselves on the road toward Concord, and took their stations so as to intercept any expresses which might be sent from Boston to alarm the country. Gage hoped to manage the affair so skilfully, that the Americans would be completely taken by surprise. The grenadier and light infantry companies were taken off duty on the pretext of learning a new exercise, and at eleven o'clock at night, eight hundred picked men embarked from the west side of Boston common landed near Lechmere Point, and marched rapidly towards Concord.

But it was impossible to evade the jealous vigilance of the Bostonians. Every movement of the troops had been watched, and no sooner had they entered the boats, than a beacon light blazed from the tower of the north church, and spread the alarm into the country. On all the roads leading from Boston, the inhabitants were roused, took to their arms, and collected at different points, not knowing in what direction the enemy were proceeding. The inhabitants of

Lexington received intelligence from Dr. Warren, a little after midnight, that the British were on their march to that town.   The militia immediately assembled, and as the day began to dawn, the royal troops, on entering the town, were met by a body of about sixty Americans, drawn up on the green.   The British advanced upon them with loud shouts, and Major Pitcairn, their commander, cried out, "Disperse, you rebels; throw down your arms, and disperse!"   He then fired his pistol, and this was followed by a heavy volley from his men.   No resistance could be offered by the provincials against so superior a force, and they immediately scattered, leaving eight of their number dead on the ground, and having ten wounded.

Such is the history of the rencounter in which the first blood was shed in that memorable war which put an end to the British empire within the present territory of the United States.   The royal troops gave three cheers, and pursued their march to Concord.   A guard of about one hundred militia was posted at the outskirts of the town.   Early in the morning, the British were discovered advancing by the Lexington road.   The sun shone with uncommon splendor, and the arms of eight hundred men, glittering in his bright beams, formed a novel, imposing, and alarming sight to this small band of undisciplined rustics.   At first, they determined to face the enemy, and abide the consequences; in this they were encouraged by the clergyman of the town, Mr. Emerson, who had turned out at the first alarm to animate the people by his counsel and example.   "Let us stand our ground!" said he; "if we die, let us die here."   "No," said another, "it will not do for *us* to begin the war." They did not then know what had taken place at Lexington. Finally, it was decided to retire and wait for reinforcements. The British marched in, and took possession of the town. The greater part of the stores had been secreted, so that the main object of the expedition was frustrated. The British staved about sixty barrels of flour, knocked off the trunnions of three iron cannon, burnt four carriage-wheels, and threw five hundred pounds of ball into the mill-pond and wells; but before their work of destruction was completed, the sounds of the alarm bell and the sight of numbers of people gathering on the surrounding hills, warned the British commander that he was in danger of having his retreat cut off, and he hastily took up his march for Boston.

But it was now broad day, and the alarm had spread throughout the neighborhood. From every village, hamlet and solitary farm-house, the people came thronging to the scene of action; and three hundred armed men had collected at Concord as the British marched out of town. Near the bridge, several shots were fired from the British ranks, by which two of the Americans were killed, and two more wounded. The Americans immediately poured in a volley, by which three were killed and eight wounded on the side of the royal troops. Scattering shots continued to fall upon the British from flank and rear, and as they retreated, the fire of the Americans increased. From behind fences, stone-walls, trees, and houses, flashes of musketry apprized them that a daring and indefatigable enemy had determined to avenge

the blood spilt at Lexington.   Every step increased
the number of the provincials, and the alarm of the
British ; these, exposed to the incessant fire of a cloud
of expert marksmen, whom they could neither escape
nor repel, saw their ranks thinned by invisible enemies, and were compelled to hasten their retreat, leaving the road behind them strewed with their dead
and wounded companions.   General Gage, in the
mean time, had received at an early hour the news of
the affair at Lexington, and was informed that the
country was rising.   Feeling alarmed for the safety
of the detachment, he sent out another body of nine
hundred men, with two pieces of cannon, for their
relief.   To show their contempt for their enemies,
these troops marched out with their band playing a
tune which had lately been composed in derision of
the Americans, but which subsequent events have
raised to uncommon fame and honor.   As they filed
through the streets of Roxbury, a smart boy cried
out in the hearing of Lord Percy, who commanded
the detachment, "*You march out with Yankee Doo-
dle, but you will dance home with Chevy Chase.*"   It is
added, that this sally was not out of his lordship's
head for the whole day.

The arrival of this timely reinforcement saved
Pitcairn's troops from being completely overwhelmed.
They made a short halt at Lexington, to take breath ;
but the number of the Americans continually increasing, they were still in danger of having their retreat
cut off.   Constant skirmishes took place ; the militia
hung upon their flanks and rear, and their numbers
being now formidable, the annoyance which they gave

the retreating troops was excessive.   To add to their
embarrassments, the wind, which blew strong from the
south, was uncommonly warm, and the road being
dry, they were blinded by clouds of dust, and exhausted with their rapid march under a hot sun.
Major Pitcairn was obliged to abandon his horse, which
was taken with the pistols in the holsters.   Such was
the confusion and panic among the ranks of the
British, that the soldiers pointed their guns over the
stone walls and fired when there was no enemy in
sight.   In this manner, they continued their retreat
with an accelerated pace, and had the good fortune to
reach Charlestown just as the shades of night were
gathering around them.   A delay of an another hour
would have caused the capture or dispersion of their
whole body.   They were completely exhausted by the
excessive fatigue of this march, and had suffered a loss
of two hundred and seventy-three in killed, wounded
and prisoners.   The loss of the provincials in killed,
wounded and missing, was eighty-eight.   Several
houses, also, were set on fire by the British in their
retreat.

Such was the memorable affair of Concord, which
is known in American history by the less appropriate
name of the Battle of Lexington.   Seldom has a
military action produced so instantaneous and momentous an effect.   The news of it ran through the country like an electric shock, and in all quarters the
inhabitants rushed from their houses as the messenger
of war swept by them: the husbandman abandoned
his plough; the mechanic threw down his tools; the
tradesman quitted his shop; the churches poured forth

their congregations at the tidings that blood had been shed; and the spirit of war was now sweeping over the country. The first moments of panic and amazement were succeeded by courage, resolution and decisive action. One single determination now seemed to inspire all New England, to avenge the blood of Concord and Lexington. Unsummoned and self-impelled, old and young rushed to arms; in three days the roads were covered with files and companies of men, marching upon Boston, and within a week the town was invested by an army of twenty thousand men. From the heights of that capital, the British commander espied with astonishment the watch-fires of his enemies. which studded the horizon for miles in a long sweep around his encampment, and completely enclosed him in a narrow space. It was then that he became sensible of the momentous character of the deed he had done, and perhaps repented of his rashness. But it was too late; the decisive blow had been struck, and the flame was kindled which was destined to sweep over the land, and blaze, till the British empire in these states was no more.

The provincial army, which, like the progeny of the dragon's teeth, seemed to have sprung at once out of the earth, immediately intrenched themselves on the heights of Roxbury, Brookline, Cambridge and Charlestown. Seldom have troops been apparently more poorly qualified for the business of war. Few among them had ever seen the face of an enemy; fewer still knew anything of discipline; and fewer yet, of military science as it had been taught in the armies of Europe. Their equipments were of the most heterogeneous character: rusty muskets and fowling-pieces were the weapons of such of the infantry as possessed fire-arms; they had no cavalry; bayonets were hardly known among them; and their artillery consisted of four cannon of the smallest size. Such command over them as existed, was exercised by a deacon of the church—General Ward. From what quarter they were to obtain ammunition, nobody knew; but these men, inspired by an ardent resolution to avenge the blood of their countrymen, and face their insolent enemy in his strong-hold, undertook to besiege a powerful and well-equipped British army, commanded by the most skilful and experienced officers, and assisted by a strong fleet of ships of war, lying in the harbor. If General Gage's first sensation was that of astonishment, it soon subsided into contempt for his enemy, in whom he saw nothing but a disorderly rabble, whom he imagined he could disperse by the first movement of his veteran columns. As soldiers, the Americans were despised by the British, whose obstinate self-conceit had not yet been subdued. In the campaign against Louisburg, thirty years before, the awkward discipline and uncouth engineering of the New England troops, excited the hearty merriment of the officers of the royal navy, who pronounced such an army unable to capture a cow-yard. The Yankees made no answer, but they took the town.

General Gage continued inactive for some weeks, expecting every day that the provincials would disperse of their own accord, and leave him at liberty to range the country at his pleasure. But, to his surprise, no indication of such a design was perceptible.

His surprise was redoubled by discovering, on the morning of the 17th of June, an intrenchment, which had risen during the preceding night, on the summit of Breed's Hill, the most advanced of the heights on the peninsula of Charlestown. No part of this peninsula had before been occupied by the American forces; but on the 16th of June, a detachment of a thousand men, under Colonel Prescott, was ordered to take post and throw up works on Bunker Hill, a loftier and steeper eminence, farther from Boston. Either mistaking the locality, or stimulated by a desire to approach as near to the enemy as possible, the Americans advanced to the heights nearest to Boston, and, during the shortest night of the year, labored with such industry that by the dawn of day they had thrown up a redoubt of earth eight rods square. Several ships of war lay in the river, close to the hill; yet such was the extraordinary silence with which the work was prosecuted, that the British heard nothing of the noise and bustle of a thousand men at labor with their intrenching tools. As soon as dawn revealed what had been done, a brisk fire was opened upon the redoubt from one of the ships; but the Americans took no notice of it, and continued their labor with the coolness of veteran soldiers. The cannonade upon them soon increased; the other ships and floating batteries added their fire, and the British works on Copp's' Hill, in Boston, which directly faced the Americans, poured upon them an incessant shower of shot and shells. Only one man was killed by all this cannonading and bombardment; and the works on the hill were pursued till a breastwork had been carried down from the east side of the redoubt nearly to the foot of the eminence. But the Americans had no time to complete their lines of defence; they were stopped in their work by the approach of the enemy's troops.

In the affair of Bunker Hill, neither the Americans nor the British were guided by the rules of sound military tactics. The possession of the post which they occupied was of no value to the Americans, as, from their want of heavy artillery, it gave them no additional means of annoying their enemy. The British general, on the other hand, had no adequate object in driving them from this post, for the same reason; and, in addition to this, he had it in his power, by taking possession of Charlestown Neck, to cut off their retreat and starve them into a surrender. The true cause of the battle was, that both sides were eager to come to blows. In spite of the lesson which they had received at Concord, the British still remained under the impression that the American militia were cowards, who would not stand the fire of regular troops, and they wished, as a pastime, to meet and scatter an army of them, in revenge for the inglorious nineteenth of April. The Americans, in their turn, were resolved to improve the first opportunity of trying their strength. In this situation of things, a speedy conflict was unavoidable. Gage issued immediate orders to drive the provincials from the hill. Between four and five thousand men, the choicest troops in the army, were detached upon this service, and a little before one o'clock, the greater part of them landed in Charlestown, and formed for the attack. Generals Howe and Pigot had the command; they were well supplied with field artillery, and all sorts of ammunition. The Americans amounted, in all, to fifteen hundred men, a third part of whom arrived during the engagement. Prescott seems to have exercised the command. Dr. Warren, president of the provincial congress, had just received a commission as general; but he refused the command at Bunker Hill, and served as a volunteer. General Putnam, according to the testimony of many good witnesses, was also in the battle. Yet this point of history is involved in strange contradictions. As new companies dropped in from time to time, they took their stations and acted probably without much regard to the orders of any commander. Two light pieces of cannon were mounted in the redoubt, but that work had no embrasures, and the artillery-men were without skill in gunnery. There was but a small quantity of powder among the Americans, and that chiefly in powder-horns; no measures had been taken for a supply, and very few of the guns had bayonets. Such was the relative condition of the two armies, which exhibited a disparity of force that must astonish every one who contemplates the result of the battle.

At the first movement of the British troops in Boston, their batteries on the Neck opened a heavy fire upon the American works in Roxbury, in order to direct the attention of the provincials from the main point of attack, and prevent them from sending reinforcements to Charlestown. The Copp's Hill batteries and the shipping increased their fire as the troops formed and advanced against the American lines on Bread's Hill. The tremendous roar of cannon and the preparations for the approaching battle wrought up the inhabitants of the town and neighborhood to the highest pitch of excitement. It was, indeed, a moment full of awful suspense and anxiety. The hills of Boston, the housetops and steeples, the heights which surround the town, were covered with people, breathless with expectation, and every stirring emotion. The British troops advanced slowly up the hill, facing the American breastworks, in excellent order, and halting occasionally, to give time for the artillery to fire. The scene now became grand and awful in the highest degree. Charlestown, a cluster of five hundred wooden houses, was set on fire by the British, and rose in a huge pyramid of flame to the sky. The roar of the conflagration, the thunder of the British artillery, and the shower of bombs and shot which rained upon the Americans, might have appalled the most hardened veterans ; but, with the utmost courage and coolness, they maintained their post, reserving their fire till the British had arrived within point blank shot, when they took deliberate aim, and poured upon their advancing lines so destructive a volley, that in an instant they were brought to a stand ; unable to support it beyond a few minutes, they gave way, and retreated down the hill. At full speed, and in great disorder, they gained the landing-place, and some of them took refuge in their boats. The officers were seen running after them, attempting to rally and encourage them, and even goading them backwards towards the enemy with their swords.

By great efforts, the royal troops were rallied, and led a second time against the lines. Again the provincials waited their approach with the most determined coolness, and again did a vigorous and well-directed fire mow down the British ranks, and put them to flight. Such was the carnage, that General Howe was left standing almost alone amid heaps of the dead; and such was the dismay caused by this terrible slaughter, that the officers exclaimed against the orders to renew the attack, and pronounced it a "downright butchery." But in the mean time, Gage, from the opposite shore, had witnessed the unexpected discomfiture of his troops, and hastened to strengthen them by a reinforcement. With this help, a new effort was made to face the Americans, though the soldiers evinced the utmost repugnance to be led again to battle. The united and strenuous efforts of their officers succeeded in once more animating them to the conflict. At the third attack, the powder of the Americans began to fail, and their fire was not kept up with the usual spirit. This revived the courage of the assailants; the cannonade from the ships, batteries and field-pieces was redoubled, and the imperfect nature of the breastwork enabled the British to get in the rear of it on the left wing, and bring several pieces of cannon to bear, so as to rake it on the inside from end to end. No position is tenable when it becomes thus exposed: the breastwork was abandoned, but those in the redoubt held out. The British followed up their success, and encouraged their soldiers to attack the redoubt. Three sides were assailed at once by a furious charge with the bayonet. The Americans, overpowered by numbers, with neither powder nor bayonets, nevertheless made an obstinate resistance with the butt ends of their muskets, till the redoubt being half filled with the enemy, and all further opposition a useless waste of life, they gave up the contest and retreated. General Warren was just at this moment struck with a bullet in the head, and killed within the redoubt.

The possession of the battle-field rested with the British; but the enormous loss which they sustained, and the unexpected courage and obstinacy with which the Americans had fought, took away all reason for exultation on the part of the victors. One thousand and fifty-four of their number were killed or wounded, and the officers killed amounted to eighty-nine. The American killed and wounded did not exceed four hundred and twenty. On the other hand, the firmness with which the provincials had resisted the attack, and the execution which they had made among the ranks of their enemies, were accounted by them as equivalent to a victory. The result of that day gave them high confidence, dismayed their antagonists, and proved an effectual stop to the advance of the British into Massachusetts. The consequences, moreover, were felt in more distant quarters. Washington, who had just been appointed commander-in-chief, was duly sensible of the hazardous nature of the contest between the raw militia of the colonies, and the well-disciplined veterans of Britain. When he was informed that a battle had been fought between the British troops and the New England militia, he eagerly asked whether the latter had stood the fire of the regulars; on hearing the battle described, he clasped his hands together, and exclaimed with energy, "*The liberties of America are safe!*"   23*

ARNOLD'S MARCH TO QUEBEC.

WHILE the American army were blockading Boston, in the autumn of 1775, a scheme was projected by congress for the invasion of Canada. Favorable accounts had been received from that country, and it was believed that neither the Canadians nor the Indians would take up arms against the Americans. The scheme was approved by Washington, and it was decided that a strong force should advance upon Quebec by the way of Lake Champlain, while another body should be detached from the army at Cambridge, and march upon the same point through the wilderness of Maine, by the way of the river Kennebec. Generals Montgomery and Schuyler were entrusted with the command of the former, and Colonel Arnold with that of the latter division of the invading army.

Arnold's undertaking was deemed hazardous, but it was beset with far greater perils than any one imagined. There were few settlements in Maine at any great distance from the seacoast, and the district to be traversed was a desolate wilderness, of which hardly anything was known; but Arnold, who was courageous, of a sanguine temper, and little accustomed to prudential calculations when a new and attractive enterprise presented itself to his ambition, readily accepted the command of the expedition. His force consisted of ten companies of New England infantry, and three companies of Virginia and Pennsylvania riflemen. They amounted in all to eleven hundred men. The field officers, in addition to the commander, were Colonels Greene and Enos, and Majors Bigelow and Meigs. The riflemen were commanded by Captain Daniel Morgan, afterwards so celebrated as a partisan officer. The famous Aaron Burr served in this expedition as a lieutenant.

On the 13th of September, 1775, the detachment marched from Cambridge for Newburyport, where, six days after, they embarked in ten transports for the Kennebec. Two days' voyage brought them to the mouth of this river, and they ascended it as far as Gardiner. A company of boat-builders had previously been despatched to that place from Cambridge, to construct batteaux; and they labored with such industry, that in fourteen days from the time the first orders for the drafting of the troops were issued at Cambridge, the whole body were embarked on the Kennebec in two hundred boats, completely equipped and provisioned. They sailed up the river and rendezvoused at Fort Western. opposite the site of the present town of Augusta.

Hitherto they had proceeded without any adequate conception of the difficulties that lay before them: but the perils of the undertaking soon began to appear. The cold season was approaching, and the winters of Maine are uncommonly severe. Eleven hundred men, with their arms, ammunition and provisions, were to find their way through an unknown region, wild, rugged, and without inhabitants. There were craggy mountains to traverse, how lofty and steep no one knew.   Nothing like a road existed in the vilderness.   Rapids and cataracts obstructed the navigation of the rivers, and they were not only compelled to force their batteaux against swift currents, but were exposed to the labor of constantly unlading them, and transporting them and their cargoes round the waterfalls.   More than two hundred miles were to be travelled through all these difficulties, before they reach the French settlements on the frontiers of Canada.   Arnold had but slight knowledge of the country to direct his movements.   Colonel Montresor, a British officer, had passed over this route fifteen years before, and an imperfect copy of his journal had fallen into the hands of the American leader, who relied chiefly upon it for his guidance.   Some Indians had furnished additional information ; and Arnold secretly despatched two persons forward as an exploring party.   These men, on reaching the head waters of Dead River, met an old Norridgewock Indian, the last of his tribe, who had his wigwam in that neighborhood.   The crafty savage, being probably in the interest of the British, contrived to terrify them with bugbear stories, and they dared not advance any further, but wrote back to Arnold, who received their communication at Fort Western.

From this post, the army proceeded up the river in four divisions, keeping a day's march between them, that they might not interfere with each other in passing rapids and cataracts.   Morgan, with his riflemen, led the van, and Enos brought up the rear.   As they advanced, the rapidity of the stream increased, and the bed and shores grew still more rocky.   On the first of October, the forward party reached Norridgewock. Here, a little below the falls of the river, formerly stood the Indian village where the celebrated missionary Rasle lived twenty-six years, and built a chapel. The ruins of the latter were still visible, as Arnold's troops passed the spot. Their curiosity was also interested by another object; this was a child fourteen months old, the first white person ever born in that place. At the Norridgewock falls, it was necessary to unlade the batteaux, and transport them, with all their effects, a mile and a quarter by land, over a rough and rocky country. On examining their provisions, they were now found to be much damaged, particularly the bread. The boats, from the hurry in which they had been constructed, proved leaky, and had constantly suffered from accidents in ascending the rapids. It cost the little army seven days' labor to repair their injured craft, and get them round the falls. Passing more of these obstructions, they reached the Great Carrying Place at the head of the Kennebec. The fatigues which they had encountered were extreme, having been obliged to wade in the river for half the distance, dragging the boats against the swift current. Much sickness prevailed among them, reducing their effective force to nine hundred and fifty men.

The expedition had now reached the extreme point of navigation on the main stream of the Kennebec. From this spot, the Great Carrying Place extended fifteen miles to Dead River, one of the head streams of the Kennebec. They had yet fifteen days' provision remaining, and Arnold was confident of reaching

B

the Chaudiere, which falls into the St. Lawrence, in eight or ten days. It was necessary to transport the boats, provisions and baggage, on men's shoulders, the greater part of the distance, as the Carrying Place had only three small ponds to relieve them of the labor through its whole extent. A steep and rugged ascent of three miles caused them a march of painful toil to the first pond, where they again embarked. Beyond this, their course was impeded by craggy ravines and morasses; but by unwearied efforts they made their way through every impediment, and, after six days' incessant labor, they reached Dead River on the 16th of October. The ponds were stocked with abundance of fine salmon trout, which afforded a most welcome supply of food after this laborious march. Two blockhouses were built at different points on this route, as depositories for the sick, and for a stock of provisions which had been ordered from Norridgewock.

Before they reached Dead River, Arnold sent forward one of his men with two Indians. The latter carried letters to General Schuyler, and some persons in Quebec, who were supposed to be well affected toward the Americans. The other individual was directed to explore the French settlements on the Chaudiere, ascertain the feeling of the inhabitants, and return with such intelligence as he could obtain. It appears that Arnold had not sufficient proof of the fidelity of the Indians to warrant his entrusting them with so important a mission, for they betrayed their trust, and carried the letters to the lieutenant governor of Canada. The expedition now advanced up the gentle stream of the Dead River, which, however, was interrupted in several places by falls of short descent. The meandering course of the river made their progress a very slow one. Near a bold and lofty mountain, capped with snow, the army halted for rest, two or three days. A tradition has prevailed that Major Bigelow ascended to the top of this mountain, in the hope of discovering the hills of Canada and the spires of Quebec; and from this circumstance it has obtained the name of Mount Bigelow.

The provisions now began to fall short, and a detachment of ninety men were sent back to hasten the march of the rear division, which was better supplied than the rest. Arnold and Morgan pushed forward with the first and second. Heavy rains fell, and for three days every man and all the baggage were drenched with water. Violent floods pouring down the ravines of this mountainous region, exposed them to constant danger. One night, having encamped on shore at a late hour, they were suddenly roused by a mountain torrent, which burst upon them with such fury that they had barely time to escape, before the spot on which they had lain was completely overflowed. These incessant rains caused the river to swell, and in nine hours the water rose eight feet. The rapidity of the current was increased, and the stream, expanding, flooded the low grounds along the banks of the river, and entangled the batteaux among the driftwood, bushes, and other obstructions. Seven of them were overset, and all their cargoes lost. By this disaster their slender stock of provisions became further reduced, and a council of war being called, it was decided to send back all the sick and debilitated. Orders were therefore despatched to Greene and Enos, who were yet in the rear, to push forward with as many of their men as they could supply with fifteen days' provision, and send the remainder back to Norridgewock. Enos disobeyed this order, and, instead of continuing his march, abandoned the enterprise, and retreated with his whole division of three companies to the seacoast, from whence he returned to the army at Cambridge.

The other divisions continued their toilsome course up Dead River, ignorant that they were abandoned by their comrades. So many difficulties were encountered, that they made but twenty-one miles' progress in three days. Arnold led the van with sixty men, designing to make a forced march to the Chaudiere, and send back provisions to the main body. The fatigues and sufferings of the soldiers augmented daily; the cold increased; the rain changed to snow; the rivers and ponds froze, and they were obliged to drag the batteaux through the ice. At length, on the 27th of October, the advanced party reached the highlands, which separate the head streams of Maine from those of Canada, having passed seventeen falls on Dead River, and made their way through an immense number of ponds and morasses, choked with logs and other obstructions. They were now near Lake Megantic, the source of the Chaudiere; a sheet of water thirteen miles long, and three or four broad, and surrounded by lofty mountains. They encamped on its eastern shore, where they fortunately discovered a

.arge Indian wigwam, which afforded them comfortable quarters.

At this spot, they found Lieutenants Steel and Church, who had been forward to explore the country, and clear paths at the portages. Arnold was gratified to find also in their company Jakins, the individual who had been sent into Canada with the Indians. He had explored the French settlements, and brought a very favorable account of the people, stating them to be friendly to the Americans, and rejoiced at the approach of the army. Arnold now detached Captain Hanchet with fifty-four men, to march by land along the shore of the lake, and himself, with sixteen others, embarked in five batteaux and a birch canoe, to gain the settlements as speedily as possible. In three hours they reached the northern extremity of the lake, and entered the Chaudiere, which dashed its turbulent waters over a rocky bottom, boiling and foaming with great fury. The batteaux were swept down the stream with fearful rapidity; and they had no pilot. They shortly fell among rapids; three of their batteaux were upset and dashed to pieces against the rocks, with the total loss of their cargoes. Six men were for some time in imminent danger of drowning; but, after struggling a long time in the water, they succeeded in saving their lives. This disaster, however, saved the party from destruction. For no sooner had the men dried their clothes and reembarked, than one of them, who had walked forward, cried out, "A fall ahead!" But for this discovery, the whole of them must have been hurried to instant death. This providential escape taught them caution, but their whole course down this dangerous stream was marked with every species of peril. Rapids and falls were continually occurring. The canoe ran upon the rocks and was lost. At a portage of above half a mile, they were fortunate enough to find two Penobscot Indians, who assisted them in passing round. After escaping a multitude of dangers, they arrived, on the 30th of October, at Sertigan, the first French settlement on the Chaudiere, seventy miles from Lake Megantic, by the course of the stream.

In the mean time, the main body were advancing with all possible speed under the excessive fatigues and privations to which they were exposed. Their sufferings were now augmented to an alarming degree. Incessant toil amid cold, rain, snow and ice, had almost exhausted their strength; their provisions gave out, and famine stared them in the face. The few dogs in the army were killed, and afforded the hungry soldiers the last meal apparently within their reach. Then the hides of the dogs were devoured. After this, their moose-skin moccasins, cartridge-boxes, breeches, shoes, and other articles of leather, were boiled, and eaten, to save them from absolute starvation. Amid such incredible sufferings, they crossed the highlands, and proceeded down the Chaudiere; but, exhausted by famine, they were unable to prevent the total destruction of their batteaux in the rapids of that river. At last, on the third of November, at the very point of starvation, they were transported with joy at the sight of a party of their own men, who had been sent back by Arnold with a supply of provisions. The next day, they arrived at a French house, where they were hospitably received. This was the first dwelling they had seen for thirty-one days. In this unparalleled march they traversed a distance of more than three hundred miles through a wilderness, against rapids and falls, through tangled woods, swamps, and morasses, and over craggy hills and mountains. All their powder, except what they carried about them in cartridges and horns, was lost.

The whole army, emerging in detached parties from the forests, was thus assembled in Canada, and appear quickly to have forgotten their losses and sufferings, in their ardor to prosecute the great enterprise which they had undertaken. The Canadians received them in the most friendly manner; they supplied them liberally with provisions, and seemed to wish them success in their undertaking. The sudden appearance of such a body of men, issuing in this unexpected manner from the bosom of an almost impassable wilderness, struck them with surprise and astonishment. The exploit served to realize the tales of romance; and the old Canadians, who dwell in the remote and sequestered valley of the Chaudiere, recount to their children at this day the marvellous tale of the " descent of the Bostonians," as the great event that has marked the history of that region.

The heroic courage, firmness and resolution of this famous band, were not rewarded with a proportionate degree of final success Ten days after their arrival at Sertigan, Arnold reached Point Levy, on the St. Lawrence, opposite Quebec, and the whole army rendezvoused at that place on the 13th of November. The approach of the Americans had already become known in Quebec; yet so great was the panic occasioned in that city at the sight of Arnold's troops, that an immediate *coup de main* would doubtless have carried the place. The British, however, had secured all the boats on the river, and the Americans, although in sight of the grand object of their expedition, were unable to strike the important blow. After some delay, thirty or forty birch canoes were collected, and Arnold prepared for an attack. But during this space, the British had time to recover from their surprise; Quebec was put in a state of defence; the exaggerations respecting the force of the Americans were exposed, and Arnold had the mortification to discover that his men had now not above five cartridges of ⁓der apiece. After summoning the city in vain to surrender, he marched eight leagues up the river, to await the arrival of General Montgomery from Montreal. The unfortunate events which followed, form a mournful page in the history of our revolutionary struggle.

THE DECLARATION OF INDEPENDENCE.

John Hancock.

To what individual the idea of the independence of the British North American colonies first seriously suggested itself, never can be known. It has been said, we do not recollect upon what authority, that, before the breaking out of the revolutionary troubles, Franklin, then on a visit to England, was one day observed sitting on the bank of the Thames, and gaz-

24 *

ing pensively upon its waters.   On being questioned
as to the subject of his meditations, he replied, " I was
thinking of the strange fact, that all the noble rivers
of America are subject to this little stream."   This is
supposed to be evidence that at that early period he
indulged in grave speculations as to the desirableness
and probability of separating the colonies from the
mother country.

The wishes and the schemes of individuals, however, are not always to be referred to as the causes of
important events of this nature ; they lie much deeper ;
they originate in more general springs of action, and
owe their full development to nice and critical con-
junctures.   When the American colonists first took up
arms against Britain, there was no thought of independence ; they entered into the contest for the preservation of their ancient rights, and not to overturn
their existing government ; they combated in the first
instance upon conservative and not upon revolutionary
principles.   The mother country was the original inno-
vator ; the colonists resisted innovation.   The British
ministry entered into a deliberate design to alter the
government of the colonies without consulting them ;
the colonists were reduced to the alternative of either
changing their government by their own hands, or
submitting to a change imposed upon them by others.
It was perfectly natural that they should make choice
of the former.

That the plot of the British cabinet against the
liberties of the colonies was deeper and more deliberate than has generally been imagined, is apparent
from the following anecdote.   The celebrated Metho-

dist preacher Whitefield, being at Portsmouth, in New Hampshire, on the 2d of April, 1764, sent for Dr. Langdon and Mr. Haven, the Congregational ministers of the town, and in a private interview with them made the following statement: "I cannot in conscience leave the town without acquainting you with a secret. My heart bleeds for America. O, poor New England! There is a deep-laid plot against both your civil and religious liberties, and they will be lost. Your golden days are at an end. You have nothing but trouble before you. My information comes from the best authority in Great Britain. I was allowed to speak of the affair in general, but enjoined not to mention particulars. Your liberties will be lost."

The stamp act excited the liveliest indignation in the colonies, and, being considered illegal, was openly resisted. The violent opposition of the Americans caused its repeal the next year; but this opposition, being founded upon the persuasion of its unconstitutionality, was not considered by them as partaking of a revolutionary spirit; there were yet no thoughts of revolution or rebellion. The aggressions and vexations which followed, did not prevent the colonists from continuing to style and believe themselves the "loyal and dutiful subjects of the king." But their remonstrances to the British parliament were unavailing; their petitions for redress were spurned from the throne; aggression followed aggression, exhibiting a settled design on the part of the British ministry to force their unconstitutional measures on the colonists at all hazards, even at the point of the bayonet. The colonists took up arms; the British poured their troops into the country; hostilities broke out; battle after battle was fought, and the Americans found themselves arrayed in martial strife against the government to which they professed allegiance. The royal authority had ceased in all the colonies, and was replaced progressively by that of the people, expressing their views through conventions assembled in the several colonies.

Samuel Adams was perhaps the first to suggest independence. It is remarkable that this distinguished leader, as early as his twenty-first year, when he commenced Master of Arts at Harvard College, in 1743, proposed this question for debate : " Whether it be lawful to resist the supreme magistrate if the commonwealth cannot otherwise be preserved." He maintained the affirmative. When the affair of Lexington took place, he pronounced an opinion that the contest would result either in the independence or slavery of the colonies. John Hancock may share the celebrity with him. The following language must surprise us by its boldness, when we consider that it was uttered by Hancock in public at Boston, when that town was garrisoned by a strong body of British troops : it is from an oration commemorative of the fifth of March. " Some boast of being friends to government. I am a friend to righteous government,—to a government founded upon the principles of reason and justice ; but I glory in publicly avowing my eternal enmity to tyranny. And here suffer me to ask, what tenderness, what regard have the rulers of Great Britain manifested in their late transactions for the security of the persons or property of the inhabitants of these colonies? Or rather what have they omitted doing to *destroy* that security? They have usurped the right of ruling us in all cases whatever, by arbitrary laws. They have exercised this pretended right by imposing a tax upon us without our consent, and lest we should show some reluctance at parting with our property, their fleets and armies are sent to enforce their mad and tyrannical pretensions. The town of Boston, ever faithful to the British crown, has been invested by a British fleet. The troops of George the Third have crossed the Atlantic, not to invade the enemy, but to assist a band of traitors in trampling on the rights and liberties of his most loyal subjects; those rights and liberties which, as a father, he ought ever to regard, and, as a king, he is bound in honor to defend from violations, even at the risk of his own life. Dark and designing knaves! murderers! parricides! how dare you tread upon the earth which has drunk the blood of slaughtered innocence shed by your hands? How dare you breathe the air which wafted to the ear of Heaven the groans of those who fell in a sacrifice to your accursed ambition?"

Hancock and Adams, the two chief leaders in the revolutionary movements in Massachusetts, although their political principles were the same, and their devotion to the liberties of the people equally ardent, differed most remarkably in manners and appearance. Adams was poor throughout his life, and while occupied with the most important and responsible public duties; his wife was laboring with her hands for the maintenance of his domestic estab lishment. He was a man of incorruptible integrity; and when the British minister inquired of Governor Hutchinson, why he was not bought off from the opposition by an office, he replied, " Such is the obsti nacy and inflexible disposition of the man, that he never can be conciliated by any office or gift whatever." In his dress and manners, he exhibited the utmost simplicity and plainness.

Hancock, on the other hand, was one of the richest men in the country. He maintained a splendid equipage, altogether surpassing in state and magnificence anything of the kind known at presen in the United States. His dress was sumptuously embroidered with gold and silver lace, and all the other showy decorations fashionable among men of fortune at that time. On public occasions he rode out in his coach, drawn by six beautiful bay horses, and attended by servants in livery. His manners were graceful and prepossessing, and he was devoted to what were deemed the refined and elegant pleasures of life,—to dancing, music, routs, assemblies, card-parties, rich wines, social dinners and festivities, all which things the austere republican virtue of Adams regarded with indifference, if not with contempt. Such were the men who were combined in the common enterprise of giving a direction to the first popular feeling which displayed itself on the subject of revolt and independence. They were both at Lexington when the British marched upon that town, having been specially excluded from the king's mercy by the proclamation of General Gage. As they withdrew together after the conflict at that place Adams exclaimed with enthusiasm,

"Oh! what a glorious morning is this!"—in the belief, it is supposed, that it would eventually lead to independence.

Such a persuasion, however, did not immediately take possession of the public mind. To throw off at once all nominal subjection to Great Britain, was a bold and fearful step, and one for which the minds of men were by no means prepared. We must not apply to the conduct of the people of that day a standard of judgment taken from our own times. The history of the whole of the present century has been little more than a series of revolutions; we are familiarized with such events, and they by no means wear that desperate and momentous aspect which formerly characterized them. But the colonists had no examples to encourage and guide them; they drew back with fear and distrust from the contemplation of so bold, novel and hazardous a project as that of setting up an entirely new and independent government. Still, the increasing exigencies of their condition brought them nearer and nearer to a crisis, and before long they became prepared for the decisive step by certain considerations, which are lucidly set forth in the following language of a writer who exercised a vast influence among the colonists at that time,—the author of a series of papers signed "Common Sense."

' We had no credit abroad, because of our *rebellious dependency*. Our ships could obtain no protection in foreign ports, because we afforded them no justifiable reason for granting it to us. The calling ourselves subjects, and at the same time fighting against the prince we acknowledged, was a dangerous precedent to all Europe. If the grievances justified our taking up arms, they justified our separation; if they did not justify our separation, neither could they justify our taking up arms. All Europe was interested in reducing us as rebels; and all Europe, or the greater part at least, are interested in supporting us in our independent state. At home, our condition was still worse. Our currency had no foundation, and the state of it would have ruined whig and tory alike. We had no other laws than a kind of moderated passion; no other civil power than an honest mob; and no other protection than the temporary attachment of one man to another. Had independency been delayed a few months longer, this continent would have been plunged into irretrievable confusion, some violent for it, some against it; all in the greatest cabal; the rich would have been ruined, and the poor destroyed. The necessity of being independent would have brought it on in a little time, had there been no rupture between Britain and America. The increasing importance of commerce, the weight and perplexity of legislation, and the enlarged state of European politics, would daily have shown to the continent the impropriety of continuing subordinate; for, after the coolest reflection on the matter, this must be allowed, that Britain was too jealous of America to govern it justly, too ignorant of it to govern it well, and too distant from it to govern it at all."

These reasons were apparent and convincing to the more sagacious and clear-sighted among the popular leaders; but these men, who were now bent on throwing off all allegiance to Great Britain. had many obstacles to surmount in the execution of this design, notwithstanding the zeal and promptness with which their measures had been seconded by the people. The multitude approved resistance, but were appalled at the thought of openly asserting their independence. For this reason, those individuals who had the chief direction of affairs, fearful of injuring their cause by too much precipitation, were compelled to observe great circumspection, and unfold their designs gradually. Massachusetts, which had been the first colony to offer resistance to the British government, was also the first to take strong ground in favor of independence. A provincial congress of this colony assembled at Watertown, and, without formally discarding all allegiance to Britain, organized an entire new government. The other colonies displayed much backwardness in following this example, but ere long the same movements took place in various parts of the country. Massachusetts even went so far as to vote unanimously, "that if congress shall think proper to declare the colonies independent, this house will approve of the measure."

But the general congress at Philadelphia had now taken up the subject, and before the Massachusetts resolution was known to that body, the question of independence had been decided. "John Adams," to use the language of Mr. Jefferson, " was the pillar of independence on the floor of congress ; its ablest advocate and defender against the multifarious assaults which were made against it. He was our colossus on the floor ; not graceful nor elegant, not always fluent in his public addresses, but he always came out with a power, both of thought and expression, that moved us from our seats." On the 6th of May, 1776, Mr. Adams brought the subject to a trial by moving a resolution that the colonies should form governments independent of the crown. This was in substance a declaration of independence: and on the 10th of the same month, the resolution was adopted in the following shape: "That it be recommended to all the colonies which had not already established governments suited to the exigencies of their case, to adopt such governments as would, in the opinion of the representatives of the people, best conduce to the happiness and safety of their constituents in particular, and Americans in general." The way being thus prepared by this bold step, a proposition for the formal declaration of independence was introduced by Richard Henry Lee, on the 7th of June. After some discussion, it was postponed for final decision to the 2d of July, and in the mean time a committee was appointed to prepare a declaration of independence. This committee was composed of the following persons: Thomas Jefferson, John Adams, Benjamin Franklin, Roger Sherman and Robert R. Livingston.

The instrument was drawn up by Jefferson, Adams and Franklin. The original draft was executed by Jefferson; some modifications were introduced by the other members of the committee, and it underwent a slight revision in congress while under discussion; but none of these alterations affected the general character of the document, and the merit of the performance as a state paper fairly belongs to Jefferson. On the 2d of July, a resolution, declaring the colonies independent, was passed in congress, and on the ever memorable 4th, the Declaration of Independence, as it now stands on the page of history, was formally and unanimously adopted.* We subjoin an extract from Mr. Websters's eulogy, in which he represents the style of Mr. Adams' oratory, and the arguments by which he enforced this great measure.

" Sink or swim, live or die, survive or perish, I give my hand and my heart to this vote. It is true, indeed, that, in the beginning, we aimed not at independence. But there's a Divinity which shapes our ends. The injustice of England has driven us to arms; and, blinded to her own interest, for our good, she has obstinately persisted, till independence is now within our grasp. We have but to reach forth to it, and it is ours. Why then should we defer the declaration? Is any man so weak as now to hope for a reconciliation with England, which shall leave either safety to the country and its liberties, or safety to his own life and his own honor? Are not you, sir, who sit in that chair, is not he, our venerable colleague near you, are you not both already the proscribed and predestined objects of punishment and vengeance? Cut off from all hope of royal clemency, what are you, what can you be, while the power of England remains, but outlaws? If we postpone independence, do we mean to carry on, or to give up the war? Do we mean to submit to the measures of parliament, Boston port bill and all? Do we mean to submit, and consent that we ourselves shall be ground to powder, and our country and its rights trodden down in the dust? I know we do

* This celebrated document, which may be considered as our Bill of Rights, was signed by all the members of congress present, and we give a *fac simile* of their signatures.

Tho? Stone Samuel Chase Rob? Treat Payne
George Wythe Mathew Thornton
Geo? Clymer Th? Jefferson Benj? Harrison
Th? Nelson Phil. Livingston
Lewis Morris Abra Clark Cæsar Rodney
Arthur Middleton Fra? Hopkinson
Geo Walton Carter Braxton James Wilson
Richard Henry Lee Tho? Heyward jun?
Benjamin Rush John Adams Rob? Morris
Lyman Hall Joseph Hewes Button Gwinnett
Francis Lightfoot Lee Edward Rutledge Jos. Smith

William Ellery

25*

not mean to submit.   We never shall submit.   Do we intend to violate that most solemn obligation ever entered into by men, that plighting, before God, of our sacred honor to Washington, when, putting him forth to incur the dangers of war, as well as the political hazards of the times, we promised to adhere to him, in every extremity, with our fortunes and our lives?   I know there is not a man here, who would not rather see a general conflagration sweep over the land, or an earthquake sink it, than one jot or tittle of that plighted faith fall to the ground.   For myself, having, twelve months ago, in this place, moved you that George Washington be appointed commander of the forces, raised or to be raised, for defence of American liberty, may my right hand forget her cunning, and my tongue cleave to the roof of my mouth, if I hesitate or waver in the support I give him.   The war, then, must go on.   We must fight it through.   And if the war must go on, why put off longer the declaration of independence?   That measure will strengthen us.   It will give us character abroad.   The nations will then treat with us, which they never can do while we acknowledge ourselves subjects, in arms against our sovereign.   Nay, I maintain that England herself will sooner treat for peace with us on the footing of independence, than consent, by repealing her acts, to acknowledge that her whole conduct towards us has been a course of injustice and oppression.   Her pride will be less wounded, by submitting to that course of things which now predestinates our independence, than by yielding the points in controversy to her rebellious subjects.   The former she would regard as the result of fortune; the latter she would feel as her own deep disgrace. Why then, why then, sir, do we not, as soon as possible, change this from a civil to a national war? And, since we must fight it through, why not put ourselves in a state to enjoy all the benefits of victory, if we gain the victory?

" If we fail, it can be no worse for us. But we shall not fail. The cause will raise up armies; the cause will create navies. The people, the people, if we are true to them, will carry us, and will carry themselves, gloriously through this struggle. I care not how fickle other people have been found. I know the people of these colonies, and I know that resistance to British aggression is deep and settled in their hearts, and cannot be eradicated. Every colony, indeed, has expressed its willingness to follow, if we but take the lead. Sir, the Declaration will inspire the people with increased courage. Instead of a long and bloody war for restoration of privileges, for redress of grievances, for chartered immunities, held under a British king, set before hem the glorious object of entire independence, and 't will breathe into them anew the breath of life. Read this Declaration at the head of the army; every sword will be drawn from its scabbard, and the solemn vow uttered, to maintain it, or to perish on the bed of honor. Publish it from the pulpit; religion will approve it, and the love of religious liberty will cling round it, resolved to stand with it, or fall with it. Send it to the public halls; proclaim it there; let them hear it, who heard the first roar of the enemy's cannon; let them see it, who saw their brothers and their sons fall on the field of Bunker Hill, and in the streets of Lexington and Concord, and the very walls will cry out in its support.

"Sir, I know the uncertainty of human affairs, but I see, I see clearly, through this day's business. You and I, indeed, may rue it. We may not live to the time when this Declaration shall be made good. We may die; die, colonists; die, slaves; die, it may be, ignominiously, and on the scaffold. Be it so. Be it so. If it be the pleasure of Heaven that my country shall require the poor offering of my life, the victim shall be ready, at the appointed hour of sacrifice, come when that hour may. But, while I do live, let me have a country, or at least the hope of a country, and that a free country.

"But, whatever may be our fate, be assured, be assured, that this Declaration will stand. It may cost treasure, and it may cost blood; but it will stand, and it will richly compensate for both. Through the thick gloom of the present, I see the brightness of the future, as the sun in heaven. We shall make this a glorious, an immortal day. When we are in our graves, our children will honor it. They will celebrate it with thanksgiving, with festivity, with bonfires and illuminations. On its annual return they will shed tears, copious, gushing tears, not of subjection and slavery, not of agony and distress, but of exultation, of gratitude, and of joy. Sir, before God, I believe the hour is come. My judgment approves this measure, and my whole heart is in it. All that I have, and all that I am, and all that I hope in this life, I am now ready here to stake upon it; and I leave off, as I began, that, live or die, survive or perish, I am for the Declaration. It is my living sentiment, and, by the blessing of God, it shall be my dying sentiment—independence *now;* and INDEPENDENCE FOREVER!"

The prophetic spirit of Mr. Adams clearly foreshadowed the momentous consequences which were destined to flow from this decisive measure. He saw, by a piercing glance into futurity, that a great empire would in after times look back to this day as the day of its birth, and commemorate it as a national anniversary. His feelings on the occasion are best described in a letter written to his wife, on the day after the Declaration was adopted. "Yesterday," says he, "the greatest question was decided that was ever debated in America; and greater, perhaps, never was, or will be decided among men. A resolution was passed, without one dissenting colony, 'That these United States are, and of right ought to be, free and independent states.' The day is passed. The 4th of July, 1776, will be a memorable epoch in the history of America. I am apt to believe it will be celebrated by succeeding generations as the great anniversary festival. It ought to be commemorated as the day of deliverance by solemn acts of devotion to Almighty God. It ought to be solemnized with pomp, shows, games, sports, guns, bells, bonfires and illuminations, from one end of the continent to the other, from this time forward forever. You will think me transported with enthusiasm, but I am not. I am well aware of the toil, and blood, and treasure that it will cost to maintain this declaration, and support and defend these states. Yet, through all the gloom, I can see the rays of light and glory. I can see that the end is worth more than all the means; and that posterity will triumph, although you and I may rue, which I hope we shall not."

ARNOLD'S TREASON.

THE attempt of General Arnold to betray the important post of West Point into the hands of the British, is one of the most memorable events in the war of the American revolution. Had this plot succeeded, it would probably have resulted in the total ruin of Washington's army, and possibly the complete subjugation of the colonies. Five years of incessant hostilities had passed without securing any permanent advantage to the British arms, when, in a single instant, a blow was on the point of being secretly struck, which threatened the existence of American liberty. That which armies had failed to accomplish, was now about to be attempted by the machinations of a traitor; and this individual was one whose brilliant achievements had given him a high place in the annals of fame.

Arnold was a soldier of undisputed courage, but he was mercenary and unprincipled at heart. In the midst of the privations and distresses that surrounded the Americans in their heroic struggle for freedom, he could not keep his hands clear of peculation. For an act of this nature, a court-martial sentenced him to be reprimanded by the commander-in-chief. This judgment was executed by Washington, with so much delicacy, as well as dignity and propriety, that we cannot refrain from copying his words: " Our profession is the chastest of all. The shadow of a fault tarnishes our most brilliant actions. The least inadvertence may cause us to lose that public favor which is so hard to be gained. I reprimand you for having forgotten, that in proportion as you had rendered yourself formidable to our enemies, you should have shown moderation towards our citizens. Exhibit again those splendid qualities which have placed you in the rank of our most distinguished generals. As far as it shall be in my power, I will myself furnish you with opportunities for regaining the esteem which you have formerly enjoyed."

But Arnold, obstinate and vindictive, was not moved, as a man of noble sentiments and generous mind would have been, by the frank appeal of a companion in arms. His honor, in fact, was already lost. He had, previous to this event, begun secret intrigues with the enemy, under a feigned name, with the design of acting according to circumstances, and to take his revenge, should the court-martial decide against him. Love of country, regard for his fame, virtue, sincerity, truth—all were now cast to the winds. The execrable scheme of betraying his country became the sole object of his thoughts, and he delayed his treason only till he had studied how to strike the most effectual blow, and reap the highest reward for his guilt.

Practising a deep dissimulation, he continued to feign a fervent zeal in the cause of independence and was restored to his rank in the army. During the summer of 1780, he asked leave of absence, on the pretence that his private affairs required his attention. Washington readily granted this request, and Arnold took up his residence in Philadelphia. As he had represented himself to be incapacitated by his wounds for the services of an active campaign, congress gave him the command of the forces in that city, and he plunged at once into every species of extravagance. He hired a magnificent house, formerly occupied by the Penn family, and furnished it in the most sumptuous manner. His play, his table, his balls, his concerts, his banquets, would have exhausted an ample fortune. His own funds, and the emoluments of his office, being far from sufficient to support him in his profusion, he soon became involved in debt, and his credit speedily declining, he was driven to new means for the indulgence of his prodigal habits. He betook himself to commerce and privateering; but his speculations proved unfortunate, his debts accumulated, and his creditors tormented him. A new and more audacious plan for replenishing his purse was now projected, and he hoped to do this by means of the public treasury. He presented accounts to the government more worthy of a shameless usurer than a general, and such as the commissioners appointed by congress refused to allow until they had been reduced one half.

Nothing was now left for him but to carry into effect the scheme of treachery which he had long meditated. This was accelerated by a domestic affair which occurred at Philadelphia. He had not been many weeks in that city when he became acquainted with a young lady of great beauty, named Shippen; belonging to a family which remained in Philadelphia after the retreat of the British, although they were disaffected to the cause of independence. This lady was lively and ambitious, and had been much admired and flattered by the British officers. Her acquaintance with Major André, was on so familiar a footing, that she maintained a correspondence with him after his departure with the British troops to New York. Arnold was smitten with her charms, and she was no less fascinated by the splendor which surrounded him. They were married, and this connection brought him into constant intercourse with several persons in the British interest. Nourishing vindictive feelings towards congress, these were inflamed by the arts of those around him, who exaggerated his grievances, and plied every argument that might hurry him on to revenge. His wife continued to correspond with André, and this afforded a convenient medium of communication with that officer. Arnold, through the hands of André, made certain advances to Sir Henry Clinton, the British commander at New York. He did not disclose his name, nor rank, but gave sufficient evidence that he was a man of consequence among the Americans, and had a knowledge of the secret springs by which their affairs were regulated. The correspondence continued for eighteen months, and Arnold, who began by merely announcing his disaffection to the American cause, from that proceeded to transmit valuable information, and at length made a direct offer to surrender himself, in such a manner as to perform a most important service to the British. Up to this moment he had not revealed himself to his confederate; his handwriting was carefully disguised, and he called himself

Gustavus. Clinton, however, after weighing all the circumstances, had before this arrived at the conclusion that his unknown correspondent was General Arnold.

West Point, a strong and commanding fortress on the Hudson, was a post of such importance as to be denominated the "Gibraltar of America." Arnold cast his eyes upon this place as the most valuable object which he could betray into the hands of the enemy. To gain the command of the fortress, he represented to Washington that his wounds were not so far healed as to enable him to render good service in the field or remain long on horseback, and that West Point was the only post at which he could do justice either to himself or the army. Washington whose forces then occupied the eastern bank of the Hudson, and who had a prospect of soon fighting the enemy, had already appointed Arnold to the command of his left wing. He was now struck with surprise at his behavior, so inconsistent with all that was known of the character of the man, and could ne conceive how an officer of his known courage enterprise, and love of distinction, could, in the heat of a busy campaign, wish to shut himself up in a garrison, where there was little scope for his military talents. He had previously disregarded several hints which Arnold had thrown out, indicating a desire to obtain this command. Surprised as he was, however, not the slightest suspicion of treachery occurred to his mind, and Arnold was entrusted with the garrison at West Point.

Clinton now saw the most important military post

of the Americans nearly within his grasp, and eagerly urged forward the scheme proposed by Arnold. That crafty traitor had yet observed the most extraordinary precautions to avoid detection. His treasonable design was opened to the British commander, under the disguise of a commercial speculation; so that if any of his letters had been intercepted by the Americans, they would have seen nothing in them but a mercantile correspondence. Before taking any further steps, he determined to stipulate for the reward of his treason; and the letter from *Gustavus* to *John Anderson*, the assumed name of André, in which he drops a hint that could not be mistaken, that he must have gold for his crime, contains the following passage. He speaks of himself in the third person. " He is still of opinion that his first proposal is by no means unreasonable, and makes no doubt, when he has a conference with you, that you will close with it. He expects, when you meet, that you will be fully authorized from your house; that the risks and profits of the copartnership may be fully and clearly understood. A speculation might at this time be easily made to some advantage with *ready money.*"

Both sides proceeded with caution. Clinton would risk nothing till he could be made as sure as possible of his object; and Arnold was resolved to keep back till a sufficient sum of money was offered, and all the terms were agreed upon. These points could be settled only by an interview between Arnold and some one in the confidence of the British commander. The person whom Clinton selected for a service which was attended with such melancholy results, was Major

John André, Adjutant-General of the British army,
and his own aide-de-camp, a young and accomplished
officer, of amiable manners, who appears to have been
universally beloved in the army.   André, as we have
already stated, was the medium through which the
intrigue was commenced, and it was by Arnold's
express solicitation that he was selected for the conference.   About the middle of September, 1780, Washington having left his head-quarters for Hartford, where
some affairs demanded his presence, this opportunity
was seized for bringing about the interview.   The
British sloop-of-war Vulture had been stationed a little
below West Point, to facilitate the communication
between the parties.   Arnold's evil conscience had
nearly betrayed him, just before the departure of
Washington.   The commander-in-chief, with his suite,
were crossing the Hudson in Arnold's barge, and
passed within full view of the Vulture.   While Washington was looking at her through his glass, and conversing in a low tone of voice to those near him, Arnold
manifested great uneasiness and emotion; a circumstance which was afterwards called to recollection.
This was not the only instance in which he came
near exciting fatal suspicions.   The French fleet,
under the Count de Guichen, was daily expected; and
as the conversation turned upon that topic, Lafayette
jestingly remarked, " General Arnold, as you have a
correspondence with the enemy, you must ascertain
as soon as possible what has become of Guichen."
This was only an allusion to an exchange of news-
papers which was carried on between West Point and
New York; but Arnold, taken unawares, manifested

great confusion, and hastily demanded what he meant. However, he immediately controlled himself, and the boat came to the shore. It is evident that he thought his plot was detected, and that this occasion had been chosen for arresting him.

On the 21st of September, André landed from the Vulture, under cover of the night, near Haverstraw, on the west bank of the Hudson. He found Arnold waiting for him alone in a thick piece of woods. A person named Smith, who owned a house in the neighborhood, acted as the go-between in this affair, having been inveigled into it by Arnold, who, as he affirms, kept him in ignorance of its true character. Arnold and André passed the whole night in the woods, and the dawn surprised them before they had made all their arrangements. They adjourned to Smith's house, where they had no sooner arrived, than a heavy cannonading was heard down the river. An incident had occurred which had an important effect in giving a turn to the business in hand. Colonel Livingston, who commanded the American fort at Verplanck's Point, received intelligence that the Vulture lay within cannon-shot of the shore, and that the inhabitants were afraid her boats would land and commit depredations. He accordingly sent a party down the eastern bank with cannon, who opened a fire upon her. André, from the window of Smith's house, saw the Vulture enveloped in smoke and flame, and it was believed she was on fire. He betrayed great emotion, but at length the firing ceased, and he resumed his wonted composure. But the affair had resulted fatally for him. The Vulture, unable to

T 26*

drive the Americans from their position, was compelled to fall down the river, out of the reach of their shot.

Arnold and André remained in an upper chamber of the house through the day, and here the whole scheme was settled, and the terms agreed upon. The plan was as follows : a strong body of British troops, already embarked at New York under the pretext of an expedition to the Chesapeake, was to be kept in readiness to ascend the Hudson at a moment's warning. Arnold was to make such arrangements as to weaken the garrison of West Point, and compel it to surrender at the first attack. This was to be done by scattering and dividing his troops in such a manner that they could not act in concert, nor move in any direction, by which any effectual resistance could be opposed to the advancing bodies of the British. Arnold furnished André with several papers describing the fortifications at West Point, giving the number of the troops and furnishing directions as to the manner in which the fortress might be taken. He gave also descriptions of the several forts, redoubts and batteries on the river, and a report of a council of war lately held at head quarters, comprising hints respecting the probable operations of the campaign. Departing from his usual precaution, Arnold had drawn up all these documents in his own hand-writing, without any attempt at disguise. It was a singular fatality that he should have exposed himself in this fool-hardy manner at the most critical point of the transaction, when it seems there was not the slightest necessity for it; and that his prudence, craft, and foresight should have abandoned him at a moment when they were most essential for the completion of his plot.

As the scheme was contrived in secret, and the British government could derive no honor by publishing the details of so foul a transaction, we know little more of the stipulations which Arnold made in his own favor than the fact that in case of success he was to be paid a large sum of money. Every point being settled, he departed for West Point, and left André to return on board the Vulture; but, in the mean time, that ship had returned up the river nearly to her former station, and when André urged Smith to send him on board in his boat, that person positively refused, alleging that he was suffering from a fit of the ague; though the true reason was that he was afraid she would again be fired upon from the shore. André passed a day of much anxiety, looking from his window across the wide expanse of Haverstraw Bay, and wishing himself on board the Vulture. It is singular how many unforeseen incidents combined to defeat this momentous plan of treason. But for the cowardice of Smith, André might in an hour or two have been safe on board the ship, and West Point had been irretrievably lost. André at length, finding Smith obstinate in his refusal either to go himself or let his boat go, saw himself under the necessity of proceeding to New York by land. Arnold had furnished him and Smith with passports, and the latter agreed to accompany André a portion of the way, till he should be out of danger.

André had come on shore in his uniform, and it was necessary to disguise himself. He therefore threw off his regimental coat, and put on an old one of Smith's; with this, and a dark great coat which had a wide cape buttoned close to the neck, he judged himself sufficiently transformed.   He then set off, just before sunset, accompanied by Smith and a negro servant.   They crossed the river from Stony Point to Verplanck's Point, and were not interrupted, till about nine in the evening, when, near Crompond, they were stopped by a sentinel, and carried before Captain Boyd, who commanded a patrolling party.   He questioned them very closely, and appeared not to be satisfied with the account they gave of themselves.   André began to be alarmed; but the sight of Arnold's passport in a great measure removed the suspicions which had been excited.   Boyd spoke to them of the danger of travelling by night, and advised them to turn back to a house at a short distance, where they might rest till morning.   With this counsel they deemed it prudent to comply.   Early the next morning, they resumed their journey, and having got beyond the reach of the patrolling party, André, who had previously been thoughtful, reserved and anxious, became suddenly animated, cheerful and talkative.   He thought himself now completely out of danger.   No person accosted the party, and at Pine Bridge they breakfasted at the house of a Dutch woman.   Smith, believing all the hazards of the journey over, parted from André at this place, and, with his servant, hastened back.   According to his own story, he was ignorant up to this moment of the name of his companion, but supposed him to be Mr. John Anderson.

The eastern shore of the Hudson, between the British and American lines, was during the war infested by gangs of marauders, who plundered the whole

debatable territory. Those above called themselves
" Skinners," and those below were denominated " Cow
Boys." The former professed an attachment to the
American cause, and the latter claimed British protection ; however, they were all banditti, and plundered
friends and foes. André was, in fact, so far from
being secure, that thirty miles of his journey now lay
through the territory of these prowlers. Smith had
advised him to take the route through White Plains,
which in truth was much the safest, but André chose
the latter, through Tarrytown, believing it to be frequented by the British party.

Between nine and ten in the morning of the 23d
of September, as André had approached within half
a mile of the village of Tarrytown, he was suddenly
stopped by three men, who sprang out from among
the bushes, and presented their muskets. They were
Americans, who belonged to a larger party, and had
taken that station to intercept stragglers, deserters,
and droves of cattle that might be going to New York.
André asked them to which side they belonged ; they
answered, " The Lower Party." " So do I," returned
he. " I am a British officer, out on particular business, and I hope you will not detain me a minute." In
proof of this assertion, he pulled out a gold watch. The
American officers, we infer, were supposed not to possess articles of such value. The men ordered him to
dismount, which he did, and exhibited Arnold's pass,
which was in the following words : " Permit Mr. John
Anderson to pass the guards to the White Plains, or
below if he chooses, he being on public business by
my direction. B. Arnold, M. General " The men

would have allowed him to proceed at the sight of
this, had he not previously declared himself a British
officer; his imprudence and want of foresight in doing
this are most remarkable. The three men, whose
names were John Paulding, David Williams and
Isaac Van Wert, were convinced that something was
wrong. "We took him into the bushes," says Williams, "and ordered him to pull off his clothes, which
he did; but on searching him narrowly, we could
not find any sort of writings. We told him to pull
off his boots, which he seemed to be indifferent about;
but we got one boot off and searched in that boot, and
could find nothing. But we found there were some
papers in the bottom of his stocking next to his foot;
on which we made him pull his stocking off, and
found three papers wrapped up. Mr. Paulding looked
at the contents and said he was a spy. We then made
him pull off his other boot, and there we found three
more papers at the bottom of his foot within his stocking. Upon this, we made him dress himself, and I
asked him what he would give us to let him go; he
said he would give us any sum of money. I asked
him whether he would give us his horse, saddle,
bridle, watch, and one hundred guineas. He said
'Yes,' and told us he would direct them to any place,
even if it was that very spot, so that we could get
them. He said he would give us any quantity of dry
goods, and any sum of money, and bring it to any
place that we might pitch upon, so that we might get
it. Mr. Paulding answered, 'No; if you would give
us ten thousand guineas, you should not stir one step.'
I then asked the person who had called himself John

Anderson, if he would not get away if it lay in his power. He answered, ' Yes, I would.' I told him, I did not intend he should. While taking him along, we asked him a few questions, and we stopped under a shade. He begged us not to ask him questions, and said when he came to a commander he would reveal all."

André was immediately conducted to North Castle, where a military post was established under the command of Lieutenant Colonel Jameson. That officer, on examining the papers, found them to be in the handwriting of Arnold ; yet, with such plain proofs of that person's treachery before him, Jameson seems not to have suspected it. He despatched André, under a guard, to Arnold, with a letter, stating that the papers taken upon him were, he thought, " of very dangerous tendency," and that he had sent them to General Washington. Jameson, in Washington's opinion, was, either on account of his "egregious folly or bewildered conception, so lost in astonishment, as not to know what he was doing." He afterwards, at the urgent entreaty of Colonel Tallmadge, the second in command, recalled the prisoner, but, continuing in his blunders, sent on the letter, informing Arnold that André was taken. Arnold was seated at breakfast, with his family and aids-de-camp, when this letter arrived at head quarters. He opened and read it, instantly. Thunderstruck at the intelligence, he yet had sufficient control over his feelings to conceal them from the persons at table. He told his aids-de-camp that his immediate attendance was required at West Point and ordered a horse to be got ready. He then rose hastily, went to Mrs. Arnold's chamber, and sent for her. In a few hurried words, he told her that they must instantly part, perhaps forever, and that his destruction was inevitable, unless he could reach the British lines undiscovered. At this intelligence, so abruptly communicated, she fainted, and fell senseless on the floor. Leaving her in that state, he ran down stairs, sprang upon a horse, and galloped to the bank of the river; there he entered a boat, manned by six rowers, and ordered them to pull out into the middle of the stream. The men promptly obeyed his orders, and Arnold informed them that he was going on board the Vulture with a flag, and was in great haste, as he expected Washington at his house. The boat reached the Vulture without being molested, and Arnold was safe.

A letter written by Colonel Hamilton the next day, vividly describes the afflicting situation of the traitor's wife, who was frantic with distress, and seemed on the verge of distraction. She, for a considerable time, entirely lost herself. General Washington went up to see her, and she upbraided him with being in a plot to murder her child. One moment she raved, another she melted into tears. Sometimes she pressed her infant to her bosom, and lamented its fate, occasioned by the imprudence of its father, in a manner that would have pierced insensibility itself. All the sweetness of beauty, all the loveliness of innocence, all the tenderness of a wife, and all the fondness of a mother, showed themselves in her appearance and conduct. We have every reason to believe that she was entirely unacquainted with the plan, and that the first knowledge of it was when Arnold went to tell her he must banish himself from his country and from her forever. She instantly fell into convulsions, and he left her in that situation.

"Whom can we trust now?" exclaimed Washington, when Arnold's treason became known. The news of this event caused universal amazement throughout the country. The people could scarcely credit the treachery of a man in whom they had so long placed the utmost confidence. The hazard which they had run filled them with consternation; the happy chance by which they had been saved appeared a prodigy. Washington apprehended at first that the plot might have more extensive ramifications, and not knowing on what individuals to fix his eyes, was much embarrassed in the midst of his distrust. He feared also lest the contagion of example might incite even those who were strangers to the conspiracy, to entertain rash desires for a new order of things. But his apprehensions fortunately were not realized, and nothing occurred to show that Arnold had any accomplices.

André, having been captured within the American lines in disguise, was tried by a court-martial, on the charge of being a spy; he was pronounced guilty, and, agreeably to the laws of war, condemned to be hanged. Great efforts were made by the British commander-in-chief to save him, and Washington would gladly have spared him, if Arnold could have been taken, or exchanged for him. But Clinton refused to surrender the traitor, and a scheme for his capture, which we shall hereafter relate, having failed, André's execution was a matter of stern necessity. No spy captured by the

British had been spared during the conflict, and the
sacrifice of André was a melancholy, but a just retaliation.   His fate wrung tears of compassion even from
his judges.   His frankness and amiability had won
universal esteem, and he was treated with a forbearance, kindness and delicacy in his misfortunes
which called forth his warmest acknowledgments.
Finding his fate inevitable, he prepared himself for
death with fortitude and calmness.   He entreated
that he might die like a soldier, that is, by being shot,
rather than hung like a malefactor ; but the stern command of the military code prescribed the halter, and
he could not be gratified in his last request.   He was
executed at Tappaan, on the Hudson, October 2d,
1780.   His last words were, " Bear witness that I die
like a brave man."   ,
  Such was the termination of a treacherous plot
without a parallel in the history of the United States.
The momentous interests connected with it, and the
immeasurable infamy of the man by whom it was
projected, combine to make it a story of the deepest
interest.   Arnold, steeped in guilt and dishonor, received from the hands of Sir H. Clinton six thousand
three hundred and fifteen pounds sterling, in part payment for his crime.   He did not scruple to practise a
fraud to obtain the money, and made the British
commander believe that he had lost such an amount
of property by abandoning the Americans, while in
fact he left little behind him, except his debts.   His
wife was permitted to join him at New York, and we
believe she continued to share his fate during her life.
Arnold was made a brigadier general in the British

service, and distinguished himself by several marauding expeditions against his own countrymen in Connecticut and Virginia. At the conclusion of the war he went to England, and subsequently to New Brunswick and the West Indies; in all which places he lived the object of general disgust and contempt. He died in London, where he had resided several years, with a British pension, June 14th, 1801, at the age of sixty-one.

The treason of Arnold gave rise to a very bold undertaking by a subaltern officer of the American army, which deserves mention in this sketch. Shortly after Arnold's flight, Washington conceived the project of capturing him by stratagem, with the intention of saving André if he should succeed. Accordingly he sent for Major Henry Lee, and addressed him as follows: " I have sent for you in the expectation that you have some one in your corps who is willing to undertake a delicate and hazardous project. Whoever comes forward will confer great obligations on me personally, and in behalf of the United States he shall be amply rewarded. No time is to be lost; he must proceed, if possible, to-night. I intend to seize Arnold." Lee bethought himself a moment, and designated a sergeant in his corps, by the name of Champe, a Virginian of tried courage and inflexible perseverance. Champe was sent for, and the plan laid before him. He was to desert, and escape to New York, where he was to distinguish himself in professions of zeal for the royal cause. In the mean time he was to keep a watchful eye upon Arnold, and, upon the first favorable opportunity, to make himself master of his person, and conduct him to an appointed place on the river, where boats were to be in readiness to convey them to the American side.

Champe listened to the proposal, but his first feelings were those of repugnance to the undertaking. He replied that it was not the danger nor difficulty of the enterprise that deterred him from immediately concurring in it, but his mind revolted from the ignominy of desertion, and the hypocrisy of enlisting with the enemy. To these objections it was replied, that although he would appear to desert, yet, as he obeyed the order of his commander, the act could not be considered as criminal, and if he suffered in reputation for a time, the matter would be publicly explained to his credit in the end. Moreover, to save André, which it was hoped would be one result of the successful accomplishment of the undertaking, would be a deed more than sufficient to balance an apparent wrong. The objections of Champe were at length surmounted, and he accepted the hazardous service. It was now eleven o'clock at night. With his instructions in his pocket the sergeant returned to camp, and taking his cloak, valise, and orderly-book, drew his horse from the picket, mounted, and set off.

Scarcely half an hour afterwards, the officer of the day came to Major Lee, and informed him that one of the patrol had fallen in with a dragoon, who, on being challenged, put spurs to his horse and escaped. Lee, hoping to conceal the flight of the sergeant till he had gained sufficient time, complained of fatigue, and told him the patrol had probably mistaken a countryman for a trooper. But the suspicions of the officer were not so easily quieted. He withdrew to muster his men, and on examination it appeared that Champe was missing. Lee, finding that his desertion could no longer be concealed, was forced to give orders for his recapture. "Pursue him, and bring him back alive," said he, "if possible, but kill him if he resists or escapes after being taken." Champe, in the mean time, found himself in a perilous situation. A shower of rain fell shortly after his departure, which enabled the dragoons in pursuit to mark his track, the horse-shoes being made in a peculiar fashion, and each having a private mark. He had the start of his pursuers by little more than an hour. During the night, the dragoons were delayed several times by the necessity of examining the road, but in the morning the marks of the horse's shoes were so apparent, that they pushed on with great rapidity. Their course was down the west bank of the Hudson; and as they approached the village of Bergen, on gaining the top of a hill, they discovered Champe not more than half a mile before them. Fortunately, he also descried his pursuers, and being at no loss to conjecture their object, he put spurs to his horse. By turning off the main road, he got out of their sight, but on approaching the river they again discovered him. His situation was now desperate; he lashed his valise to his shoulders and prepared to plunge into the river. The pursuers now quickened their speed, and as the sergeant gained the water's edge, the dragoons were within a few hundred yards of him. He threw himself from his horse and plunged into the river, calling aloud to some British galleys which lay at anchor not

far off.   A boat was instantly despatched to his assist
ance, and a fire opened from the galleys upon his
pursuers.   Champe was taken on board, and carried
to New York, with a letter from the captain of the
galley, describing all that he had witnessed.

The pursuing party captured the sergeant's horse
and cloak, and returned to the camp with the intelligence that Champe was killed.   The grief of Major
Lee was past description, on imagining himself the
means of the death of this faithful and intrepid soldier.
It was not long, however, before his mind was relieved
by the intelligence that Champe had gained the quarters of the enemy, where he was carried before Sir
Henry Clinton, and closely interrogated ; some of the
questions required all the ingenuity and address he
was master of, to answer without exciting suspicion.
Clinton gave him a couple of guineas, and recommended him to Arnold, who was wishing to procure
American recruits.   Champe enlisted in Arnold's
legion, but was unable to mature his plan before the
execution of André.   By watching Arnold's movements, he discovered that it was his custom to return
to his quarters about midnight, and that previous to
retiring to rest he always took a walk in the garden.
Here Champe determined to seize him, with the help
of a number of associates whom he had drawn into the
plot.   He had taken off several of the palings of the
garden fence and replaced them, so that, without noise
or delay, an opening might be effected into the adjoining alley.   Into this alley it was intended to convey
Arnold, his mouth being secured with a gag ; two
persons were to support him by the shoulders, and

thus bear him through unfrequented streets and lanes to a boat stationed for the purpose; in case of being questioned by the watch, they were to represent him as a drunken soldier whom they were conveying to the guard-house.

On the day appointed, Gen. Lee, who had received instructions from Champe, left the camp with a party of dragoons, taking with them spare horses for Arnold and his captors. Proceeding toward the bank of the river, they reached Hoboken about midnight, and concealed themselves in the woods. Lee, with three dragoons, took his station near the shore. Hour after hour passed away, but no boat appeared, and at daybreak he was forced to return to camp disappointed and chagrined. In a few days he received a letter, informing him that on the day preceding that fixed upon for the execution of the plot, Arnold had removed his quarters to another part of the city, and that the American legion had been transferred from their barracks to one of the transports, it being apprehended that if left on shore any longer they might desert. In consequence of this, Champe was detained on board the fleet, and obliged to accompany Arnold in the expedition which he shortly afterwards made to Virginia. He was under the necessity of remaining for some time longer in the British service, but at length succeeded in making his escape and rejoining his countrymen. His unexpected appearance excited great surprise in the army, but when the story became known, their esteem for him was heightened by admiration of his bold and arduous attempt, which nothing

but an unforeseen accident had prevented him from
bringing to a successful termination.

The story of Arnold is in the highest degree painful, yet it has not been without its use. It has set
before the world a lesson never to be forgotten, show-
ing the danger of profligate habits, the gulf of ruin to
which loose principles of action lead, and the everlast-
ing infamy which awaits the traitor to his country.
Nor is this all—a shadow so deep, as is furnished by
Arnold's story, serves to heighten the glorious light
which falls upon the patriots who figure by his side
on the page of history !

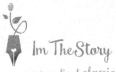